朱位蝶影

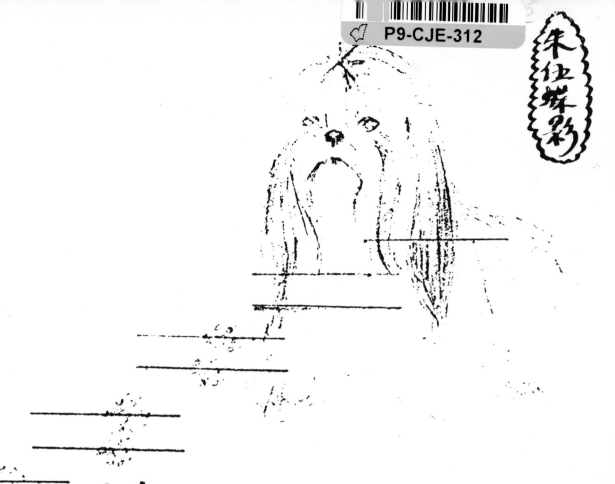

特此證明 慈母拉利英英

為亞倫依士頓夫婦所有

此狗為龍種皇族，今已

為北京皇宮來找名種

狗之第四代，來左生於

西元一九二八年五月地

兵為中國首都北京。

慈母拉利英英
好年白飛
左莫龍馬

司
N.Y. 12525
55-5295

The Book of the SHIH TZU

Joan McDonald Brearley

and

The Reverend D. Allan Easton

Front Cover:
Chumulari Ying-Ying, the outstanding champion who was the pride of the Easton's kennel. Portrait by Alton Anderson.

Back Cover:
Quang-Te v.d. Blauwe Mammouth, photographed by Alton Anderson.

Frontispiece:
Drawing by Paul Nickerson.

Distributed in the U.S. by T.F.H. Publications, Inc., 211 West Sylvania Avenue, PO Box 427, Neptune, NJ 07753; in England by T.F.H. (Gt. Britain) Ltd., 13 Nutley Lane, Reigate, Surrey; in Canada to the book store and library trade by Beaverbooks Ltd., 150 Lesmill Road, Don Mills, Ontario M38 2T5, Canada; in Canada to the pet trade by Rolf C. Hagen Ltd., 3225 Sartelon Street, Montreal 382, Quebec; in Southeast Asia by Y.W. Ong, 9 Lorong 36 Geylang, Singapore 14; in Australia and the South Pacific by Pet Imports Pty. Ltd., P.O. Box 149, Brookvale 2100, N.S.W. Australia; in South Africa by Valid Agencies, P.O. Box 51901, Randburg 2125 South Africa. Published by T.F.H. Publications, Inc., Ltd, the British Crown Colony of Hong Kong.

ISBN 0-87666-664-0

© 1980 by T.F.H Publications, Inc., Ltd.

TABLE OF CONTENTS

The Book of the Shih Tzu is dedicated to our beloved

CHUMULARI YING-YING

five generations removed from Peking Palace-bred stock, an American and Canadian champion, first Shih Tzu to win Best In Show in North America, sire of six Best In Show sons, (all from different dams), sire of 28 American champions to date, and sire of champions in Canada, Mexico, and Bermuda, grandsire of two champions in Argentina, two international champions which have won four Bests In Show in Brazil, great-grandsire of a Best In Show American champion, and winner of the Silver Award from *Showdogs* magazine in 1977 as a top sire in the breed. He was a legend in his own time.

The Eastons

It is further dedicated to Ying-Ying's daughter

CHUMULARI ME-LAH

and his granddaughter, Chumulari Tai Tai, who brought so much joy into my life as exquisite specimens of our beautiful breed and who are a credit to their illustrious ancestors!

Joan McDonald Brearley

ACKNOWLEDGEMENTS

The authors are extremely grateful to all of the fanciers who contributed to this book.

The gathering of as many photographs and as much background material as we present in *The Book of the Shih Tzu* required a maximum of time and effort, not only on the part of the authors, but by those we approached directly to supply either information or valuable photographs of their beautiful Shih Tzu.

We thank Alton Anderson for our magnificent cover photographs of Quang-Te, artist Paul Nickerson for the exquisite frontispiece and other drawings in the book, and Dr. Robert Shomer, V.M.D. for expert counsel.

Most of all, we owe our deepest appreciation to Margaret Easton for her unending quest for research and special material on our breed. Over the years, her presentation of the Chumulari Shih Tzu in the show rings has helped to endear this breed to the public. The Shih Tzu has no more devoted and successful breeder, nor a more ardent advocate—past or present—than she.

**SHIH TZU
is pronounced SHID ZOO
(singular or plural)**

ABOUT THE AUTHORS

JOAN McDONALD BREARLEY

Joan McDonald Brearley is the first to admit that animals in general—and dogs in particular—are a most important part of her life. Since childhood there has been a steady stream of dogs, cats, birds, fish, rabbits, snakes, alligators, etc., for her own personal menagerie. Over the years she has owned over 30 breeds of pure-bred dogs, as well as countless mixtures, since the door was never closed to a needy or homeless animal.

A graduate of the American Academy of Dramatic Arts where she studied acting and directing, Joan started her career as an actress, dancer, and writer for movie magazines. She studied ballet at the Agnes DeMille Studios in Carnegie Hall and was with an oriental dance company which performed at the Carnegie Recital Hall. She studied journalism at Columbia University and has written for radio, television and magazines, and was a copywriter for some of the major New York City advertising agencies working on the Metro-Goldwyn-Mayer studios, Burlington Mills, *Cosmopolitan* magazine, White Owl Cigar, Manishewitz Wine and New York newspaper accounts.

While a television producer-director for a major network she worked on "Nick Carter, Master Detective;" "Did Justice Triumph;" and news and special feature programs. Joan has written, cast, directed, produced and, on occasion, starred in television film commercials. She has written special material for such personalities as Dick Van Dyke, Dione Lucas, Amy Vanderbilt, William B. Williams, Gene Rayburn, Bill Stern, Herman Hickman and many other prominent people in the entertainment world. She has appeared as a guest on several of the nation's most popular talk shows, including those of Mike Douglas, Joe Franklin, Cleveland Amory, David Susskind and the "Today Show," to name just a few. Joan was selected for inclusion in the *Directory of the Foremost Women In Communications* in 1969, and the book, *Two Thousand Women of Achievement* in 1971. She is also a member of the Screen Actors Guild.

Her accomplishments in the dog fancy include breeding and exhibiting top show dogs, writer, lecturer and columnist on various magazines and author of over twenty books on dogs and cats, including *This Is the Irish Setter, This Is the Siberian Husky, The Book of the Doberman Pinscher,* etc. For five years she was Executive Vice-President of the Popular Dogs Publishing Company and editor of *Popular Dogs* magazine, the national prestige publication for the fancy at that time. Her editorials on the status and welfare of animals have been reproduced as educational pamphlets by dog clubs and organizations in many countries of the world.

Joan is just as active in the cat fancy, and in almost as many capacities. The same year her Afghan Hound, Ch. Sahadi Shikari, won the Ken-L Ration Award as Top Hound of the Year, one of her Siamese cats won a comparable honor in the cat fancy. She has owned and/or bred almost all breeds of cats. Many of her cats and dogs are Best In Show winners and have appeared in magazines and on television. For several years she was editor of the Cat Fanciers Association Annual Yearbook, and her book, *All About Himalayan Cats,* was published in 1976.

In addition to breeding and showing dogs since 1955, Joan has been active as a member and on the Board of Directors of the Kennel Club of Northern New Jersey, The Afghan Hound Club of America, the Stewards Club of America and the Dog Fanciers Club. She has been an American Kennel Club judge of several breeds since 1961. As a guest speaker at many dog clubs and humane and veterinary organizations she has crusaded for humane legislation for animals. She has won many awards and citations in this field which establish her as one of the best known and most knowledgeable people in the animal world. She is proud of the fact that her home-bred Ch. Sahadi Shikari was top-winning Afghan Hound in the history of the breed for several years, and still remains in the #2 position today. No other breeder can claim to have bred a Westminster Group Winner in their first home-bred litter, an honor also won by Shikari.

Joan looks forward to the near future when she will once again breed dogs at her Sahadi Kennels and Cattery to continue her line of dogs which excel in the breed rings, obedience trials, in the field and on the race tracks.

Meantime, Joan continues to write dog books (a novel about the dog fancy is in the works), continues her freelance publicity and public relations work, exhibits her needlepoint (for which she has also won awards), haunts the art and auction galleries and maintains her reputation as a movie buff! Never content to have just one interest at a time, Joan has managed to dove-tail several occupations at the same time to make for a fascinating career.

THE REVEREND D. ALLAN EASTON,
F.R.A.S., M.A., B.D., S.T.M.

Equally at home in Europe, Asia or North America, the Rev. D. Allan Easton is a Fellow of the the Royal Asiatic Society of Great Britain and Ireland and a Member of the American Oriental Society, the China Institute of America, the Tibet society of the United Kingdom and the International Platform Association which united public speakers and writers of the free world.

Born and raised in Scotland, Rev. Easton began his travels as a student when he signed on as purser on a British freighter for an eight week round trip voyage to Rio de Janeiro, Montevideo and Buenos Aires.

After completing his studies in Glasgow and New York, Rev. Easton first visited Peking in 1937, a few days before the Japanese took over the city, and thus experienced something of the fascination of pre-Pearl Harbor life in the ancient Chinese capital. From that experience he traces the beginning of his present enthusiasm for the rare little Lion Dogs from the Manchu Palace.

In 1938, while acting as Professor of Civics at an Indian college in the Himalayas, Rev. Easton became one of the few Europeans to visit the hidden land of Tibet. Made by mule and pony across a 15,000 foot mountain pass, accompanied only by a Ghurka attendant, this expedition took him to Gyantse, third largest "town" in Tibet.

Beginning with an invitation to dinner at the Royal Palace in Gangtok, where the Scottish traveller discovered that he shared a common interest in pet monkeys with the Maharajah of Sikkim, the six-week, 400 mile journey included a luncheon in a Tibetan monastery and tea parties with high ranking officials and members of nobility.

Travelling across India some months later, by sheer chance Rev. Easton found himself sharing a railway carriage with the late Mahatma Ghandi and sleeping on the berth immediately above that of the revered Asian leader. During the twenty-four hour journey, understandably, many assumed Rev. Easton to be the Mahatma's newest Western disciple.

The Rev. Easton was invited to return to Peking in 1947. Before leaving for Hong Kong two years later, he lived through the six-week siege of the city and for seven months under the Communist regime.

Spending a year as Executive Director of the Honolulu Council of Churches, Rev. Easton organized his own weekly radio program of religious news and represented the churches of Hawaii at the 1950 Mid-Century White House Conferences on Children and Youth and other important mainland conferences.

In 1951 Rev. Easton returned to Scotland. After his marriage in Ireland in 1954, he and his wife, Margaret, spent some years in an historic Scottish rural parish with ten acres of glebe or "minister's land." There they raised goats, hens, turkeys, geese and ducks in addition to having as house-pets Siamese cats, Pekingese and Tibetan Terriers. One of these Terriers was especially treasured, having been smuggled out of its homeland by an Indian disguised as a beggar, who made the journey across the mountains for the express purpose of obtaining it.

In 1960 Rev. Easton was called to New Jersey where he was Rector of St. Paul's Episcopal Church in Wood-Ridge, was also World Affairs Chairman for the Episcopal Diocese of Newark, and International Affairs Chairman for the New Jersey Council of Churches. In 1963 he was awarded a citation for "Distinguished Public Service" by the U.S. Cuban Refugee Emergency Center in Miami for his successful settlement of 97 Cuban refugees in northern New Jersey.

In 1964 Governor Richard J. Hughes of New Jersey highly commended Rev. Easton for his visit to the quake stricken areas of Alaska on behalf of the people of New Jersey, a visit which led to the Juneau Secretary of State decorating him with the "Order of the Alaskan Walrus." This six-week, 10,000 mile round trip was made together with Mrs. Easton, their two small sons, an Afghan Hound and three Shih Tzu, all of whom shared the same tent! In 1965 Governor Hughes selected Rev. Easton's church as the place of release for his official tribute to Sir Winston Churchill in which the Governor made moving reference to the importance of Anglo-American relations.

On November 30, 1970, Rev. Easton was principle speaker and guest of honor at the annual dinner of the St. Andrew's Society of Baltimore, an honor which a year before had been accorded to the British Ambassador to Washington.

In the following year Rev. Easton's name appeared among the "Two Thousand Men of Achievement" in the *Dictionary of International Biography,* published in England. This was a distinction which reflects his continuing interest in the development of better relations between the United States and the United Kingdom. Rev. Easton claims to be great-great-great-great-great grandson of Major John Pitcairn who commanded the advanced guard of Royal Marines at Lexington and Concord.

His interest in history is long-standing. At the age of eight, "having paid his freedom fine," he was admitted as a Burgess and Guild Brother of his native city of Glasgow, Scotland, thereby becoming "entitled to all the civil rights and privileges by law belonging thereto," and becoming "bound to perform all the civil duties and obligations by law incumbent on a Freeman Citizen of Glasgow." More than fifty years later, having settled in the United States, he was invited to become a member of the National Historical Society of America and an Associate of the National Archives, Washington, D.C.

On numerous occasions Rev. Easton has represented the churches of New Jersey at important meetings in Washington and other large cities and is a regular contributor to the church press. Trained at the Newspaper Institute of America, he has been Shih Tzu columnist for both *Popular Dogs* and *Kennel Review* magazines over the years.

Strangely enough, Margaret Easton was introduced to her first Shih Tzu in Ireland in the late 1940's. At the time she was visiting Miss Hutchins, a friend of her mother's who had brought specimens of the breed from China some time earlier.

The Eastons' first Shih Tzu was purchased in 1961 from the Swedish-born fancier, Ingrid Colwell of Pennsylvania. They have since imported dogs from England, Germany, Holland and Scandinavia, breeding selectively to produce their own outstanding Chumulari line which has produced three Best In Show dogs to date.

A registered nurse, trained in Edinburgh, Scotland, and serving in the Intensive Care Unit of Hackensack Hospital in New Jersey, Margaret Easton takes full responsibility for the care and feeding of their Chumulari dogs and for their magnificent presentation in the show ring. Born in India of Scottish parents, Mrs. Easton remembers camping out in the foothills of the Himalayas with the mysterious land of Tibet beyond. Ever since, dogs of oriental origin have fascinated her and she is widely respected for her detailed knowledge of Shih Tzu pedigrees.

Three times cited by the *New York Times* as leaders in the successful struggle for American Kennel Club recognition of the breed, the Eastons now breed their Shih Tzu at Tir-Nan-Og, Gaelic for Land of Heart's Desire, in the Shawangunk Mountains, Gardiner, New York.

Begun in Peking in 1947, the Eastons' guest book contains the signatures of more than 1,500 visitors from 42 American states, Canadian provinces, and 43 other countries. In recent years, the home of Ying-Ying, pride of Chumulari Kennels, has become a place of pilgrimage to which Shih Tzu fanciers travel from all over North America and as far away as Bahia, Brazil; Nairobi, Kenya; Caracas, Venezuela; and Freeport in the Bahamas. From Tir-Nan-Og, carefully selected Chumulari Shih Tzu puppies go to proud new owners all over the world.

INTRODUCTION

The authors are extremely pleased and gratified that, based on the continued success of our book, *This is the Shih Tzu*, released in 1970, our publisher requested that this new book be written so that we might bring the breed up to its present status as one of the most popular and beloved of all the Toy breeds.

The Book of the Shih Tzu contains important records and history of the Shih Tzu from its early beginnings in the orient up to its present day status all over the world. In this new volume you will find a wealth of information essential to both the newcomer and the longtime fancier, plus hundreds of photographs presenting these enchanting "little lion dogs" in all their glory!

We hope that both books will be permanent additions to your library and that you will find as much pleasure in reading this new one as we derived from writing it. *The Book of the Shih Tzu* is our personal tribute to the breed we love and admire so very much.

The Authors

Chapter 1
THE HISTORY OF THE BREED

From the earliest days when civilized people first began to select their dogs because of their distinct breed characteristics, the oriental dogs have been popular favorites. History relates the presence of shaggy little dogs resembling the Shih Tzu gamboling around the palace courtyards many centuries before Christ. This description, though vague, can readily account for this small-type dog being one of the oldest breeds or types of companion dog in the world.

While a prisoner in Genoa, Italy, the renowned Asian traveller, Marco Polo, dictated to another prisoner named Rusticiano the lengthy and detailed accounts of his travels in the orient and throughout Asia. These tales of his journey comprised eighty to ninety manuscripts, the most important of them being in the possession of the Bibliotheque Nationale in Paris. In these manuscripts Marco Polo glorifies the life and times of Kublai Khan, grandson of Genghis Khan, and a man he came to consider a friend before leaving China.

It was on his return to Venice in 1294 after years of service in the court of Kublai Khan at Shangtu, not far from Peking, that he began to take note of the great numbers of small, shaggy dogs that were such a contrast to the larger Mastiffs that stood guard outside the homes of their masters. He wrote that he believed any Mastiff could finish off a lion, should the occasion demand.

Whether it was the enormous Mastiff-type dogs that guarded homes and palaces and accompanied soldiers into war, or the chubby, middle-sized Chow Chow-type dogs bred to provide food for the masses, or the sturdy little lap and sleeve-size dogs that captured the fancy of the royal houses of Asia, the dogs of that far-off land were destined to make their way into the hearts of dog lovers in the centuries that followed their beginnings.

There were, of course, other oriental breeds during the early period. Many of them found their way to foreign lands by way of sailors on trade ships, while many others were given as gifts to visiting dignitaries. Not all survived, but those that did were to create enough curiosity and interest to lead to more specimens being brought

out of the orient by one means or another. Eventually the names of the Tibetan Terrier, Tibetan Spaniel, Pekingese, Lhasa Apso and Shih Tzu were to become known among dog fanciers and after dedicated and selective breedings they became individual breeds known and recognized for their own characteristics. Today we are better acquainted with these oriental breeds and can recognize the very definite and distinct differences which must be apparent according to precise breed standards.

The Pekingese and the Shih Tzu have been referred to as "lion dogs" in their native China. The Pekingese was said to have come into prominence in China only after an Apso-type dog had been around for quite some time. There are those who claim that the Chinese emperors actually used long-haired Tibetan dogs in their breeding programs to improve the coats of the Chinese dogs during the 19th century.

During the early part of the 20th century this slow but definite trend towards strengthening individual breeds through selective breeding continued. Exporting of the oriental dogs was virtually unheard of, due in part to a continuing reluctance on the part of the people to let go of their breeding stock.

LAST KNOWN SHIH TZU IN CHINA

The fall of the city of Peking to the Communist army in 1949 closed the door to our discovering more about the homeland of the little lion dogs. History recounts how the Shih Tzu flourished in the Imperial Palace, being bred with the most painstaking care to produce the best specimens possible—for only the best would do. Today, the tiny dogs, held in such high esteem, no longer walk the hallways of the palace, but those of the lovely palace Shih Tzu lucky enough to find their way into new homelands at the time of the invasion will perpetuate the purity of line established by the palace breeders' uncompromising efforts.

One of the last known people to breed Shih Tzu in Peking during those difficult days preceding the takeover of the city was Alfred Koehn, a Ger-

These Shih Tzu were the property of Mr. Alfred Koehn, a German author and publisher who lived in Peking during the Japanese occupation. This photograph is believed to have been taken in the late 1940's. Prevailing conditions at the time must have made selective breeding most difficult.

man author and publisher of many beautiful books on Chinese and Japanese arts and crafts.

At almost the same time as the Communist siege of the city began, a full page advertisement for these dogs appeared in the Christmas, 1948, issue of the British magazine *Our Dogs*. This advertisement showed photographs of six of Mr. Koehn's Shih Tzu beside which was stated "They are descendants of the Lion Dogs which came to China during the Manchu Dynasty as tributes from Tibet or as gifts from the Grand Lamas to the Imperial Court in Peking."

Clearly at that time it was the prevailing belief in China that the Shih Tzu were of Tibetan origin. "Dr. C. Walter Young in his monograph on *Some Canine Breeds of Asia* mentions that there is much evidence to 'support the claim that the shock-headed variety of small dog so commonly seen in Peiping are Tibetan in origin' " . . . This quote was taken from the preface of Madame Lu's *The Lhassa Lion Dogs*, originally published by the Peking Kennel Club in the mid-1930's.

From his experiences with life in the Peking palace some twenty years previously Colonel Valentine Burkhardt reached a similar conclusion. First visiting the Chinese capital in 1913, in his *Chinese Creeds and Customs* Colonel Burkhardt describes "the small dogs" which he found to be "popular" there. These are classified as the native Pekingese, the Chinese Pug, and "the Tibetan, always referred to as the 'Lion' or shih-tze kou." (Kou means Dog, Shih-Tze, or Shih Tzu, Lion).

The same opinion regarding the Shih Tzu's origin is found in articles about the breed which appeared in the Chinese English-language press. At this time the breed was just becoming known to the western world.

Those interested in historical references may consult the February, 1933, issue of the *China Journal* of Shanghai or the May, 1934, issue of the same publication, both of which are on file at the New York Public Library. On page 7 of the May, 17, 1936, issue of the *Peiping Chronicle*, and in the May, 1937, issue of the *North China Star of Tient-*

sin you will find additional information. The latter two publications can be found in the Library of Congress in Washington, D.C.

Reverend Easton was fortunate enough to spend time in Peking prior to, during and after the upheaval of the country, and he still cherishes an undying love for this land and its heritage. Late in 1948, while pastor of the Peking Union Church, an interdenominational body attended by English-speaking Protestants of many nationalities, the near approach of the Red Army made his position highly precarious.

The Secretary of the Peiping Chancery of the Netherlands Embassy in China, like many western diplomats an active member of the congregation, was anxious that Reverend Easton should not have to desert the English-speaking community at such a critical time. He made a generous offer which provided Reverend Easton with considerable security and some measure of diplomatic status. Reverend Easton still treasures the official document, written in English and Chinese and bearing the Embassy seal, which certified that he was "in the service of the Netherlands Government and as such included in the Administrative Staff of the Netherlands in China."

His responsibility was to take charge of one of the two Netherlands Embassy "compounds" in Peking, holding the Communists back at the gate, if necessary, on the grounds that the embassy was diplomatic property. For this service Reverend Easton received a nominal salary, free housing, light, heat and water. Also included were the services of a watch-dog, of uncertain origin, for which the Netherlands government granted a feeding allowance.

Since his presence on the Dutch compound was of little importance until the Red Army took over the city, to augment his finances during the six-week siege of Peking he worked by day for an American medical committee. His responsibility was to distribute supplies to the various city hospitals in order to prevent the supplies from falling into the wrong hands.

In addition, he was invited to look after the German Lutheran community, at that time left without a pastor.

For six weeks he lived in China with a British passport, maintaining a vast variety of international contacts, driving by day in a jeep flying the Stars and Stripes, sleeping by night under the Dutch tri-color, and caring for a German congregation on the side! Although his American post was of limited duration, he remained at his Dutch one for seven months after the arrival of the Communist troops. Such experiences are not readily forgotten.

So far as we know, a British diplomat who was a member of Reverend Easton's congregation is thought to have been the last person to take some of Mr. Koehn's dogs from Peking in October or November, 1948. He took a male and a female with him when he left for Hong Kong, but we have little detailed recollection of this pair except that they were probably golden and small. The only memory that Reverend Easton holds of them is of two little creatures gamboling together on the living room carpet and of picking them both up together with the greatest of ease. After that, all trace of them is lost. Mr. Koehn probably bred these dogs about a year before the Communist take-over of Peking in January, 1949*. A Shih Tzu named Wuffles was acquired by a British couple in nearby Tientsin. They took him home to England when they left North China by air immediately prior to the advance of the Red Army.

* "Peking" means "Northern Capital," the historic name of the city and that which is in use today. For a brief period between 1928 and 1949, when the capital was moved by the Nationalist Government to "Nanking" or "Southern Capital," the name of Peking was officially changed to "Peiping" or "Northern Peace."

In this book the names Peiping and Peking are used interchangeably, as was the popular custom from 1928 to 1949.

The Rev. D. Allan Easton is shown with a Chumulari puppy and an embroidered silk robe brought home with them after their stay in Tibet. The Chumulari kennels are now located in Gardiner, New York.

19

Mai-Ting and Wuffles with their daughter Pui-Yao, a black and white. Their names can be found in many pedigrees of the best English and American specimens of the breed. During their quarantine their hair was cut off, which accounts for the lack of top knot!

Described as "a most beautiful camel-colored Shih Tzu dog" with "a beautiful full coat," Wuffles was accidentally killed by a truck in early 1953, aged only four. Fortunately, he was not without progeny.

Wuffles fathered a black and white female puppy in October, 1950, through Mai Ting, an expatriate bitch whose high quality was confirmed by the British Consul General and another leading British official with extensive knowledge of Tibet and China. Through this single offspring of a single mating, Wuffles' and Mai Ting's lineage was carried on. A bitch called Jigme Jemima of Lhakang, the great, great grand-daughter of the pair, was said to have closely resembled her distinguished grandmother, Mai Ting. She became an honored member of Rev. Eastons's family after being exported from England where she was whelped in 1965. Jigme was personally selected for export by Mrs. L.G. Widdrington, leading English authority on the breed.

Mai Ting, like Wuffles, had been forced into expatriation when the Red armies invaded her homeland. The worth of this Shih Tzu from Shanghai was validated in many quarters, though her breeder was unknown. Information about the background of this little puppy, presented as a surprise gift to some British Consulate children in the summer of 1948 by their Chinese chauffeur, was not available except for the assurance that she came from the house of a "number one" Chinese family in Shanghai. The expression "number one" was used by Chinese servants to express unqualified approval. It probably made reference to a highly placed Chinese family that may well have been compelled to flee the city at that time.

A year later, in April, 1949, Mai Ting had been taken to Hong Kong en route to England via a Royal Naval vessel dispatched to evacuate citizens of the United Kingdom in the face of growing Communist threats. Though such passage constituted a unique honor for a dog and required special permission from the ship's captain, still it was not unfitting for an animal that may well have been the last native-born representative of this royal breed. She was shipped in more orthodox fashion from Hong Kong to England, where, after a three-year stay at the British Embassy in Cyprus, she finally died, August, 1962 at the ripe old age of 14½.

Another bitch is reported to have been imported into England from China in 1952, but so far we have not been able to trace any detailed reference to this story. Possibly, she originated in Taiwan or Hong Kong, as by that time it seems unlikely that it would have been possible to take dogs out of mainland China. In this regard, we may be mistaken, however, and we are still hoping for more extensive information.

Mrs. Charlotte Kauffmann's daughters pose with Leidza, and in the basket are Aidzo and over him, Schauder. This photograph was taken at the Danish Embassy in Oslo, Norway, in 1938. This charming picture was featured in the Norwegian magazine *Alt Om Hunden* in November 1976.

Mrs. Charlotte Kauffman with her black and white Shih Tzu Schauder and the gold and white Leidza. These two dogs, the first to arrive in Norway, were originally registered as Lhassa Terriers in 1940. Mrs. Kauffman was one of the pioneer breeder-owners in that country.

These last imports from China are of particular interest since the breed must be presumed to be extinct in that country today. This presumption is strengthened by a letter dated July 1, 1966, written by the Honorary Secretary of the Hong Kong Kennel Club. Published in the British Magazine, *Shih Tzu News,* in December of the same year, this letter expresses interest in securing Shih Tzu from the West, both "pet and exhibition type," for members who apparently could not find them in Asia.

EARLIER SHIH TZU EXPORTS FROM CHINA

Of course, the Shih Tzu had reached the West some twenty-five years before the Communist Revolution, a few having been brought to Great Britain, Ireland and to Scandinavia during the early 1930's, others following to Great Britain some years later.

The Scandinavian imports were of particular interest, being brought home by Mrs. Henrik Kauffman, wife of the Danish Minister to China who was later his country's Ambassador in London and Washington. Since the Kauffmans were transferred from Peking to the Danish Legation in Oslo, the three Shih Tzu were registered with the Norwegian Kennel Club, a fact ascertained from a letter written by Mr. Turid Moen, Secretary of the Norwegian Kennel Club, to Miss Astrid Jeppesen, and dated September 14, 1965.

An interesting story is attached to the Kauffmans' first acquisition of a Shih Tzu. It is said that Mrs. Kauffman saw some dogs in Peking which were to be burnt, possibly in connection with a funeral ceremony, although normally the burning of wood models made of paper or cypress twigs was regarded as sufficient to ensure that the real thing would be at the disposal of the deceased in the after-world.

Feeling sorry for the innocent victims, Mrs. Kauffman begged that their lives be spared, finally taking one home to the Danish Ministry with her. As a result, she took such a liking to the breed that two others of the same type were added to her household later, one from the Imperial Palace, the other from Shanghai.

Although strange, this vivid account comes to us from Mrs. Adele Heyerdahl of Oslo, who was given one of the Kauffmans' first Norwegian-born puppies and who remained an ardent Shih Tzu breeder until her death thirty years later. Since Mrs. Heyerdahl helped Mrs. Kauffman to register her imports with the Norwegian Kennel Club in 1934, her knowledge of their story seems likely to be accurate.

The Norwegian Kennel Club account runs: "The names of the dogs which were imported from Peking by the wife of Minister Kauffman are: 'Aidzo' 12180, 'Leidza' 12182, and 'Schauder' 12183.

" 'Aidzo' was born in Peking in March 1930; his father was 'Law-Hu,' his mother, 'Lun-Geni.'

'Leidza' was born in the Imperial Palace in Peking in May 1928; her father was 'Chintai,' her mother, 'Wu-hi.' 'Schauder' was born in Shanghai in December 1931; her father was 'Aidzo-Huh,' her mother 'Hu-Luh'."

Since missing numbers raise questions, it should be explained that NKC 12181 was Lingen, a male Shih Tzu bred by the Kauffmans in Norway. Although obviously some years younger, in the process of registration Lingen was given a lower number than two of the imports from which he was descended.

Quarantine restrictions kept the Kauffmans from taking their Shih Tzu to London, but one wonders whether or not they accompanied them to the United States. We do know that a puppy of this line was presented to Queen Elizabeth, then Duchess of York in 1933, and was later used at stud in England.

Followed later by his grandson, Ching, this dog quickly became one of the British royal family's favorite pets, accompanying them on their visits to their Scottish summer home and elsewhere on their travels.

"We called him Choo-Choo," King George VI once explained, "because when he first came to us he made noises exactly like a train!" The King would jokingly refer to Choo-Choo as "the animated dish-cloth" or "the hairy monster."

Keeping himself aloof from the five other dogs in the royal household, as though aware of his unique lineage, Choo-Choo enjoyed one very special privilege. Whenever the Queen took him up in her arms, as she frequently did, the self-assured Shih Tzu would solemnly nibble her corsage. "Without comment Princess Elizabeth would pick another sprig of jasmine, and with equal gravity Choo-Choo would chew that also—and once again only a cluster of stalks would adorn the Queen's jacket."

As might be expected, the association with royalty did much to draw favorable attention to the breed in the United Kingdom, particular notice being taken of the fact that the Shih Tzu had also enjoyed a privileged place at the Chinese court. The breed's Tibetan ancestry created widespread interest, especially when it was reported that in Tibet dogs of this type had been trained to turn prayer wheels for those unwilling to undertake this responsibility for themselves. Such wheels, or drums, were filled with written prayers which were believed to ascend to heaven with each revolution of the container. These could be turned by dogs in the same way as dogs were used to turn cooking-spits in old England.

Since he was getting old and blind and liable to

The Royal Family relaxing with their dogs at Windsor. The Queen Mother (right) holds Choo-Choo the Shih Tzu, who was bred by Mrs. Henrik Kauffmann.

be upset by gunfire, during World War II Choo-Choo was evacuated to the Queen's family home and birthplace which had been turned into a military hospital. A moving story is told of his reunion with his royal mistress (now the Queen Mother) when she paid a visit to the soldier invalids.

"The soldiers were gathered in the large drawing-room when the Queen came in. Choo-Choo was asleep on the hearthrug.

"Suddenly he sat up and sniffed the air. Then practically turning a somersault in his eagerness, he hurled himself across the room at the beloved mistress whom he had not seen for so many months.

"The Queen was taken off her guard. In a moment she was kneeling on the floor, with the little lion-dog throwing himself ecstatically upon her, pulling her hat and her hair in his eagerness.

"It was as if both had forgotten there were any others in the room. Then the Queen stood up and laughed apologetically as she picked Choo-Choo up and carried him around in her arms throughout the inspection."

An equally moving account is given of the reunion of the present Queen (then Princess Elizabeth) with the royal Shih Tzu after a forced separation during the war years.

While Shih Tzu fanciers take a natural pride in such stories of royal recognition, they can hardly be expected to be surprised. Somehow, it seems only right that the pride of the Peking court should similarly be honored at Buckingham Palace. American fanciers may be permitted to wonder when the little aristocrats will be permitted to grace the White House with their presence.

In our opinion, there are sound historical reasons for considering the Shih Tzu brought to Scandinavia as more representative specimens of the imperial lion dogs than those brought to England at the same time.

In those days the Chinese felt the British to be especially responsible for the "unequal treaties" forced on them thirty years previously that gave westerners a privileged position in China. Since they particularly resented the foreign troops stationed in their country, it seems unlikely that the Chinese would have made the best of the treasured little dogs available to the high-ranking British military officers who brought most of the first ones home to England. Indeed it may be strongly suspected that they would derive considerable satisfaction from misleading them.

For an explanation of Chinese feelings towards the British at this time we need only read *A History of the Far East in Modern Times,* by Harold Vinacke. Here it is described how the Chinese leaders "singled out England as the principal target against imperialism . . . The national propagandist needed concrete acts undertaken by particular states to focus attention on as evidence of imperialism . . . These were at this time supplied him by the British."

What this meant in practice is vividly described in *Chasmu Shih Tzu, International Newssheet, No. 4,* where an English traveller, Mrs. Audrey Fowler, describes how she was led to believe the Chinese would go to any length to prevent her Shih Tzu from leaving the country with her.

Handing over to the care of the ship's butcher two puppies she had acquired through the Countess d'Anjou and was taking home to England, Mrs. Fowler was "horrified" to be told that they would only live for a few days. When she asked why, she was told, "The Chinese always give their puppies powdered glass just before they leave as they do not want them to leave the country." "How thankful I was," Mrs. Fowler exclaimed, "I had not bought them from a Chinese."

A similar account of her experiences is given by the Countess d'Anjou who, as a Frenchwoman, also came from a nation which had its troops stationed in China and enjoyed the other special concessions. The Countess gives a colorful description of her difficulties in securing Shih Tzu during this period, and of the extraordinary obstacles placed in her way by the Chinese.

"At first I bought grown females and they had never had puppies," she reminisced sadly. "They had certainly done something to keep them from having them. The Lamas in the temples behind

One of the main courtyards in the Imperial Palace (the Forbidden City) in the heart of Peking. Within these walls only the nobility and the imperial eunuchs were permitted. Generation after generation of Shih Tzu shared in the life of the court. The banisters are marble; the lions at the foot of the steps are bronze.

Leidza, right and Aidzo, photographed in Norway in the early 1930's after their arrival from China. Leidza, described as a brown female, was born in the Peking Imperial Palace in May, 1928. Aidzo, black and white, was also born in Peking in March, 1930. Both were small. This photo was taken in the garden of Mr. and Mrs. Henrik Kauffman at the Swedish Ministry in Oslo, Norway.

Peking also bred them but refused to sell them."

Fortunately she secured the co-operation of the Paris-educated Princess Der Ling, who was in a unique position to help her, having been for two years a lady-in-waiting to the Empress Dowager.

We were particularly interested to discover the evidence regarding the Princess' French schooling in the *China Weekly Chronicle*, dated October 13, 1935, on page 22. The Countess' account of her difficulties in securing Shih Tzu, and of the help given to her by the Princess, will be found in her *Description of the Shih Tzu* written in Peking in 1938 and published in England in the booklet *Chasmu Shih Tzu*, edited by Mrs. Fowler, though no date is given.

No such Chinese ill-feeling placed difficulties in the way of the Danish diplomat and his wife, since they were in a wholly different situation. They represented a small country which had no troops stationed on Chinese soil, and which in 1928 had expressed readiness to accept the abolition of the privileged status of westerners in China. Under such circumstances it seems reasonable to suggest that the Chinese were far more likely to make the best dogs available to them.

There is an interesting piece of evidence to substantiate this suggestion. As early as 1927 we know that a British General and his wife discov-

ered that Shih Tzu in Peking "were not easy to find and some were very large." This was reported in the U.S. magazine *Shih Tzu News'* Christmas, 1966, issue. Aware that "the few surviving palace eunuchs were supposed to have some," but apparently never being permitted to see any of them, the English couple finally secured one of their two dogs from a French doctor who was returning home.

We have not been able to find any reference to the source from which the other dog was acquired, but there is nothing to suggest that either of them came from the palace, a fact which would hardly have been overlooked when their story subsequently came to be written. What is stressed is that the two Shih Tzu were secured only with difficulty and after the most painstaking study of specimens found with White Russian, French and other breeders of unspecified nationality in Peking.

For those readers wishing to delve further into this aspect, see the English magazine, *Dog World*, of September 25, 1959, page 1751, an article also reproduced in condensed form in the American *Dog World* magazine of November, 1967, page 111, and in the American *Shih Tzu News* magazine, December, 1966, on page 12.

A very few years later the Danish diplomat and

24

his wife secured two small Peking-born Shih Tzu, one of them, named Leidza and subsequently bearing the Norwegian Kennel Club No. 12182, being the only known palace-born Shih Tzu to reach the West.

Leidza was born in the Peking Palace in May, 1928, thus proving conclusively that breeding was still continuing there at the time when the British couple were having such great difficulty in finding good Shih Tzu anywhere in the city. Proof of Leidza's place and date of birth is to be found in the aforementioned letter to Miss Jeppesen from Mr. Turid Moen, Secretary of the Norwegian Kennel Club.

Leidza's great-great-great grandson has been in the Eastons' possession, having inherited the magnificent coat which the early Scandinavian imports have bequeathed to so many of their descendants. Bred for the Eastons in Germany, Chumulari Ying-Ying won his Canadian Championship in August, 1967, and—although whelped only in late January, 1966—has made a big name for himself in his adopted homeland. Also in the direct line from Leidza is Ch. Ying-Ying's mother, Ch. Tangra v. Tschomo-Lungma, who is also in the Eastons' possession now. Retired from the show ring, she is making a highly successful career in obedience training. Tangra was sent to the Eastons on the personal recommendation of Miss Astrid Jeppesen of Denmark, a leading European authority on the Shih Tzu.

Margaret Easton and her beloved American and Canadian Ch. Chumulari Ying Ying, the magnificent dog that did so much to establish the Shih Tzu breed in America.

Swiss, Czechoslovakian and Canadian Ch. Tangra v. Tschomo-Lungma, the first triple champion in North America in our breed. Bred in West Germany by Mrs. Erika Geusendam, Tangra was imported in 1966 by Rev. and Mrs. D. Allan Easton. Tangra was personally selected by Astrid Jeppesen of the Bjorneholms Shih Tzu in Denmark. At the 1965 FCI World Show in Brno, Czechoslovakia, Tangra was declared Best of Breed and awarded the title "World Winner" by Madame Nizet de Leemans, one of the best-known Toy judges in Europe and president of the Standards Commission of the Federation Cynologique Internationale.

The Empress Dowager of China, seated, surrounded by her attendants. The imperial eunuch appears in center background.

A Swiss, Czechoslovakian, and Canadian champion, Tangra had already become famous before leaving Europe. She was awarded the title "World Winner" at the 1965 Brno Show in Czechoslovakia, the largest World Show for dogs since World War II and the first major one behind the Iron Curtain. This show was arranged by the Federation Cynologique Internationale, a Brussels-based international organization uniting the different national kennel clubs in continental Europe.

Importing Tangra in whelp, Rev. Easton wrote, "Now thousands of miles from her lovely ancestral home in Peking, Ch. Tangra brings with her a royal heritage, full of international overtones, romantic, exciting and mysterious, tragic in the light of recent events, but not without hope as she helps to introduce her breed to the new world across the seas." Tangra crossed the Atlantic in early 1966 and her son, Chumulari Ying-Ying was born a few weeks after her arrival.

Sometimes we like to picture the scene in Peking Palace some forty years ago, as the surviving eunuchs tried to breed the finest lion dogs possible while their accustomed way of life ebbed to its close. When they gave their treasured Leidza to the distinguished visitors from far-off Denmark, did they fully understand that she would be taken away to make her home in a strange land among

strange people? How proud they would be if they could see her descendants today, most especially the gorgeous American and Canadian Champion Chumulari Ying-Ying, who has brought to the North American show rings so much of the charm and dignity of imperial China.

LAST DAYS OF PALACE BREEDING

Some charming accounts of the palace dogs are given by Miss Katherine Carl, an American artist commissioned to paint the Empress Dowager's portrait in 1903. Miss Carl is said to be the first westerner to stay at the Peking court.

She gives a very moving account of her discovery of a number of small tombstones "in a beautiful shady corner, near the stables" that marked the last resting places of the favorite dogs and horses of one of the Imperial Princes. "Each stone had an inscription with a name, and extolled the virtues of the favorite whose bones lay beneath it."

"The dogs at the Palace are kept in a beautiful pavilion with marble floors," Miss Carl wrote. "They have silken cushions to sleep on, and special eunuchs to attend them. They are taken for daily outdoor exercise and given their baths with regularity."

According to this talented artist, a very close

26

relationship existed between the royal mistress and her dogs, which were kept apart from all others. They all obeyed her implicitly, while she was possessive toward them in a very tender way.

"The day we first met the dogs in the garden was the first time I had seen them," Katherine Carl writes. "They rushed up to Her Majesty, not paying the slightest attention to anyone else. She patted their heads and caressed and spoke to each of her favorites. After a while they seemed to notice that a stranger was present, and they bounded over to me ... I bent down to caress them, and forgot my surrounding in my pleasure at seeing and fondling these beautiful creatures.

"I glanced up, presently, never dreaming Her Majesty had been paying any attention to me, as I was standing at a little distance behind her, and I saw on her face the first sign of displeasure I had noticed there. It seems her dogs never noticed anyone but herself, and she appeared not to like her pets being so friendly with a stranger at first sight.

"Noticing this, I immediately ceased fondling them, and they were presently sent away. It was but a momentary shadow that passed over her face, and I quite understand the feeling. One does not like to see one's pets too friendly with strangers, and I had been tactless in trying to make friends with them at once.

"A few days later, on another of our walks, some young puppies were brought to be shown the Empress Dowager. She caressed the mother and examined critically the points of the puppies. Then she called me up to show them to me, asking which I liked best. I tried not to evince too much interest in them this time, but she called my attention to their fine points and insisted upon my taking each of them up. She seemed to be ashamed of her slight displeasure of the day before, and to wish to compensate for it."

Later a eunuch brought a little dog to Miss Carl, placing it in her arms and saying that Her Majesty had ordered that it should be presented to her from the royal kennel. The Empress told Miss Carl to call the dog "Me-lah" (Golden Amber), from the color of his spots.

"Her Majesty and the Princesses were all much amused at the way he followed me around, not leaving my side for an instant, nor paying any attention to their frequent efforts to attract his attention," Miss Carl recounts proudly. "From that day, he became my constant companion and faithful friend."

According to Miss Carl, the Empress Dowager had "some magnificent specimens of Pekingese pugs and a sort of Skye Terrier." We can be sure that the "sort of Skye Terrier" was actually Shih Tzu, particularly when we remember that Skyes were considerably smaller in those early times.

"The Empress Dowager has dozens of these pets," Miss Carl continues, "but she has favorites among them, and two are privileged characters. One of these is of the Skye variety, and is most intelligent and clever at tricks. Among other tricks, he will lie as if dead at Her Majesty's command, and never move until she tells him to, no matter how many others may speak to him."

"Her other favorite she loves for his beauty. He is a splendid fawn-colored Pekingese pug, with large pale-brown, liquid eyes. He is devoted to her, and she is very fond of him, but as he was not easily taught, even as a puppy, she called him 'Shadza' (fool)."

The puppy given to Miss Carl is described as "a Pekingese pug," so it was not a Shih Tzu. Does this mean that the Shih Tzu were too precious to give away? If that was the case, it would bear out the contention of Mr. Pinkham who is emphatic that he frequently heard the Princess Der Ling say that the shaggy little Shih Tzu Kou were the most treasured of the royal dogs.

Oddly enough, the Empress Dowager had a strong dislike for cats. Although some of the eunuchs had some very fine specimens, they had to be kept carefully out of sight of the royal eyes!

Another noteworthy recipient of royal dogs was Mrs. Sarah Pike Conger, wife of Major E.H. Conger, American Minister to China during and after the Boxer Rising of 1900. In a letter to her daughter Laura, written in the American Legation, Peking, and dated March 25, 1902, Mrs. Conger describes a luncheon to which she was invited by some of the court princesses. Also invited were ten other American ladies and Mrs. Uchida, wife of the Japanese Minister to China.

"We made arrangements for all to go together and went in chairs, carts, and on ponies. There were six chairs with eight bearers each, seven carts with their escorts, and each lady had two or three outriders and two or three amahs. We had nearly one hundred servants, but we were obliged to have them in order to conform to Chinese custom.

"The Princesses met us in the court and welcomed us most graciously. Each took one of us by the hand, escorted us into the house, and tea was served. We had not been there long before two eunuchs entered, each with a pretty new basket with a red satin pad upon which was a beautiful little black dog. Around the neck of each was a rich collar of gold bells, tassels, and other ornaments in a most fanciful arrangement. There

Lung-Fu-Ssu, begging, was one of the first three Shih Tzu known to have been brought to Europe from Peking to Ireland in 1930 by Miss E. M. Hutchins. Lung-Fu-Ssu was black and white and described as having a "coarse coat with an inclination to waviness. Head possibly bigger than the other two original imports, but a heavier dog. Tail did not curl well." This photo, taken at the 1933 Cheltenham show in England, appeared in the famous *Hutchinson's Popular Illustrated Dog Encyclopedia*.

was also, for each dog, a gold-mounted harness with a long silk cord and gold hook.

"One little dog was placed in my lap and the other in Mrs. Uchida's and we were told that the Empress Dowager had sent them to us. I have been wanting one of these dogs and to think of its coming in this way I was delighted. He is a bright little fellow, full of life, not at all afraid, and he now rules the household."

Later, Mrs. Conger was given another dog by the Empress Dowager and she describes what a warm welcome the two little dogs gave her and Major Conger when they returned to the Legation in Peking after a lengthy official trip to the Philippines and Japan. Called Lao Hu and Mo Moi Yu, these dogs travelled with the Congers when they left Peking for good in April, 1905, after seven years in charge of the U.S. Legation. At that time Major Conger became U.S. Ambassador to Mexico.

We have traced present day descendants of Major and Mrs. Conger who are justifiably proud of their unique accomplishments, but among the family heirlooms no photographs or items of information regarding their dogs has yet been found. Some day we hope something will turn up. In the meantime, we can only speculate what type of dogs these were. Although we do not know the color of Mrs. Conger's second dog, it is probably significant that the first one was black. It may well be that the old Empress Dowager was not very

fond of that color and was not reluctant to give them away. When we read of the lengths to which she would go to ensure that her private train was painted yellow, locomotive, coaches, and all, we can be confident that her dogs of imperial gold occupied a very special place in her heart right up to the day of her death on November 15, 1908.

Describing court life eight years later, as the princes and attendant eunuchs desperately strove to maintain a semblance of the old regime, a sympathetic observer, Juliet Bredon, calls it a "make-believe kingdom, curious and infinitely pathetic, too, this last stronghold of mystery in once mysterious Peking!"

Shih Tzu and other palace dogs continued to be bred during this twilight period, we are told, but the imperial eunuchs were largely left to their own devices as—unlike the old Empress Dowager—their lonely young master was not greatly interested. He is said to have abhorred the court pets on account of "the mess they made," and to have been only too happy to give them away to anyone. Under such circumstances, mating of the royal dogs was "rather haphazard."

In these early days, we are told, a Shih Tzu came into the possession of a British military attache at a time when dogs were excluded from the Legation for fear of rabies. An exception was quickly made in this case, however, the little dog being officially classified as a cat!

An Italian diplomat, Daniele Vare, paints an

amusing picture of his visit to the Forbidden City, as the Imperial Palace was called, on the day after it first became open to the public. Accompanied by their Fox Terrier, Tricksy, he and his Scottish-born wife joined a large number of Chinese in strolling around and "gaping" at precincts which previously had been the jealously guarded preserve of the privileged few.

"Some eunuchs watched us from the adjoining pavilions," Vare writes. "The fact that the 'stupid people' can now penetrate into the courts of the palace must seem to them a sign of impending doom. One of the eunuchs had a little dog with him, a Pekingese. It seemed pleased to see Tricksy even though she does belong to a foreign devil."

The Italian writer adds thoughtfully that he supposed his Fox Terrier, brought with him from Europe, to have been the first western dog ever to have smelt the smells of the Forbidden City!

Although thoroughly familiar with life in Peking in 1912 and for some years after, it is interesting to note that Vare makes no mention of the little Shih Tzu Kous with their Tibetan history. Were they still kept very much in the background, being the most precious of the Imperial Lion Dogs? To this we may never know the answer and it seems likely to remain an open question, although we have not yet heard any alternative explanation of the fact that they appear to have been so late in becoming known to the western world.

Up until 1923 there are said to have been well over 1000 eunuchs employed in the palace, but in that year most were summarily dismissed. This was due to a disastrous fire for which the eunuchs were believed to have been responsible in order to cover their large-scale theft of palace treasures.

Only about fifty were allowed to stay because the three remaining dowager consorts, "when they learned that their indispensable and more or less faithful eunuchs would no longer be there to anticipate every want and obey their lightest whispers, were filled with woe and dismay." Many more were probably allowed to return later, especially the old and crippled who knew no other home.

One of the dowagers died in the palace not long after and the remaining two were turned out on November 21, 1924, some days before the flight of the young Emperor to Tientsin. A number of eunuchs must have remained, however, doubtless having nowhere else to go, and Lion Dog breeding clearly continued in some measure for several years. Regarding this we have been able to get little information apart from the fact that Leidza was whelped in the Peking Palace in May,

1928—and that in itself is an important milestone in the history of the breed.

Monsieur Graeffe, Belgian Ambassador in Peking in the 1930s, is said to have been able to acquire six Shih Tzu descended from a pair bred in the palace in the 1920s, by name Lize and Kwanine. He was well thought of because he represented a small nation which had taken a lead in the move to abolish the privileged status of westerners in China.

Monsieur Graeffe was transferred to Iran and took his Shih Tzu with him to the Belgian Embassy in Teheran where, in 1940, he gave four male puppies to Mrs. Sheila Bode. One of these puppies was run over by a car in Teheran, another died of pneumonia at an early age. The two survivors lived much longer, one dying while undergoing an operation in Paris in 1949 or 1950, the other of a heart attack in Brussels in 1954.

Presumably because of quarantine difficulties, none of these dogs accompanied Mrs. Bode when

This 1948 import from China, Shebo Schunde of Hungjao, was a black dog bred by Major-General A. Telfer-Smollett and owned by Mrs. Sheila Bode. A son of Ishuh Tzu, Shebo was said to be "quite small and with a very arrogant carriage." When Shebo was bred to a liver and white, Mao-Mao of Lhakang, they produced the first solid gold and apricot-colored puppies bred in England.

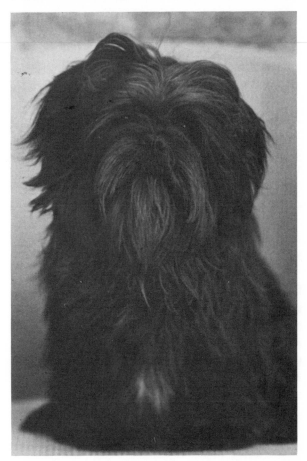

she returned to England in 1944 or 1945. She became an ardent fancier of the smaller type of Shih Tzu and a founder of the Manchu Shih Tzu Society.

We later learned from Mrs. Bode, who then resided in Spain, that these four puppies were the offspring of her Pekingese bitch bred to one of Madame Graeffe's Shih Tzu. This step was taken because the Belgian Ambassador's only bitch had died of distemper and there were no other Shih Tzu bitches available in wartime Teheran.

The four male puppies resulted from this mating. Mrs. Bode writes, "When adult they resembled their father—the only Peke points being a somewhat shorter nose and diminutive size. They had the profuse Shih Tzu coats and temperament."

When Mrs. Bode had to return to England suddenly in 1944, owing to her husband's illness, she left the two surviving dogs with Madame Graeffe, who took them to Europe after the end of the war, "when dogs were allowed to travel." One was given to a friend of Madame Graeffe's in Paris, the other to a friend in Switzerland. This explains the fate of the line of Shih Tzu brought out of Peking by Madame Graeffe.

THE FIRST IMPORTS TO THE BRITISH ISLES

In expressing the opinion that the Scandinavian imports were nearer to the direct imperial line, we cannot emphasize too strongly that we are in no sense criticizing those who brought the first Shih Tzu to the British Isles at approximately the same time. Unquestionably, these early English and Irish fanciers acted in accordance with the best knowledge available to them and went to very great trouble to secure the finest possible specimens of the breed. It was most certainly no fault of theirs if it be true that political circumstances closed doors for them which were readily opened to the Danish couple—as is clearly suggested by the fact that the latter alone were able to bring home a palace-born Shih Tzu.

An interesting photograph of these pioneers from England and Ireland with their dogs, as they appeared at the Cheltenham Show in 1933, is to be found in Hutchinson's *"Popular and Illustrated Dog Encyclopedia," Volume II,* page 1137. At that time the Shih Tzu were mistakenly described as Apsos in England, the distinction between the two breeds not being made until the following year.

Lack of detail in the photograph makes it impossible to get an altogether clear picture of the dogs, but they would appear to be delightfully characteristic "shaggy mops" and it is small wonder that they seem to have made a highly favorable impression. Of the six Shih Tzu portrayed, four show distinctly bowed fore-legs, a feature which would seem to distinguish them from those in the Scandinavian line. Although not identified in the caption, standing behind the dogs are the importers, General Sir Douglas and Lady Brownrigg of England and Miss E.M. Hutchins of Ireland.

In the same volume other similarly attractive photographs of these first Shih Tzu in the British Isles appear on pages 1134, 1143 and 1146. In one instance, as in an early photograph of the Scandinavian imports, a Shih Tzu is sitting up on its hindquarters in that fascinating pose which comes so naturally to the breed, and which they must have inherited from their palace ancestors.

In their *Pekingese Scrapbook,* Elsa and Ellic Howe refer to this in the chapter headed *The Princess Der Ling at the Royal Kennels.* Here the Princess is quoted as describing how, on command from the eunuch in charge, "all the dogs sat on their haunches and waited . . . Of course, some of them were awkward and had to keep trying, and the eunuch waited until all were erect, when he spoke sharply again: 'Ga Leo Fo Yea, bai bai!' which meant something like 'give greetings to Her Majesty, the Old Buddha!' The dogs barked and waved their front feet as though waving them at Her Majesty."

In the British *Kennel Gazette* of March, 1934, an illuminating glimpse is given of the problem confronting judges in England at the time when it was gradually coming to be realized that the Shih Tzu was not the same as the Apso and should be judged separately.

Reporting on his experiences with the "Apsos, Tibetan Terriers and Spaniels" at Crufts in 1934, Mr. G. Hayes writes, "One white dog which took my fancy in the ring very much at first glance, I could not place on examination. The round eye, domed head and flat face, also the tail, made it of different type altogether, the outlook being nearer to that of the Japanese Spaniel or Pekingese. Though I did not know this at the time, I ascertained afterward this dog had been bred from a dog and bitch imported from China."

Later that year, it was ruled by the Tibetan Breeds Association that the dogs from China were not Apsos. After consultation with Mr. Croxton Smith, then Chairman of the Kennel Club, the name Shih Tzu was selected for them. The sponsoring body for the separate breed was first called the Shih Tzu (Tibetan Lion Dog) Club, but in

Importers of the first three Shih Tzu in Britain are pictured at the 1933 Cheltenham show. Left to right: Lady Brownrigg with Hibou, dog, Yangtse and Shu-Ssa, bitches; Miss Hutchins of Ireland with Lung-Fu-Ssu, bitch, and Tang, dog; General Sir Douglas Brownrigg with Hzu-Hsi; and Miss Wild with a Lhasa Apso.

1935 the name was shortened to the Shih Tzu Club.

At a meeting of the General Committee of the British Kennel Club on May 1, 1934, it had already been decided that "dogs must be registered under the heading of Any Other Variety, Shih Tzu, and that those now registered as Apso could be altered without charge." Six years later, at a meeting held on May 7, 1940, a separate register was granted to the breed which was then placed on the official list of breeds and made eligible for championship certificates.

In those early days, we are told, the appearance of the new breed aroused much interest and curiosity, newspaper reporters and photographers surrounding them whenever they were shown. First to judge a Shih Tzu in the British Isles was Mr. Jimmy Garrow who officiated at the Scottish show where the breed made its debut. Remembering the size and type of the original imports, to the end of his life Mr. Garrow put them up over the larger offspring which were soon to become increasingly evident on the British scene.

Two other especially noteworthy Shih Tzu were brought home in 1937 by an Englishwoman who visited Peking briefly in the course of an extensive world tour. Both bitches, these dogs were undoubtedly small in size. The English *Our Dogs* in the Christmas, 1961, issue carried an advertisement which stressed that their "weight, when fully grown," was 12 pounds. So far as we have yet been able to discover, this is one of the clearest pieces of documentary evidence we have regarding the weight of the early Shih Tzu imports to the British Isles.

Although one appears to have been bred by Miss Frances Bieber, an American expert on Chinese folklore and on the sacred lion of Buddha, both these little Shih Tzu evidently came from the Countess d'Anjou's stock. They are described as being respectively "golden and white," and "honey" in color.

A photograph of the two puppies on board the liner *Empress of Britain,* en route to England via Canada and the United States, suggests that both were liberally marked with white. This advertisement in the English *Dog World Annual* of December, 1962, page 31, states that the two were

Top left:
Judy Merrill, a pre-Pearl Harbor "Army brat" and traveller in Asia, is another fancier to which our breed owes so much. This photograph was taken in Nara, Japan, in 1938.

Top right:
Mrs. R. Laurenz with her two Lhassa Terriers, Mei Mei, the bitch on the left, and Mo'er, dog, on the left. Mo'er was the First Prize winner at the 1930 China Kennel Club Show in Shanghai. These Lhassa Terriers were classified as "Tibetan Poodles." This photograph appeared in an August, 1930 issue of the *China Chronicle*.

Left:
One of the pioneer breeders in Norway, Mrs. Klaveness is shown at the Norwegian Kennel Club's show at Oslo, in June, 1934. These Shih Tzu include her own Lingen, and three owned by Mrs. Charlotte Kauffmann: Leidza, a bitch, Aidzo, a dog, and Schauder, a bitch. They were the first Shih Tzu in that country.

"purchased in Peking for the Countess d'Anjou," the word "for" presumably being a printer's slip in place of "from." In any event, the Peking Kennel Club registration certificates indicate that the dam of one was owned by the Countess, the dam of the other by Miss Bieber.

Since the Countess d'Anjou was assisted by the Princess Der Ling in the selection of her stock, enabling her to overcome the obstacles placed in the way of other western fanciers by the Chinese, we may be quite sure that these two little bitches were worthy representatives of the imperial Shih Tzu at its very best. That neither of them ever had any puppies must be a matter of deep regret to all western lovers of the breed.

Although we have not yet been able to trace the reference, we are reliably informed that a Peking newspaper—almost certainly the English language *Peiping Chronicle*—carried a glowing account of the excitement which these two little Shih Tzu aroused when they were first seen in England.

According to the information we have received, and we have every reason to believe it to be accurate, under the heading *Today's Lions*, the report ran:

"The Lhassa (sic) Lion or 'Shih Tzu' is a breed very little known in Europe and America. They have been shown in London and New York for the last few years and have created a great deal of interest. Countess d'Anjou has been breeding these dog in Peking for the last three years and has had quite a success with them. Two of her dogs were taken to England last year by Mrs. Fowler of Yew Tree House, Winchelsea, Sussex, and shown at Crufts Dog Show in February (1938).

"Mrs. Fowler writes that they created quite a sensation. The other dogs shown in London were much larger and mostly black and white—very few of the honey-colored ones. It is interesting to know that the certificates issued by the Peking Kennel Club were accepted at Crufts, and that the Lhasa Lions bred here [in Peking] more than held their own with those bred in England."

The above bracketed explanations are by the authors.

Presumably based on information sent by the English importer in a letter to someone in Peking, the article is said to have been accompanied by two photographs. One showed the Countess with a pale-colored Shih Tzu in one hand and a cup in the other, smiling gaily; the other showed two heavily coated Shih Tzu, apparently light in color with dark ear-tips.

These were not the two bitches brought to England, we understand, but others belonging to

Toddie in the front, with Ting-a-Ling and Galloping, representing very early imports abroad. Galloping, who was born in 1938, had as a sire the early arrival, Aidzo, and his dam was Ting-a-Ling.

the Countess in Peking. To illustrate the article, the Chinese newspaper obviously had to use whatever photographs it had on file. We have not yet seen them ourselves, but we eagerly look forward to finding them among the other fascinating material still hidden on microfilm in the library.

As has already been suggested, in our opinion the clue to the whole situation lies in the fact that the Princess Der Ling was a graduate of the Sacred Heart School in Paris, her father having represented the old Chinese Empire in several different western countries. Further details will be found in the *China Weekly Chronicle*, October 13, 1935, and the whole story makes fascinating reading, most especially when we are told that the opportunity of entering Vassar College in the United States appealed to the young princess more strongly than that of becoming one of the ladies-in-waiting to the Empress Dowager. In spite of her familiarity with European ways, in this regard she was overruled by her father, who counselled her to accept without question the commands of the Empress.

Wholly unique for one who was later to become an important attendant at the Manchu Court, this educational background explains the close friendship which appears to have sprung up between the Princess and the Countess d'Anjou. They must have had much in common, not least being a shared love for the French capital. This friendship, in turn, opened doors for the Countess which had previously been closed to her, secured answers to questions which had hitherto been politely evaded and made it possible for her to overcome the difficulties placed in her path as she strove to obtain the best possible breeding stock.

On board the steamship Empress of Britain in March, 1937, were Niu San, bred by the Countess d'Anjou and Fu Tzu, bred by Miss Bieber. Both these Shih Tzu were registered with the Peking Kennel Club and acquired by Mrs. Audrey Fowler while visiting Peking. Unfortunately, neither was ever bred.

Zizi's King Po, owned by Baronesse van Panthaleon van Eck-Klasing in the Netherlands. King Po poses with an oriental lion dog owned by the Baronesse.

Exquisite watercolor of our oriental breed depicted in a typical Chinese mandarin setting. The lovely painting was done by Mrs. Annette Mellinger, of the World-Vu Kennels, Matawan, New Jersey.

The Countess could have selected no better advisor, for the Princess had made it clear that her knowledge of the royal dogs was derived from the mouth of the Empress Dowager herself. Describing how she was first introduced to the personal pets of the old ruler, the former lady-in-waiting explained, "we went around the Ten Thousand Years Hill to the kennels, which were near the terrace where silk was dried in the sun, and on the way the Empress Dowager told me something about the dogs we were to see."

Apparently, the dogs were very well trained by the attendant eunuchs and were "plainly very happy to see Her Majesty," a fact which naturally delighted the old woman. What appears to have struck the young Princess most were the dog's intelligent eyes, fixed on their Royal Mistress. "One could not see all of the eyes, because of the long hair, but when the sun shone on them they were like tiny lights peering through the darkness."

Regrettably, the Countess died in 1965 at her daughter's home in Canada. Details of her death were reported on the front page of the British *Shih Tzu News* in February, 1966, and co-author Easton paid great tribute to her memory in the May, 1966, issue of *Popular Dogs* magazine in his Shih Tzu breed column. In June of that year there was also news of her passing in the *British Manchu Shih Tzu Society Newsletter*.

A letter dated September 19, 1968, from Stan Goldberg, a California Shih Tzu fancier, stated that the Princess, who was teaching at the University of California, had been hit by a car and killed "several years ago." Pathetically, the letter adds that the press report of the accident was "very small in a world that had long forgotten her and the grandeur of the court of China."

As we have discovered even more recently, however, the Princess is by no means wholly forgotten. Among those who remember her with gratitude and affection is Mr. Ed Pinkham, a Shih Tzu fancier from Rhode Island, who tells us that he followed her eagerly when she lectured in New England some forty years ago. Although it was a long time ago, Mr. Pinkham insists that he clearly recalls the Princess Der Ling emphasizing more than once that the little Tibetan Shih Tzu Kou were the most precious of all the royal dogs. If this be so, we can be confident that she made sure that the best possible specimens were made available to her French friend when she returned to Peking after her lecture tour.

Acquired from the Countess d'Anjou in 1937, the two 12 pound bitches which took London by storm in the following year, must probably be classed among the finest specimens of the breed to have reached the shores of the United Kingdom by that time. In the light of their background in Peking and their link with the Princess, these Shih Tzu may well have fallen very little short of equalling in quality those brought home to Scandinavia from the palace by Mrs. Henrik Kauffman a few years earlier. It is by no means inconceivable that they were of similar high caliber.

Unfortunately, this unique little pair died without leaving issue. The importer, Mrs. Fowler, has written that she was too occupied to think of breeding puppies, due to the outbreak of war in 1939, and "then one was run over by an army lorry (truck) and the other too precious to mate." Had they only left descendants by a carefully selected sire of similar, or preferably of smaller, size (assuming such to have been available in England at the time) this pair of 12 pound bitches might well have exercised a decisive influence on the whole subsequent course of Shih Tzu history in the United Kingdom and beyond.

In a letter to Reverend Easton dated January 7, 1966, Mrs. Fowler, the importer of the two Shih Tzu concerned, wrote, "I brought these back, and when they came out of quarantine they weighed fourteen to sixteen pounds respectively." Obviously this is a lapse of memory, as evidenced by the emphatic statement in the Christmas issue of the English magazine Our Dogs five years earlier. The caption below the photograph of these two Shih Tzu read "weight when fully grown, 12 pounds."

While the mistake is understandable, it does illustrate sharply that the unaided human memory is subject to error after the passage of nearly thirty years. While great experiences do stick in our minds, details have a way of becoming blurred astonishingly quickly. Since undocumented recollections can lead to confusion regarding figures and dates, in such matters it is wise to rely only on such written evidence as is available.

Known Bloodlines From Which the Present-day Shih Tzu Descend

A. Scandinavian Imports

Aidzo (d)
Schauder (b)
Leidza (b)

All three were imported in 1932 by Mr. and Mrs. Henrik Kauffmann. Mr. Kauffmann was the Danish minister in Peking.

Whelped in May, 1928, Leidza is the only known palace-born Shih Tzu to reach the West.

B. United Kingdom and Irish Imports

Hibou (d)	1930	Imported from China by Lt. General Sir Douglas and Lady Brownrigg.
Shu-Ssa (b)	1930	ditto ditto
Lung-Fu-Ssu (d)	1930	Imported from China by Miss Hutchins of Ireland.
Tashi of Chouette (b)	1938	Imported from Canada by Rt. Hon. the Earl of Essex. Parents from China.
Ming (b)	1939	Imported from China by Lt. General Telfer-Smollett, Lord Lieutenant of Dumbartonshire, Scotland.
Ishuh Tzu (b)	1948	Imported from China by Lt. General Telfer-Smollett.
Wuffles (d)	1948	Imported from China by Mr. and Mrs. Fraser Buchanan.
Mai-Ting (b)	1949	Imported from China by Mr. and Mrs. Roland Morris.
Hsi-Li-Ya (b)	1952	Imported from China (Taiwan or Hong Kong?) by Mr. R.P. Dobson.

d = dog b = bitch

Wei-Honey Gold of Elfann, bred by Miss E. M. Evans of England, and imported into the U.S. by Rev. and Mrs. D. Allan Easton, in 1963. Honey is the mother of Chumulari Trari, and was sired by Si-Kians Tashi.

Chapter 2
THE SHIH TZU IN AMERICA

In an article in the September, 1961 issue of *Popular Dogs* magazine, Mr. Philip N. Price, first president of the Shih Tzu Club of America, wrote " . . . in the years prior to 1954 a number of pedigreed Shih Tzu were exported by the British breeders to the U.S., but since the breed was not recognized by the American Kennel Club, they were unregisterable and unshowable. It has been difficult to trace them." If it was almost impossible to trace the first Shih Tzu imports in the U.S. up until 1961, the intervening years have made it even more difficult!

From British records we do know that at least seven Shih Tzu were brought over from England before 1952. These seven imports include Dingling of the Mynd and Wuffy of the Mynd, two bitches bred by Mrs. Harold Eaden which are said to have come from England in 1938 and which undoubtedly travelled by sea. According to Mrs. Audrey Dadds, these dogs were the first English-bred Shih Tzu to enter this country. There is no reference to them in the first stud books and it seems likely that this line died out long before the day of American Kennel Club recognition in 1969.

If these two bitches were the first English Shih Tzu to cross over the Atlantic, they must also have been among the last to do so prior to the outbreak of World War II in 1939. The War represented a serious delay in the arrival and development of the breed in North America. We can assume they were among the last to travel by sea, because following the conclusion of hostilities in 1945 the growing use of air transportation made the shipping of dogs much easier and quicker. While the rapid growth in numbers of Shih Tzu imports can be directly related to the development of air transport, the fact that it is easy to import dogs in quantity has by no means always proved to be in the best interests of the breed.

The position of the early English imports was complicated by the fact that several of them—mistakenly or otherwise—were registered with the American Kennel Club as Lhasa Apso. Unlike the Shih Tzu, the Lhasa Apso was recognized at the time. Among others, whose names have not been verified, were Fardale Fu Ssi, Yah Shih of Shebo and Linyi of Lhakang, all three of which were registered as Shih Tzu in England but as Lhasa Apso in the United States!

According to one story, this was done deliberately by the importers who knew of no other way of getting them into the ring other than "representing them as Lhasa Apso and registering them as same." Another story has it that "a man in the registration department made an error and registered the Shih Tzu as Lhasa Apso." There had been similar confusion in England not long before, and as the two breeds, though very different, have much in common, either explanation is understandable and the first explanation not necessarily as deceptive as it might seem.

Being registered as Lhasa Apso, the dogs concerned were treated as Lhasa Apso in the United States and their subsequent history does not concern us here. Although we must say a few of the Apso fanciers protested strongly, the vast majority accepted the situation when convinced that it would inflict no lasting damage to their breed.

Perhaps the best commentary on this unusual incident was that of Mr. John A. Brownell, Assistant to the American Kennel Club Executive Vice President, who wrote some time later, on February 20, 1963: "When the American Kennel Club first started to register (the Lhasa Apso) there were no dogs of the breed with pedigrees issued by any organization in the world whose pedigrees would normally be acceptable to us. Each dog was registered on its own merits and, as with any breed in this situation, there were some among them that we might now wish we had never registered. Among these were three or four dogs which were registered by the Kennel Club in England as Shih Tzu, and those dogs have probably caused more unjustified talk in the breed than any others, although I don't believe there is any evidence that their influence on the quality of the breed would justify any such view."

The early setback resulted from the six dogs exported to the United States that were bred extensively as Lhasa Apso. As we have noted, they were actually Shih Tzu and registered as such in the country of their origin. However, we must recall that in their native land the Apso dogs were all under one classification, which is one of the reasons why the standards for these breeds are so precise today, since many of the newcomers to each breed can easily become confused.

This situation occurred in the late 1930's, when when Mr. William Patch, the son of a United States Commander at Pearl Harbor, purchased two long-haired dogs from the Holly Heath Kennels of Mrs. Harvey Hill in Shanghai. The dogs were represented as being two Lhasa Terriers. Named Ming Tai and Tai Ho, the two little dogs created much publicity and interest, and subsequently more dogs were imported from Mrs. Hill.

While negotiations for these imports were under way, Tai Ho whelped three bitch puppies (sired by a dog named Rags) while in quarantine in Hawaii. Rags happened to be Tai Ho's sire as well. Ming Tai and Tai Ho were littermates sired by Rags out of a bitch named Peggy. Another of the imports, named Shanghai, was sired by Rags out of a bitch named Betty. An imported bitch named Lhassa was the get of Monk and Prim, and she and Shanghai were both bred to Hamilton Sigme, a Lhasa Apso. It is with these matings that Shih Tzu breeding was introduced into the Lhasa line and created the problem.

It was also the breeding of Ming Tai and Tai Ho that produced the bitch, Ch. Ming Lu, which became the foundation of Judge Lloyd's Ming Kennel, one of the earliest and best of the Lhasa kennels in this country. Once the mistake was discovered it was rectified in all future breedings, but nevertheless, the names of Shih Tzu can be found behind many of the early and best Lhasa Apso in this country. This has remained a sore spot among breeders for years and no doubt will continue to be.

Many orientals considered the controversy "much ado about nothing" since, as we have pointed out before, the Lhasa, Shih Tzu, Pekingese and all of the other Tibetan breeds were crossbred down through the centuries in their countries, not only on the streets but in royal palaces as well.

From the point of view of the Shih Tzu admirers, the grave importance of this episode is that it undoubtedly delayed the day of official recognition by the A.K.C., that organization being rightly anxious to avoid the slightest possibility of any further confusion of this kind. When World War II ended in 1945 it again became possible to import Shih Tzu into the United States, but for a considerable time records remained unclear.

In the first Stud Book, prepared in 1961, by far the oldest Shih Tzu recorded are a brother and sister, bred in France by the Countess d'Anjou

Capa's Benji Bear of BoRu is owned by Charles Ballard of Camden, Ohio. The sire was HeeShe's Tank ex Arcuragi's Sen-Soo Yein. Breeder was Carol Arcuragi.

and whelped on October 2, 1953. Named Chi Kuai and Chin Tze, this dog and bitch were the offspring of Golden Fi Lock and Fe Shaing, and were imported by A.S. and M.J. Burns. There is no further reference to them in the Stud Books, so it is doubtful they were ever bred, and we can be quite certain that they played no significant part in the development of the breed in this country.

If only these two little Shih Tzu, bred by the Countess, could have been widely shown at that time, it would have let the American public see the true palace type. Exhibiting these dogs would have been of immeasurable help to the small band of fanciers (specifically Mr. and Mrs. Charles Gardner of San Antonio, Texas) who were following the pattern set by the English Manchu Shih Tzu Society by trying to bring home the fact that the breed should be small in size.

As it was, this crucial fact regarding Shih Tzu size did not become widely known in the U.S. until *after* the American Kennel Club recognition and *after* the preparation of the American Stan-

Ch. Heavenly Dynasty's Mei Boi Toi, owned by Elizabeth and Mel Johnson, is pictured with Toi's sister, Ch. Heavenly Dynasty's Hsi Hsi Te, owned by Rosalie Becker. Bred by Jo Ann White, they were sired by Heavenly Dynasty's T'ai Tzu out of Ch. Heavenly Dynasty's Pasha. Toi has several group placements to his credit.

Chumulari San Pai Yin Te Yin, 11 week old puppy owned by Dorothy Nelson of Stratham, New Hampshire.

Side Waters Cornish Ambrose, English import owned by Mrs. James Ellison of Blue Bell, Pennsylvania.

dard for the breed. This explains the attitude of Brigadier General Frank Dorn, U.S.A. (Retired), author of *The Forbidden City, the Biography of a Palace,* and a widely recognized authority on life in the old time Chinese court. Knowing more about the subject than anyone else in North America, General Dorn wrote wistfully in 1971, two years after the adoption of the present American Standard:

"As far as I have been able to find out, the imperial ideal was larger than the expression 'sleeve dog' implies, but smaller than the so-called 'standard' of this country. The generously wide sleeves of the imperial court were wide enough to provide space for any small dog.

"But based on what I was told in Peking in the middle 1930's," the General concluded, "my guess is that the imperial ideal for these dogs was about half way between the American Toy Pekingese and the Standard Pekingese. I agree with you that breeders in this country do lean toward building up a larger animal than the original Chinese dogs."

When we recall that the miniature Pekingese runs from six to eight pounds, while the Standard permits the larger ones to go up to fourteen pounds, it will be realized that the General's statement means that the court idea for the Shih Tzu averaged approximately ten to twelve pounds. Had the two dogs bred by the Countess d'Anjou been widely exhibited, the ideal Shih Tzu size would have become known to the American fanciers at a much earlier date. Once seen, the small palace-type Shih Tzu are not easily forgotten.

39

Although there is no reference to them in the Stud Books, another especially interesting pair of Shih Tzu are said to have reached the United States in or around 1950. According to Mr. Will C. Mooney, these two little dogs, which he does not name, were imported by Colonel and Mrs. Harry Atkinson. In the service of the U.S. Air Force, the Colonel apparently succeeded in getting these dogs out of China at the time of the Communist take-over.

The Atkinson's two Shih Tzu, being the only known China-bred Shih Tzu to reach our shores, are of exceptional significance. The Air Force couple settled in Louisiana, but when his wife died the Colonel abandoned the breeding program. Unfortunately, it was not taken over by those to whom he gave the dogs. They were probably unaware of the dogs' unique value. What an influence this little pair of Shih Tzu might have had on the development of the breed in the United States! As it turned out, we are left with yet another lost opportunity in the Shih Tzu history.

OTHER EARLY IMPORTS

In 1952 it was reported in England that there were "seventeen Shih Tzu in the U.S., either of British stock or bred from it, and, of course, many others, especially on the Pacific Coast, imported from China." The reference to the existence of Shih Tzu on the West Coast, brought directly from China, comes up again at a later date in breed records, but always on a hearsay basis and without evidence to support it. It is debatable if there were any such Shih Tzu and it is quite certain that they had no influence on the shaping of the breed in America.

The Shih Tzu acquired some measure of status in America in 1955 when the American Kennel Club officially accepted the breed as a separate and distinct breed, making provision for it to be shown in the Miscellaneous Class at American Kennel Club-approved shows. Judges were given a description of the breed to assist them in judging the dogs and were also supplied with a very carefully detailed list of the differences between the Shih Tzu and the Lhasa Apso. Unfortunately, the average weight for the Shih Tzu was given as around sixteen pounds. This resulted in some of the top-winning Shih Tzu of that period being very large and coarse.

In the Miscellaneous Class, the Shih Tzu was competing with Akitas, Chinese Crested, King Charles Spaniels and other breeds which were equally rare, if not more so. The big drawback was that breeds in this class were not able to

Jaisu Mont Taj and Ch. Gin Doc's Pocohanas, owned by Mrs. Sue Miller of Green, South Carolina.

Ch. Hayohan V. Buruf, Dutch import owned by Dr. and Mrs. Roland Wicks of Kansas City, Kansas.

become champions, the highest possible win being a pink First Place ribbon. A reporter for a New York City newspaper described the Miscellaneous Class as "a dog show's leper colony, performers have the limbo-like listing of 'miscellaneous' in the program." He went on to reveal, "Putting it another way, you are welcome in the lodge but you have no voting privilege and you can't sign the chits."

Although there were drawbacks, competing in the Miscellaneous Class did benefit the Shih Tzu immensely by making it possible for the breed to be seen by the public from coast to coast, certainly more widely than ever before. Fanciers were quick to take this delightful little breed into their hearts, and within a few years the Shih Tzu almost "took over" the Miscellaneous Classes. Specimens of the breed were being shown in many parts of the country and greatly admired.

The tremendous gain in interest and enthusiasm can be seen by reading a report in the

Jemima of Lhakang was one of the most important bitches in Rev. and Mrs. D. Allan Eastons' Chumulari Kennels. "Jigme," a compact 10 pound bitch bred in England, was imported by the Eastons in 1965. She is said to resemble strongly her great, great grandmother, Mai-Ting, the last known Shih Tzu to come out of China. By special permission of the captain, Mai-Ting left Shanghai on a British naval vessel in 1949 at the time of the Communist takeover.

February 18, 1962 edition of the *San Francisco Examiner:* "Shih Tzu look so like a Lhasa or a Peke that even another Shih Tzu has trouble telling the difference. Nonetheless, the Shih Tzu is a distinct breed, recognized by the American Kennel Club and exhibited at shows in the Miscellaneous Class, a sort of limbo for pure-breds which aren't numerous enough to rate a full-fledged AKC approval.

"Shih Tzu have coats just about identical to those of Lhasas or of parti-colored Pekes. They also weigh around 10-12 pounds, further compounding the identification problem.

"The principle difference, if it can be called that, is that the Shih Tzu is sort of in between the two other lion types, having a Peke-like head, but more of a Lhasa type coat.

"In any event, if you're in an identification contest, guess it's a Peke first. Your chances are roughly 70 to 1 it will be a Peke rather than a Lhasa, and much better than that against a shaggy dog being a Shih Tzu. Or in a pinch just ask one of 'em. They're all very smart dogs."

Along with the steadily growing number of

Shih Tzu being exposed to the public at the dog shows, another important development was taking place . . . Shih Tzu fanciers were beginning to congregate at the shows and were getting to know one another. Up until this time, the few scattered fanciers were virtually unknown to each other. The time had come for them to meet at ringside and to linger after the judging and discuss their mutual interest in this darling new breed. Tentative plans for the recognition and the betterment of the breed was progressing nicely, along with their popularity.

In those early days the fanciers were predominantly Americans who had travelled overseas and brought Shih Tzu home with them. Among these pioneer fanciers was Mr. Philip Price of Swarthmore, Pennsylvania, who purchased a dog, Golden Se Wen, while spending the winter of 1954-1955 in London. Bred by Mrs. Audrey Fowler and whelped on August 4, 1954, Golden Se Wen was imported to the United States at an early age. As his name implies, this little dog was gold, it being the color Mrs. Fowler has always promoted as the correct imperial shade.

In December, 1955, Mr. and Mrs. Price arranged for a bitch to be shipped to them from London, and quite possibly this was the first Shih Tzu to cross the Atlantic by air and was unaccompanied in this journey. Named Ho-Lai Shum of Yram, the little bitch was bred by Mr. and Mrs. A. Haycock and whelped on May 6, 1955. Obviously, the Prices' imports were the forerunners of many other Shih Tzu which would follow in the years to come.

On January 22, 1957 Mr. and Mrs. Price's imports produced a litter of two puppies. The proud breeder-owners asserted that this was possibly the first pure-bred Shih Tzu born in America, a claim which is in all probability true.

These two little males, Hsung Chu of Ting Chia and Fei Ling of Ting Chia, were given by Mr. Price to his aunt, Miss Maureen Murdoch, who joined her nephew in a breeding and exhibiting program which was to make their Shih Tzu well-known not only in the Philadelphia area but far beyond. At the Philadelphia Kennel Club Show in February, 1957 the Prices' showed three of their Shih Tzu in the Miscellaneous Class, claiming it to be "the first public appearance of the breed, on the East Coast at least."

Mr. Price further stated, "We understand that Shih Tzu were occasionally seen in the Miscellaneous Class at western dog shows." This statement of deliberate vagueness clearly indicated that Mr. Price was passing along hearsay, but accepting no responsibility for its accuracy. Even today it remains to be proven that such West Coast Shih Tzu ever existed.

Late in 1957, the Shih Tzu Club of America was founded with the proud assertion that it was the first club devoted to furthering the interest of the Shih Tzu in the United States. Primarily made up of fanciers in the Philadelphia area, and under the leadership of Mr. Price, this club set up a Stud Book and registry service in the hope of acting as a repository of pedigree information until such time as the American Kennel Club established the Shih Tzu in the championship classes and opened its own Stud Book to the breed. Meanwhile, the breed remained in the Miscellaneous Class and was promoted by a steadily growing band of dedicated fanciers with the dream of ultimate recognition by the A.K.C.

The chances of this dream becoming a reality seemed far in the future when the *Baltimore Sun*, in reporting the 1960 Maryland Kennel Club's 47th Annual Dog Show, described the three Shih Tzu entries as "oriental aristocrats which were the outcasts of the show!" It went on to quote Mr. Charles Le Bouitillier, then vice-president of the

Terry Fowler of Mt. Pleasant, South Carolina, poses with some of her Su Chun Shih Tzu.

American and Canadian Ch. Fang of Shang T'ou is pictured at 4 months of age. Owned by Mary Hollingsworth, Fang Chu Shih Tzu, Lancaster, Ohio.

American Kennel Club, as saying, "We know all about their record as palace dogs in China and Tibet. But until the A.K.C. gets more in their pedigrees, we can't allow them a separate class here. These records may be hard to get to. I don't think we recognize the Kennel Club of Tibet and we don't recognize any kind of a club in Peking."

These were discouraging words, to say the least.

These words reflected the fear of confusion with the Lhasa Apso, recognized by the American Kennel Club in 1935, and a fear which had complicated the breed's recognition in Great Britain some years before. Fortunately, the owner of the three Shih Tzu on display at the 1960 Baltimore show was neither surprised nor shocked by this snubbing of her dogs.

"We know we have a long hard battle to get these dogs recognized as a separate class in this country," Miss Maureen Murdoch of Philadelphia told us, "but I'm confident that a dog with as long and illustrious a history can't be excluded from a separate class forever. It may take us years, but we'll be recognized."

Miss Murdoch was right. It was to be more than nine long years before the dream of American Kennel Club recognition came true.

The *Baltimore Sun* went on to describe them as "small, long-haired dogs that resemble miniature English sheepdogs." It was further reported that the little dogs had been shown at dog shows throughout the country for the past two years, having "garnered between them five blue ribbons, five second places and one third place." But the truth of the matter is they had only won *pink* ribbons in the Miscellaneous Class, which further attests to the 'accuracy' of the *Sun* reporter! In spite of the negative reporting, Miss Murdoch's entry of three, Chin Tee (which translated means Golden One) Hsaio Hun Tsai (Little Cabbage) and Chouette (Littlest Cabbage), did much to rouse interest in the breed in the large crowd which attended the show.

It was at this same Baltimore show in January, 1960 that Miss Murdoch told the reporter that while there were only fifteen known Shih Tzu in the United States, she and all the other fanciers were making every effort to locate more. Just as she predicted, their numbers did increase. By September, 1961, when Mr. Philip Price retired from the presidency of the Shih Tzu Club of America, the group was able to account for no fewer than thirty-seven Shih Tzu registered with that Philadelphia-based organization.

At the same time this club was making their presence felt, Shih Tzu, and clubs dedicated to establishing the breed, continued to crop up in other parts of the country. Servicemen returning from duty overseas were bringing the dogs back home with them and were beginning to show and breed them.

Colonel and Mrs. James Lett brought their Shih Tzu with them from England when they settled in Texas. Their interest led to the formation in 1960, of the Texas Shih Tzu Society; the club headquarters were set up in San Antonio. Colonel Lett served as its first president. The Charles Gardners, who had settled earlier in Texas with their English imports, later imported a pair of Shih Tzu from Sweden. The dog, Jungfaltets Sing-Ling, and the bitch, Jungfaltets Mi-San-Li, bred by Mr. Carl Olof Jungefeldt, were the first Shih Tzu to enter the United States from Scandinavia.

These were followed by a carefully-selected English bitch of the smaller type, Shu Shih of Elfann. The Gardners were the first American breeders to stress—even in their advertising—that they "specialized in under 12 pound stock," and in the breeding of what they described as the "under 12 pound miniature type." These were the first "shots" in what was to become a long, drawn-out—and not yet wholly successful "battle"—to keep the Shih Tzu in the United States from becoming too large in size.

Late in arriving on the American scene, and relatively few in numbers, it took some time for the Scandinavian type, introduced by the Gardners, to play a dominant part in bringing the Shih Tzu breed to its present day high standard in the United States.

The late Mrs. Ingrid Colwell with some of her well-known Scandinavian line of Shih Tzu. Born in Sweden, she later came to the United States as an Air Force Bride. This photo was found among her papers after her death in a fire, in January 1968, at just 40 years of age.

Chapter 3
THE INFLUENCE OF INGRID COLWELL

Of all the fanciers who helped to make the Shih Tzu known and loved in the United States, none did more for the breed than Ingrid Colwell, a native of Sweden who settled in Pennsylvania upon her arrival in this country. For her dedication to their cause, Ingrid's name should be forever remembered with gratitude by all lovers of Shih Tzu in North America. Her contribution has never been surpassed nor equalled, nor is it likely to be in the foreseeable future.

Born and reared near Stockholm, Ingrid was the daughter of Mrs. Ingrid Engstrom, whose Pukedal's Shih Tzu were at that time well known and admired in Scandinavia and in all continental Europe. Ingrid was therefore familiar with the Shih Tzu breed from her earliest days.

Although she is unlikely to have seen Leidza and the other imports brought to Denmark by Henrick Kauffman, Ingrid, being very young at that time, must have heard all about them from fanciers who knew them well. She was certainly very familiar with the direct descendants of the imports, some of which she used in her own breeding program and brought across the Atlantic with her to the United States.

Recognizing that they had a contribution to make, Ingrid was prepared to use carefully chosen English-line dogs in her breeding program, such as Fu-Ling of Clystvale and Fu Chang of Chasmu. Fu-Ling was the dog bred by Mrs. Longden and brought from England to Sweden in 1958 by Mrs. Erna Jungefeldt. Bred by Mrs. Audrey Fowler of London, Chang was owned by Miss Suzy Solidor, a famous French singer and restaurant owner.

Yet, Ingrid's stock was almost 80% Scandinavian in background and she took a special pride in a very carefully compiled pedigree which traced her dogs' ancestry right back to the palace-born Leidza and to Aidzo, who was born in the city of Peking.

When Ingrid married William Colwell, a sergeant stationed with the U.S. Air Force in Europe, they moved to Chateauroux Air Station in France, and then eventually to Olmsted Air Force Base, near Middletown, Pennsylvania. Accompanying the Colwells on their travels were

three Shih Tzu: two bitches, Pukedal's Do That and Jungfaltets Jung Wu, and a dog, Inky Dinky.

Pukedal's Do That had been bred by Mrs. Engstrom, Ingrid's mother, in Sweden. Do That was whelped December 5, 1958, by Fu-Ling of Clystvale ex Shepherd's Si-Kiang. Jung-Wu, called "Kia" and a special favorite of Ingrid's, was bred in Sweden by Mrs. Erna Jungefeldt and whelped January 1, 1958, by Bjorneholms Wu-Ling ex Bjorneholms Pippi. Inky Dinky was bred in France by Ingrid herself, whelped September 18, 1959, by Fu Chang of Chasmu ex Pukedal's Do That.

From these small beginnings Ingrid derived her distinctive Si-Kiang line, which was to become the best known and most highly-respected Shih Tzu name in North America in its time.

In addition to her own stock, in January, 1958, Ingrid brought a male from Sweden, Pukedal's Ding-Dang. Brother to Pukedal's Do That, Ding-Dang was destined for Yvette Duval, another Air Force wife whom Ingrid had succeeded in interesting in the breed. In keeping with the international pattern already noted, both the Duvals were French Canadian in background, having grown up in the province of Quebec.

Shown by Ingrid and Yvette in Paris, Bordeaux, Chateaureux and elsewhere in France (as well as in various other places in Europe), Ding-Dang and Kia became French champions. They caused a sensation when they were both awarded their titles at the prestigious Paris show in 1960. Undated clippings from the Air Force base newspaper give a colorful picture of Ingrid's activities during this period.

Under the headline "International Show Attracts 5,000. Ten Chateauroux Entrants. King/Colwell Takes Firsts" we read, "Chateauroux's first International Dog Show in almost twenty years hosted a crowd of 5,000 canine enthusiasts and more than 500 dogs, representing 70 different breeds, last Sunday at the Avenue de Deols Public Garden. The weather, although threatening at times, was custom-made for the event, being cool and cloudy bright.

"Amid hundreds of impatient pooches of all sizes, shapes and descriptions, and masters of equally varied temperaments, American participation was marked with gratifying success. Of the ten dogs entered by Chateauroux Air Station personnel, at least seven took home the coveted 'blue card' for first or second place wins. None of these entrants received less than a 'very honorable' mention.

"A small Tibetan Tsi-Shu (sic), owned and shown by Mrs. Ingrid Colwell, walked away with first place in her class. The pooch was rated 'excellent' and 'best of breed.' "

The reference in the headline to the name "King" referred to another highly successful American entry, a Pekingese owned by a Mr. Gordon King. Another quote was "Kia Winked, Paris Judges Pinked, Then Named Her Best of Breed." This headline was followed by "Spaghetti, as a main dish, followed by cooked beets, and marshmallow for dessert, rates mighty high with Kia, a prize-winning Shih Tzu dog, recently crowned French Champion, owned and shown by Mrs. Ingrid Colwell, wife of Sgt. William Colwell of the Transit Alert Section.

"Mrs. Colwell recently entered Kia in the yearly Paris dog show. Here Kia strutted before the judges, who studied her every move and step. They rated her 'excellent' and 'Best of Breed' and she was awarded the title Champion of France.

"But this high standard of performance was par for Kia. Her first showing took place in the public garden at the Chateauroux Dog Show in the summer of 1959. Kia stole the show in her class and took first prize with a rating of 'excellent' and 'Best of Breed'. This show was just the beginning for the two-year-old Oriental beauty. She followed through that autumn and was crowned top dog at the show in Vichy.

"One wall of the Colwell apartment is covered with first prizes won at dog show competitions.

"Sgt. and Mrs. Colwell, who will leave for the States in August (1960), say, 'Feeding the Shih Tzu is no problem, but they do have their own special likes. We'll be all right if the commissary doesn't stop stocking marshmallows and spaghetti!' "

When Ingrid Colwell finally came to the United States in the fall of 1960, the Shih Tzu was still being shown in the Miscellaneous Class, a big difference when compared to the status they enjoyed in France. Nevertheless, the breed had "caught on" sufficiently to arouse a great deal of interest among the American public and all kind of questions were being asked about the breed. Unfortunately, very few fanciers in the States were in a position to answer all these questions, as very little research had been done on them and no

Ingrid Colwell (top) with French Champion Jungfaltets Yung-Wu and Yvette Duval with French Champion Pukedals Ding-Dang. Yung-Wu, or Kia as she is called, and Ding were the first champions of any foreign country to enter the United States.

documented account of the breed was available prior to the publication of *This Is The Shih Tzu* in 1970.

As a result, before that date, interested parties had to rely on snippets of information, not always accurate by any means, which were passed on unchecked from one to another. Fortunately the erroneous information in no way discouraged interest in the breed. One small but easily-disproved instance of this type of "information" was the story that at the time of the Communist Revolution in China, "members of the Royal Family" cut their dogs' throats, before committing suicide themselves, rather than have them fall into the hands of the Communists.

Although this gruesome story has circulated widely, in a variety of versions, and although it is repeated in a somewhat garbled form in the American Kennel Club official dog book, this story is totally fictitious. Similar stories about the breed circulated in the United States in Ingrid's

46

time, but the stories became even more complicated and exaggerated because there was no authoritative source by means of which the accuracy could be checked. Not many Americans had the opportunity to talk with anyone who had actually seen the breed in Peking for themselves.

The result was a great deal of confusion about the Shih Tzu and a great deal of misinformation was passed along in writing and by the spoken word. Since both China and Tibet were quite inaccessible to the western world at that time, and since there were relatively few people in North America or Europe who knew much about them, even the wildest statements about the little Tibetan Lion Dogs from old Peking were unlikely to be challenged.

The position was further complicated by the fact that the American public's increasing interest in the breed was encouraging breeders of a new type to make their appearance. Not all of them were of the same caliber as the little band of pioneers who had struggled so hard to win a place in the American show ring for the Shih Tzu, and some of these newcomers showed little apparent interest in the unique background and history of the breed.

It was a big day for the Shih Tzu when Ingrid Colwell came to settle in the United States in 1960, bringing with her, in addition to her dogs, the fruits of her labor after years of experience with the breed in Europe. Her unique knowledge of the breed quickly became apparent, and so much so that within eight months she had been invited to become president of the Shih Tzu Club of America, the Philadelphia-based group which had been founded under the leadership of Mr. Philip Price a few years previously.

This club was going through a process of reorganization and it turned for help to the recently arrived fancier, a singular honor for a very new immigrant from Sweden who still had considerable difficulty expressing herself in English. The language barrier would have been an insurmountable barrier to many, but in Ingrid's case the situation was solved by the fact that she so obviously knew what she was talking about that those who were really concerned about learning took the necessary trouble to listen and understand.

With wholehearted enthusiasm, Ingrid Colwell set herself to the task of clearing up the existing fallacies and confusion, and introduced to the American public the Shih Tzu as she had known them for so many years. To do this, Ingrid was prepared to travel far and wide to get her dogs into the show ring where they could be seen and admired by as many people as possible. Probably her longest trip was to San Antonio, Texas, where she showed three Shih Tzu on March 12, 1961.

Ingrid had only been in the United States some six months at this time, and this long trip must have been quite an undertaking since it followed two strenuous days at the Westminster Kennel Club Show in New York City. Her readiness to travel often such distances, with so little to be gained without the dogs' official recognition, proves her enthusiasm for establishing the breed in this country.

A fascinating account of Ingrid and her beloved dogs during those early days in this country was carried in an article which appeared in the *Olmsted Orbiter*, published at Olmsted Air Force Base in Pennsylvania, and dated November 8, 1962. Written by Rickie Comitz, it is in many ways strangely similar to some of those articles written about the Empress Dowager and her palace dogs. Under the headline "Originated in Tibet. NCO's wife at Olmsted Raises Rare Breed of Far-East Dogs," the article begins:

"Don't be alarmed if you're in the Meade Heights Area of the Base and you hear a lovely female voice, with a bit of Swedish accent, calling, 'Jung Wu, Mitzi, Dudo That, Ai Lan, Jenn Ling, To Be Or Not To Be.' It is only Ingrid Colwell's chow call for her seven Shih Tzu dogs." Referring to their appearance and carriage, the reporter went on to say that they had a top-knot hairdo that Ingrid had devised that could compete in any hair stylist's show. He mentioned that the dogs' hair was teased up in a very attractive and comfortable manner and they could easily be thinking "...

French Champion Jungfaltets Jung-Wu, lovely bitch bred by Mr. and Mrs. Jungefeldt, and imported to the United States by the late Mrs. Ingrid Colwell, one of the most famous fanciers in the history of our breed.

Swedish Champion Junfaltets Jung-Wu-Pi, an 11 pound gold and white bitch bred by Mr. and Mrs. Carl-Olof Jungefeldt of Sweden. She went Best of Breed and Best Toy All Breeds at the Swedish Kennel Club International Show in Stockholm in May, 1963. Wu-Pi was also Best of Breed at another large Stockholm Show five months earlier, where she was handled by the Jungefeldts' 11 year old daughter.

just washed my hair and can't do a thing with it!"

After a glowing reference to Ingrid's trophy room, filled with ribbons, certificates and prizes, he added that with her enthusiasm and charm Ingrid had obviously done a good job of selling the breed to the public.

"Stockholm, Sweden, is home to me," she told him, "and my family always had dogs. In fact, I was practically raised by the family's old shepherd dog."

The article went on to reveal that Ingrid had interests other than dogs. She was a skilled painter, worked in ceramics, knitting and sewing. She was also the chairman of the social committee for the NCO wives' club at the base. With all her zeal for the Shih Tzu, Ingrid still managed to keep her other interests alive, which helped her remain placid under the stresses of dog show travel and care, stresses which often caused others to lose their sense of proportion as well as their sense of humor.

Through her contact with her mother in Sweden, Ingrid remained in a unique position to secure the best possible breeding stock from overseas to enhance her breeding program. In addition to the three already mentioned which Ingrid brought with her, she later imported seven other Shih Tzu from Scandinavia. Three of the earliest were, according to the stud books, Do That, Jung-Wu, and Inky Dinky. These were all males, officially named Bjorneholms Tja-Ha, bred by Astrid Jeppesen in Denmark; Stefengardens Jenn-Ling, bred by L. Svensson in Sweden, and Jungfaltets Wu Po, bred by Carl Olof Jungefeldt in Sweden. There were four females, Pukedal's Ai Lan, bred in Sweden by Ingrid Engstrom, her mother; Jungfaltets Pi-Dhona, bred in Sweden by Carl Olof Jungefeldt; Min-My-Shih, bred in Sweden by M. Berg; and Rosengardens Ragna-Toy, bred in Sweden by L. Grenalt.

Those who witnessed it will not easily forget Ingrid's excitement when she announced proudly that another good dog was arriving "from home." To the end of her life Ingrid was intensely proud of her stock and was determined to do her best to use these dogs to the best possible advantage so that she might present the very best Shih Tzu to the American public.

This program which she had begun in Sweden was, however, only to last seven years. It was brought to a halt with her sudden death. The last litter whelped by one of her bitches was on November 9, 1967. This was a short time after the first American litter of another of Ingrid's bitches came upon the scene on October 29, 1960, just less than two months after her arrival in this country. American fanciers were greatly deprived of a very important line and contribution to the breed.

During these seven years, however, the records show that Ingrid bred 79 Shih Tzu, an average of eleven a year. This was a relatively small number, making it possible for each puppy to get individual care and attention. Yet this was enough to keep Ingrid busy and she was able to get the dogs around the country into the show rings.

INGRID COLWELL IN THE SHOW RING

Five Shih Tzu and one Akita made up the Miscellaneous Class at the Westminster Kennel Club Show on February 13 and 14, 1961, the first appearance of the Shih Tzu in the most prestigious of all show rings! The judge on this auspicious occasion was Mr. William L. Kendrick. Maureen Murdoch exhibited a bitch, and Ingrid Colwell's entry consisted of two dogs and two bitches.

A newspaper article about the show describes it best. Under the headline "Status Seekers: Shih Tzu, Akita Lead Dog's Life," a reporter wrote: "Huddled together in a large stall at the Eighth Avenue end of Madison Square Garden's benching floor yesterday were the six members of the Westminster Kennel Club's 'leper colony,' the performers with the limbo-like listing of 'miscellaneous' in the program. Nevertheless, this was one happy settlement, more companionable than most in the crowded and raucous basement. A chance visit found five Shih Tzu and one Akita getting along famously. The fact that they were sleeping, or feigning same, in no way detracted from the impression of their compatibility.

"The owners, on the other hand, were very much awake. They had to be, for their bungalow-quarters probably received more visitors in two days and nights than any other canine camp-out. Still, they made a homey group, one in which the tourist found surcease from the vocal (canine and human) scramble for best in show."

It is plain to see that Ingrid and her "helpers" were busily expounding the virtues of the breed to all comers and rightly impressed the newspaper reporter. Frequently asked if they were as brave as people say, Ingrid would reply, "Yes, they are as brave as people say but with them it's ridiculous. They see a big dog and they want to fight it. The

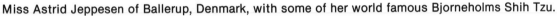

Miss Astrid Jeppesen of Ballerup, Denmark, with some of her world famous Bjorneholms Shih Tzu.

big dog looks at them and says, 'There's nothing there for me to fight! So they get away with it.'" Ingrid added, "In some circles the Shih Tzu is called the 'dog of tomorrow.' "

These were bold words back in the early 1960's, considering there were only five Shih Tzu among the hundreds of dogs at this 1961 Westminster show. We now know that Ingrid's words were not such an exaggeration as they might have seemed at the time.

On Thursday, February 1, 1962, the *New York Times* published its first full length article on the Shih Tzu. It was written by the then-dog editor, John Rendel, and was romantically headlined "Tibet to Eighth Avenue." The article drew attention to the forthcoming Westminster show and stated that at this show there would be twelve Shih Tzu on display at the Garden. Actually there were ten Shih Tzu in the Miscellaneous Class that year, plus two Akitas. At any rate, the entry represented twice as many Shih Tzu being shown as there had been the previous year. Once again the major portion of the entries belonged to Ingrid Colwell, with none of the other owners entering more than one dog each. As president of the Shih Tzu Club of America she set a marvelous example.

It was at this Westminster show that we saw for the first time a Shih Tzu being taken into the ring by a professional handler. This distinction goes to Anne Hone Rogers, now Mrs. James Clark, the all-breed judge. Within a few years, however, other top American handlers of both sexes were to play their part in exhibiting this breed to the Western world.

In his coverage of the show Mr. Rendel also pointed out that "Shih Tzu adherents are pleased when eight or nine are assembled under one roof," and added that the Shih Tzu was "the only breed known to be making a serious effort to become a member of the American Kennel Club official family."

"New breeds are accepted into the A.K.C. stud book from time to time, but admittance is by no means commonplace," the dog editor explained, adding that "nobody, including the A.K.C. officers and those of the Shih Tzu Club of America, knows when the Shih Tzu will make the grade."

John Rendel went on to caution against undue optimism in that regard, pointing out that on the previous day Mr. John Neff, the American Kennel Club Executive Vice President, had warned that "acceptance was not imminent."

"The A.K.C. requires a new breed to exist in the United States in substantial numbers (about 300 or more individual specimens) held by many different owners in scattered parts of the country," Mr. Rendel elaborated.

"The breed must be backed by a responsible club that keeps acceptable pedigrees. Usually, the process takes several years. The Shih Tzu Club of America was formed in 1957." Quoting Maureen Murdoch of Philadelphia, club secretary-treasurer, as having reported that "up to August, 1960, only eighteen members of the breed were known to be in the country," he pointed out that at the time of his writing the club president Ingrid Colwell confirmed that there were "fewer than 100 Shih Tzu in the United States.

"The total has grown rapidly, through the uncovering of additional resident and imported dogs, but still is insufficient for official approval," the dog editor concluded, emphasizing that " a major club project is to find more dogs. The work is aided by the comparable British club, which notifies the American group of dogs sent here."

This lengthy and informative article in the *New York Times* must have been an immense source of encouragement to Ingrid. Unlike most other exhibitors in the U.S., she had known the breed in France, where it was recognized and accorded the honor which she felt was its due. After "attaining the high spots" over there, the ignominy of the Miscellaneous Class must have been hard to take and the delay in gaining acceptance was immeasurably frustrating.

It should be noted that this article in the *Times* was the beginning of a singularly happy relationship between the breed and that newspaper, which continued to extoll the virtues of the Shih Tzu to the American public during the subsequent years.

The next major event in dog show entries for the breed took place three months after Westminster, on May 19, 1962, at the Western Kennel Association Show in Pittsburgh, Pennsylvania, when fifteen Shih Tzu entered in the Miscellaneous Class to be judged by Mrs. George B. St. George. In fact, there were nothing *but* Shih Tzu in this class and it was believed to be the largest turnout of the breed at any American show up to that date.

Looking back over the years, Mrs. St. George still recalls with excitement how proudly the top-knotted little Lion Dogs were presented for her evaluation. She also recalls the trepidation with which she approached the judging of those rare little dogs about which so little was known and which were so new to her.

This Western Kennel Association show marked the annual business meeting of the newly reorganized club, and while the entry hardly

Ch. Si-Kian's Mayfair Geisha, bred by Ann Hickock and owned by Patricia Durham and Peter D'Auria. Geisha was handled by Barbara Wolferman for this 1970 Harrisburg Kennel Club show.

could be called a specialty, it could be regarded as the closest thing to it under the unusual circumstances!

It is also interesting to note that although the early stud books indicate that at this period Shih Tzu brought to the United States from Scandinavia were far outnumbered by those brought from England, Ingrid's strong influence at this time is shown by the fact that the entries at this important show were predominantly Scandinavian in background. Eleven of the fifteen were of Scandinavian lines, five actually bred in Scandinavia and six bred in the U.S. of Scandinavian background stock. Of the remaining four, three

were English-bred imports, one a French-bred mixture of English and Scandinavian bloodlines.

The records show that sterling silver bowls were awarded to the winners and were won by La-Mi Li-Chang, a male, bred by Mr. and Mrs. Charles Gardner and owned by Beryl and Sidney Bashore; and by Jungfaltets Fu-Wi, a female, bred by Mr. and Mrs. Carl Olof Jungefeldt and owned by Yvette Duval.

The list of owners in the catalogue was impressive. Almost without exception, they represented the top Shih Tzu breeders in the country at the time. Most of them had first come to know the Shih Tzu overseas and had been ready to struggle

51

Ch. Ah-Kamas Kompis,
whelped in May, 1971,
sired by Swedish and
Norwegian Ch. Osprey's
Mr. Pym ex Int. and Scan.
Ch. Ah-Kamas Am-Bra.
Kompis, the winner of six
Best of Breed awards, was
bred by I. Holst, Sweden
and owned by Rita Ravn
and Christian Ravn, Den-
mark.

Ch. Yong's Tschju-Hei, whelped September 1973,
and a Best in Show winner in Denmark where he
was bred and owned by Rita Rasmussen, Kennel
Yong. The sire was Ch. Bjorneholm's Va-Tu-Ling ex
XaXa van de Oranje Manege.

Ch. Yong's Mah-Jong, Danish Best in Show winner,
bred and owned by Rita Rasmussen, Kennel Yong,
Denmark. The sire was Bjorneholm's Nu-Chi-Ling ex
XaXa van de Oranje Manege. This black-masked
golden was whelped in October 1972.

Ta-Chi's Aimee, co-owned
by Rita Ravn and her son,
Dr. Christian Ravn, of the
Ta-Chi Kennels, of Den-
mark. Aimee was sired by
Int. and Scand. Ch. Bjorneholm's Hsiao-Ping ex Ah-
Kamas Rebecca. Aimee
had just won Best of Breed
when this photograph was
taken.

and sacrifice to make the breed known in the United States.

Dr. and Mrs. Sidney Bashore from the Air University Hospital at Maxwell Air Force Base, Montgomery, Alabama; Ingrid Colwell and Yvette Duval from Olmsted Air Force Base in Pennsylvania; Charles and Helene Gardner from San Antonio, Texas; Maureen Murdoch from Philadelphia; and Brenda Ostencio from Chicago, all had made their mark on the breed.

Going through the list of names now, in the light of what was to follow, it somehow reads strangely like a last roll-call of the "old guard." With the passing time, inevitably those who had first come to know the breed overseas were outnumbered by a new generation of breeders who had first met the Shih Tzu in this country and whose knowledge of the breed was limited to such information as they had been able to glean from owners in this country.

This meant that most of these newcomers learned about the Shih Tzu history from an English point of view. Language difficulties made it hard for the Scandinavian breeders to make their view of the breed widely known in America. Ingrid Colwell, for example, became reasonably fluent in speaking English, but found it difficult to express herself in writing. Sharing a more or less common language, English breeders had no such problems and they were naturally very ready to take full advantage of the opportunities this gave them to spread the word about their interpretation of the breed.

Two paperback publications on the Shih Tzu were circulated widely in the United States during this period, both written by English authors and both illustrated with photographs of English-bred Shih Tzu. Neither made more than the briefest and most obscure references to the existence of the Scandinavian line, although one of these books gave a detailed listing of Shih Tzu brought from China to England. While these listed the names of those who imported the breed in England, neither book made any mention whatsoever of Mr. and Mrs. Henrik Kauffman or the Shih Tzu they brought with them from Peking to Scandinavia.

Although it would be unfair to regard these omissions as deliberate, they can only indicate clearly that the writers were hardly aware of the Scandinavian dogs and certainly did not attach much importance to them. This is readily understandable because dogs entering England have to pass through such a prolonged quarantine that it is almost impossible for fanciers there to have any direct knowledge of dogs in other countries. How-

Ch. Si-Kiang's I Ko Tien Shih, pictured winning under judge Isador Schoenberg, with handler Robert Sharp. Owner is Pat Durham of Duncannon, Pennsylvania.

ever, a very different situation to that is found in the United States. Obviously, both books were written with readers in England in mind, knowing that the dogs of the Scandivanian lines would never be seen in England in more than miniscule numbers. The two authors more than likely saw no point in making much mention of them. It is possible that it never occurred to them that their books would also be read in North America.

After the circulation of these two publications, when much attention was brought to light over the omissions, two later and more recent English books give a much fuller account of the Scandinavian dogs. Intentional or otherwise, the omissions did have a highly misleading effect on the breed when the first two books reached American readers. No other source of information being available to them, many fanciers in the United State were left with the distinct impression that there were no Shih Tzu of consequence other than those of English background.

Since the Scandinavian bloodlines have no spokesman to present their case, Shih Tzu of their type tended to be overlooked. Attention was temporarily focused on a larger, coarser variety which was for a time presented as the ideal for the breed.

A family group study featured on a Christmas card from the Si-Kiang Kennels.

Dralhas Ashoka, bred and owned by Inger Fallberg, Dralhas Kennels in Skollersta, Sweden. The sire was Int., Nor. Ch. Tempelgardens Chi-Co-Tzu ex Formaregardens Pi-Nhette.

The well-known Si-Kian's Tashi, part of the kennel force at the Easton's Chumulari Kennels in Gardiner, New York.

International and Scandinavian Ch. Lyckobringarens Ka-Thinka, owned and bred by Miss Margrethe Svendsen. The sire was Int. and Scan. Ch. Tempelgardens Chi-Co-Tzu ex Bey-The-Wang. She earned her title in the strongest competition at just 28 months of age.

Breed history! The first day that Shih Tzu were eligible to compete in the championship classes, Chumulari Ying Ying not only won the breed, but went all the way to Best in Show at the 1969 New Brunswick Kennel Club show under James Trullinger. Ying Ying was to become one of the most important dogs in the breed, and had a sparkling show ring career with his handler, John Marsh, after this spectacular start. On the right is club president Lemuel Strauss. Ying Ying was breeder-owned by the Rev. and Mrs. D. Allan D. Easton.

Chapter 4
BREED RECOGNITION AND EARLY STATISTICS

The news that all Shih Tzu fanciers were waiting for arrived in April, 1969. The April issue of the *American Kennel Gazette* carried the official word from the American Kennel Club. On the Secretary's Page the announcement read as follows:

REGISTRATION OF NEW BREED

"By action of the Board of Directors, the Shih Tzu breed has been admitted to registry in The American Kennel Club's Stud Book.

"Regular classification in the Toy Group may be offered at All-Breed shows held on and after September 1, 1969. Prior to September 1, Shih Tzu will continue to be eligible to be shown in the Miscellaneous Class. They may not be entered in the Miscellaneous Class at shows held on or after September 1.

"A Shih Tzu that is AKC registered before September 1, 1969 and that does not already have an ILP number, will automatically be granted an Indefinite Listing Privilege upon registration, permitting it to compete before September 1, in the Miscellaneous Class at shows, and in Obedience Trials. The individual registration number will be acceptable on entry forms in lieu of an ILP number.

"Persons approvable to judge all-breeds or all Toy breeds will be eligible for approval to judge Shih Tzu at shows held on and after September 1, 1969."

At last the mission was accomplished! Shih Tzu were ready to compete for championship status. It is a shame that Ingrid Colwell did not live to see this day.

SHIH TZU REGISTRATIONS

The American Kennel Club closed its Stud Book on the registering of foundation stock of the Shih Tzu as of June 30, 1970. After July 1, 1970 all Shih Tzu had to be registered under the regular rules and regulations set up by the American Kennel Club. This ruling applied to all foreign bred Shih Tzu as well, and there were many dogs registered very quickly.

THE BREED'S FIRST CHAMPION

The November, 1970, issue of the *American Kennel Gazette* carried the announcement in their "Champions of Record" section that the first Shih Tzu to attain the championship title was Ch. Bjorneholm Pif. Owned by Mary Wood and Norman Patton of Terre Haute, Indiana, Pif not only was the breed's first champion but tied for Top Producing Toy Sire for 1970, a dual honor to be sure! He was also noted sire of a Best In Show son, Ch. Mariljac Chatterbox, and Pif had already racked up several Group Placements for himself by the time news of his title reached print.

Pif was bred by Miss Astrid Jeppesen of Denmark and was already a champion in five European countries before the J.R. Woods imported him in 1968.

Mariljac En-Chan-Tress, bred by the Mariljac Kennels, and Dutch Champion Glenka Tzi Von Klein Vossenburg tied for the top honors as the Number One Toy Group Dam for 1970, according to the *Kennel Review* magazine statistics. En-Chan-Tress, purchased by Dr. and Mrs. J.W. Edel of Florida, was the dam of five champions in 1970. They were Mariljac Tinker Town Toi, Mariljac Tinker Town Tom, Mariljac Tinker Town Tot, Mariljac Tinker Town Tidbit and Mariljac Ta-Kuai.

Dutch Champion Glenka Tzi Von Klein Vossenburg, owned by Mrs. Jean Gadberry of the Bomshu Kennels in California, also produced five champions: Bom Shu's Dee Dee, Bom Shu's Rockette Ting, Teen Sih Shu, Misty Isle Tashi Shu, C.D. and Bom Shu's Empress Su-Ling.

It was most obvious that not only had the Shih Tzu received official recognition from the American Kennel Club, but had managed to achieve success within their own breed, and to further distinguish themselves by going right to the top of the Toy Group for their honors. Within thirty days of the breed's admittance they were ranking among the top-winning and top-producing dogs in the country.

During the second month of their new status five more Shih Tzu captured their championship titles. The December, 1969, issue of the *Gazette* printed the names of Chumulari Ying-Ying, Car-

Chumulari Li-Tzu, owned by Mrs. Marilyn M. Guiraud of Virginia. Photograph by the Furman Studio.

rimount Ah-Chop-Chop (his son), Chumulari Li-Tzu (another Ying-Ying offspring), Lakoya Princess Tanya Shu and Si Shu von de Oranje Manege, an import from the Dutch kennels of Eta Pauptit.

It is fascinating to note that Chumulari Ying-Ying's sire was the first to attain championship, and within that first 60 days three generations had won their titles. By May of 1971 Pif had produced sixteen champions: Ch. Chumulari Ying-Ying and Li-Tzu, Mariljac Ebony Emperor, Mariljac Kwang K'Whae, Mariljac Mr. Boogie Bear, Mariljac Tinker Town Tom, Mai Ling of Mountainside, Mariljac Tinker Town Tidbit, Mariljac Tinker Town Toi, Mariljac Tinker Town Tot, Mariljac Chatterbox, Vams Joss Hotei, Mariljac Ta-Kuai, Mariljac Jhon-Nhee-Rheb, Sopon Vom Tschomo-Lungma and Mariljac Kwang Ming.

THE FIRST BEST IN SHOW WINNER

At the first dog show after the official date Shih Tzu were eligible to compete in the championship classes, one of our beautiful Shih Tzu went all the way to the coveted Best In Show win. The dog was Chumulari Ying-Ying, owned by Rev. and Mrs. D. Allan Easton, and the show was the New Brunswick Kennel Club Show on September 1, 1969. Judge James W. Trullinger bestowed the honor on Ying-Ying and his handler John Marsh. His owners and everyone at ringside could not have been more thrilled!

Throughout his entire record-breaking career Ying-Ying was a super showman and this initial win was to be only the beginning of a sparkling career that would attract much attention to the breed in all the years that followed. His many champion sons and daughters also bore the same regal bearing and outgoing personalities that made them a pleasure to own and to show.

TOP CANADIAN BEST IN SHOW WINNER

One of the most significant examples of this brand of distinction was through the record and magnificence of Ying-Ying's son, American, Canadian and Bermudian Ch. Carrimount Ah-Chop-Chop, out of Can. Ch. Brownhills Yolan of Greenmoss. Not only had Chop-Chop achieved his championship in the United States during the second month the Shih Tzu were allowed to compete, but by July 17, 1971, he added another chapter to the annals of Shih Tzu history by winning an American Best In Show at the Champlain Valley Dog Club Show in Winooski, Vermont.

Chop-Chop had already won a Best In Show in Canada for his owners, Mr. and Mrs. Jeffrey Carrique, of Carrimount Kennels. Handled by William J. Trainor and Lawrence Garrett Lambert, he was already on his way to becoming the top-winning Shih Tzu in two countries. While Mr. Lambert also showed Chop-Chop to a Best In Show win in Bermuda, where it was Joan Brearley's privilege to present the Best In Show Trophy, it was not Chop-Chop, however, to claim the title of first Champion Shih Tzu in Bermuda. The honor of going down in dog show history as the first Shih Tzu to attain a championship title on the beautiful islands of Bermuda was Ch. Mar Del's Chow Mein, owned by Mrs. Margaret E. Edel of Baltimore, Maryland. Susan H. Mitchell showed the dog for the owner.

THE FIRST BEST TEAM IN SHOW

Team competition at the shows is not as popular as it used to be, and very few of the kennel clubs offer Best Team In Show awards. Fortunately for our newly recognized breed, the Kennel Club of Beverly Hills is one show-giving club that does it and it was at their January 7, 1973 show that four perfectly synchronized little Lion Dogs glided off with the top honors. Judge Maurice L. Baker gave them the top award after Mr. C.L. Savage awarded them the Toy Group win and Mrs. S.J. Fishman placed them in the breed judging.

Sue Bouchard, who co-owns the team with Lee Bouchard, trained and handled them to this win. The names of these four little 7½-month old golden puppies are Tien Tan's Mei Ching, Tein Tan's Mei Li, Tien Tan's Mei Shu Chia of Su-Le and Tien Tan's Mei Jen of Su-Le. The four were bred by the Tien Tan Kennels, sired by Ch. Tzi Tzi Shu *ex* Ch. Durga Van de Blauwe Mammouth. These four are very likely the first Shih Tzu Best Team In Show winners in the world!

Best in Show-winning American, Canadian and Bermudian Ch. Carrimount Ah-Chop-Chop, pictured in Bermuda after winning a Best in Show with his handler, William Trainor. Owners are Mr. and Mrs. J. Carrique, Canada. Bermuda News Bureau photograph.

Chumulari Ying-Ying pictured winning the Group at the 1968 Montreal Canada show under judge James Trullinger. Owner-handled by Margaret Easton, Ying Ying also won his American championship and a Best in Show on the first day Shih Tzu were eligible to compete for championship status in this country.

Ch. Si Shu van de Oranje Manege, top winning bitch in the United States for 1968, was bred in Holland by Eta Pauptit, at her famous VDOM kennels. Owned by Mrs. Eleanore Eldredge of Easton, Washington.

Mrs. Richard Logie with Janiric Kennels' 10-week-old Ruk-a-tatin' Rockie. Richard and Janice Logie's kennels are in Ontario, Canada.

Canadian Ch. Carrimount Ah Ching-A-Ling, owned by Richard and Janice Logie, Janiric Kennels in Ontario, Canada.

American, Canadian and Bermudian Ch. Carrimount Ah-Chop Chop, pictured winning one of his Bests in Show at the 1971 Greater Lowell Kennel Club show in the U.S.A. Chop Chop was shown by L. Garret Lambert for owner Mrs. J. G. Carrique of Quebec, Canada. The Breed and Group judge was Mr. V. Johnson, and the Best in Show judge was Mr. Thomas. His sire was Am. and Can. Ch. Chumulari Ying Ying ex Am. Can. Ch. Brownhills Yolan of Greenmoss. Chop Chop was the #1 Shih Tzu in Canada for 1969 and #8 Non-Sport Group in Canada for 1969. He is the sire and grandsire of many U.S. and Canadian champions, and has two Bests in Show in the U.S., 1 in Canada, and 1 in Bermuda.

Australian Champion Erintoi Panda Bear, owned by John L. Sheppard of New South Wales, Australia. Panda is one of Australia's top bitches for 1976, having gained her title at 12 months of age. She is a multiple Best in Show winner, never having been overlooked in the ring by foreign judges or breed specialists.

Ch. Bomshu No Stuffed Toi owned by Ginny Mills of Honeoye Falls, New York.

Ch. Yingin Crepe Suzette owned by Jim Jameson of Ontario, Canada. Suzette finished for championship in December 1976. The sire was Yingin Champagne ex Jaisu Mont Taj. Breeder was Mrs. Sue Miller.

Canadian Ch. Carrimount Ah Me Saucy Su pictured winning on the way to her championship under American judge Clark Thompson. Handled by Richard Logie, who co-owns with wife Janice Logie, Janiric Kennels, Ontario, Canada.

Canadian Ch. Carrimount Ah Ching-A-Ling, pictured winning Group Second under Maxwell Riddle at the 1975 Fredericton Kennel Club show. Owned by Richard and Janice Logie, Janiric Kennels, Ontario, Canada.

TOP TEN WINNERS

There were several "famous firsts" in the breed, starting with the day of recognition up to and through their first year in the championship classes. Once recognized, the Shih Tzu also fell into the category of show dogs competing for Phillips System points on their way to the "Top Ten" listings in each breed.

1970 saw the #1 winner in Ch. Sitsang Whiz Bang. A multiple Best In Show Winner, handler Rosemarie Crandahl of Livonia, Michigan, piloted Whiz Bang to the top spot for owners Dr. and Mrs. Doyle N. Rogers of Pasadena, Texas.

In 1971 it was Ch. Paisley Ping Pong that claimed the #1 honors in the breed. Bred by the late Richard Paisley and owned by Joan Cowie of the Nanjo Kennels in Kimberton, Pennsylvania, Ping also sired 12 champions in his first four years as an active stud, making him the Top Producer in the breed for 1973.

Other superstars for that year were: #2—Ch. Thalias Sidney Sidney, a dog owned by C.L. Eudy and T.P. Smith; #3—Ch. Witch's Wood Soket Tumi, a dog owned by M.M. Guiraud; #4—Ch. Carrimount Ah Chop Chop, owned by Mr. and Mrs. J. Carrique; #5—Ch. Pentaras Warrior of Lanbur, owned by W.H. Langley and W.S. Burns; #6—Ch. Bom Shu's Earth Ling, owned by R.B. and R.F. Hoffman; #7—Ch. Sitsand Whiz Bang, now owned by Rosemarie Crandahl; #8—Ch. Mariljac Chatterbox, owned by the Mariljac Kennels; #9—Ch. Sara-A-Lee Ho Chim Wali Du, owned by Mrs. H. Rand; #10—Ch. Bel Airs Tinker Toy, owned by L.R. Cole.

In 1971 Ch. Mar Del's Ring A Ding Ding won a Best In Show over the largest entry up to that time. His win at the Hunterdon Hills Kennel Club Show over an entry of 1333 dogs on August 10, 1971, became another "famous first" for the breed. Mrs. Emma Stevens judged the Breed,

Ch. Witch's Wood Soket Tumi, the #1 Shih Tzu for 1970. He was handled during his successful show ring career by John Marsh for owner Marilyn Guiraud.

Ch. Witch's Wood Yum Yum, pictured winning Best in Show at the 1972 Muncie Kennel Club show under judge Dr. Buris R. Boshell. Owners are Dr. and Mrs. J. Wesley Edel.

Group and Best In Show and carried the dog all the way to the top win. John March handled "Ringy" to this win. Sired by American and Bermudian Ch. Mar Del's Chow Mein, his dam was Mar Del's Snow Pea. By the end of 1971 Ringy had sired five champions: Mar Del's Guy Pan, Mar Del's King Kanishka, Emperor's Golden Fizz, Adair's Tek of Paisley and Ch. Paisley Ping Pong, #1 dog in the breed in 1971.

During 1972, yet another Shih Tzu superstar zoomed across the showdog horizon. Her name was Ch. Witch's Wood Yum Yum and she was owned by Dr. and Mrs. J. W. Edel. Whiz Bang had not been in the Top Ten listings up to that time, but 1972 was her year to star. As the #1 Shih Tzu in the United States for that year, she ran up a total of 14,792 points in the Phillips System. Remember, each point represents a dog defeated, and this total represented just about twice the number of points won by the #2 dog, Ch. Jaisu Hum Dinger of Loriel, owned by Dr. and Mrs. Dayle N. Rogers.

The remaining #3 through #10 listings were as follows: #3—Ch. Witch's Wood Socket Tumi, owned by S. Kovach; #4—Ch. Carrimount Ah-Tiko-Tiko, owned by Mrs. W.B. Long; #5—Ch. Choo Lang of Telota, owned by P. Frederico and W. Guzzy; #6—Ch. Sitsang Whiz Bang, the 1970 first place winner, owned by Dr. and Mrs. Dayle N. Rogers; #7—Ch. Mar Del's Ring A Ding Ding, the Edels' 1971 winner; #8—Ch. Mariljac Maripet, owned by M. L. Wood; #9—Ch. Legends Sakee Tu Yu, owned by Dr. F. G. and W. L. Addis with C. Robinson; #10—Ch. Greenmoss Golden Talon of Elfann, owned by D. Kath.

Not only was Yum Yum's accumulation of almost 15,000 points a remarkable accomplishment, but we must pay tribute to her ten Bests In Show and thirty Group Firsts. She also had twenty-five additional Group Placements to her credit. The Edels, and all Shih Tzu owners, could be justly proud!

In 1973 Ch. Witch's Wood Yum Yum held her #1 position at the top of the list. There were 17 Bests In Show for her this year with forty-eight Group Firsts and 26 Group Placements, out of seventy-eight Bests of Breed. Socket Tumi won two Bests in Show in 1973, and the #2 dog, Ch. Charing Cross Ching El Chang, and Ch. Carrimount Ah-Tiko-Tiko each won a Best In Show to earn them a spot in the Top Ten. The #3 dog was Ch. Bel Air Tigherson of Shang T'ou; #4—Ch. Jaisu Hum Dinger of Loriel; #5—Ch. Greenmoss Golden Talon of Elfann; #6—Ch. Carrimount Ah-Tiko-Tiko; #7—Ch. Witch's Wood Socket Tumi; #8—Ch. Mariljac Mari Pet; #9—Ch. Sitsang Whiz Bang; #10—Mar Del's Ring a Ding Ding.

In 1974 Ch. Witch's Wood Yum Yum held her #1 position for the third consecutive year. The tally for 1974 Bests In Show and Group Firsts for Yum Yum was 12 Bests and 42 Groups, which brought her three year #1 spot wins to a total of 39 Bests In Show, 121 Group Firsts and 90 additional Group Placements.

It was plain to see that by the end of 1974 there was a tremendous rise in the popularity of the Shih Tzu. In the relatively short period of time from the first imports to the end of the 1974 show season, the breed had grown by leaps and bounds.

American and Canadian Ch. Charing Cross Ching El Chang is a multiple Best In Show winner, owned by Lillian Phillips of Whispering Pines, North Carolina. At the time of his retirement in 1974 he was the top-winning male in the country. His total show ring tally was 7 Bests In Show, 28 Toy Group Firsts, and 60 Bests of Breed. He is the sire of two Best In Show daughters and many dogs who are about to finish their championship. Ching was handled during his ring career by Norman Patton.

Opposite top:
A "Ying Ying" double header! On January 8, 1977 Ch. Emperor's Thing Ah Ma Ying won Best in Show at the Shih Tzu Fanciers of Southern California Specialty Show. Thing Ah Ma Ying wins under judge Lucille Meystedt, and is handled by Lesley Boyes for owner Mrs. Frank Dinelli. At this same show the championship points also went to Ying's offspring.

Opposite, bottom:
Ch. Dragonwyck the Great Gatsby wins Best in Show at the all-breed Greater Daytona Dog Fanciers Association show under judge Tom Gately. Handed by Peggy Hogg for owner Robert Koeppel of New York City. The previous day, another Ying Ying son won the Shih Tzu Fanciers of Southern California Specialty Show.

According to statistics gleaned from the show results published in the *American Kennel Gazette,* there were 10,893 Shih Tzu exhibited in the show rings in 1974. This was a fantastic increase when compared with the entry of three at the 1957 Philadelphia Kennel Club Show and a total registration of 37 in 1961!

By 1975 and through the second half of the 1970's the breed was to soar even higher in both wins and registrations. Far too many dogs and bitches won Bests In Show to list them all here, though fortunately most all of them are represented in this book in photographs in which their remarkable show records speak for them. As we go to press Ch. Ying-Ying's long standing show record has been topped by Robert Koeppel's Ch. Dragonwyck The Great Gatsby, winner of the Ken-L Ration award for the most Toy Groups won in 1976.

Records are made to be broken, and the authors couldn't be happier that when the time came for Ying-Ying to relinquish his crown that it went to another of his illustrious sons. Gatsby has been capably handled throughout his career by Peggy Hogg. Norman Patton must be equally proud of this breeding and no less credit is due the dam, Ch. Mariljac Lotus Blossom.

The second half of the 1970's also saw some wonderful Best In Show wins for Ch. Chumulari Chih Te Jih, owned by Victor Joris, and Ch. House of Wu Hai-U, owned by Max W. Kerfoot and Mrs. Takako Comerford of Denver, Colorado, to name just a few. The list of Shih Tzu kennels is endless and we are gratified that so many of them appear in this book in photographs and through bloodlines representing their kennels. In the years to come there will be even more Shih Tzu fanciers working to preserve the excellence and beauty of this breed. We look forward to having them represented in yet another book we will write after another decade of progress in the breed.

At the Club VI Specialty Show in June 1976, Wendy and Richard Paquettes' Shih Tzu won Best Team—and Best Brace—in show! From left to right, Ch. Wenrick's Miss Bobbin, Ch. Wyvern M'Lord Ainslie, Ch. Wenrick's Tina Tina, Ch. Wenrick's Sweet JaiSon, all handled by their breeder/owner, Wendy Paquette. An American judge, Jay Schaeffer, presided.

Best in Show-winning Champion Chumulari Chin Te Jih takes the top award over an entry of 2,504 at the 1976 Eastern Dog show, under judge Kenneth C. Tiffin. Jane Forsyth handled for owner Victor Joris of New York. Shown on a limited basis, his record stands as of this writing at 1 Best in Show, 4 Group Firsts, 11 Group Placements and 26 Bests of Breed, including three from the classes. Bred by Margaret Easton, the sire was Am. Can. Ch. Chumulari Sheng-Li Che ex Can. Carrimount Tai-Tai Chumulari.

A classic study of Am. and Can. Ch. Chumulari YIng Ying taken by famous dog photographer Tauskey. This photo shows the quality of this great dog, who made breed history in the show ring and passed on much of his own excellence to his many champion offspring. Owned by the Rev. and Mrs. D. Allan Easton of Gardiner, New York.

Chapter 5
THE SHIH TZU STANDARD

An interesting line drawing depicting three expressions of Shih Tzu personality. At left we see the typically rounded head, wide between the eyes, and the characteristic top knot. In the center the lush hair at the top of the head is parted, rather than top knotted. And at right, a more animated expression is seen.

The Board of Directors of The American Kennel Club has approved the following Standard for Shih Tzu, to be effective September 1, 1969:

General Appearance: Very active, lively and alert, with distinctly arrogant carriage. The Shih Tzu is proud of bearing as befits his noble ancestry, and walks with head well up and tail carried gaily over the back.

Head: Broad and round, wide between the eyes. Muzzle square and short, but not wrinkled, about one inch from tip of nose to stop. *Definite Stop.* **Eyes:** Large, dark and round, but not prominent, placed well apart. Eyes should show warm expression. **Ears:** Large, with long leathers, and carried drooping; set slightly below the crown of the skull; so heavily coated that they appear to blend with the hair of the neck. ***Teeth:*** Level or slightly undershot bite.

Forequarters: Legs short, straight, well boned, muscular, and heavily coated. Legs and feet look massive on account of the wealth of hair.

Body: Body between the withers and the root of the tail is somewhat longer than the height at the withers; well coupled and sturdy. Chest broad and deep, shoulders firm, back level.

Hindquarters: Legs short, well boned and muscular, are straight when viewed from the rear. Thighs well rounded and muscular. Legs look massive on account of wealth of hair.

Feet: Of good size, firm, well padded, with hair between the pads. Dewclaws, if any, on the hind legs are generally removed. Dewclaws on the forelegs may be removed.

Tail: Heavily plumed and curved well over the back; carried gaily, set on high.

Coat: A luxurious, long, dense coat. May be slightly wavy but *not* curly. Good woolly undercoat. The hair on top of the head may be tied up.

Color: All colors permissible. Nose and eye rims black, except that dogs with liver markings may have liver noses and slightly lighter eyes.

Gait: Slightly rolling, smooth and flowing, with strong rear action.

Size: Height at withers—9 to 10½ inches—should be no more than 11 inches nor less than 8 inches. Weight of mature dogs—12 to 15 pounds—should be no more than 18 pounds nor less than 9 pounds. However, type and breed characteristics are of the greatest importance.

Faults: Narrow head, overshot bite, snipiness, pink on nose or eye rims, small or light eyes, legginess, sparse coat, lack of definite stop.

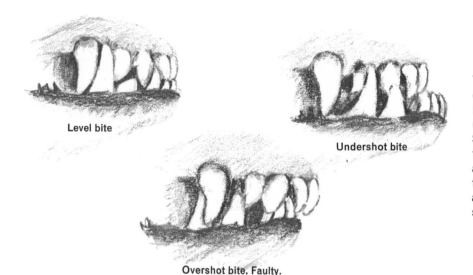

Level bite

Undershot bite

Overshot bite. Faulty.

The Shih Tzu standard calls for a level or slightly undershot bite. Shown at left are these two bites, along with one that is considered as a fault, an overshot bite.

An illustrated standard at a glance. This depiction of an "ideal" Shih Tzu specimen shows the well-plumed tail, top knot, and long whiskers and ear leathers that are the hallmarks of the breed.

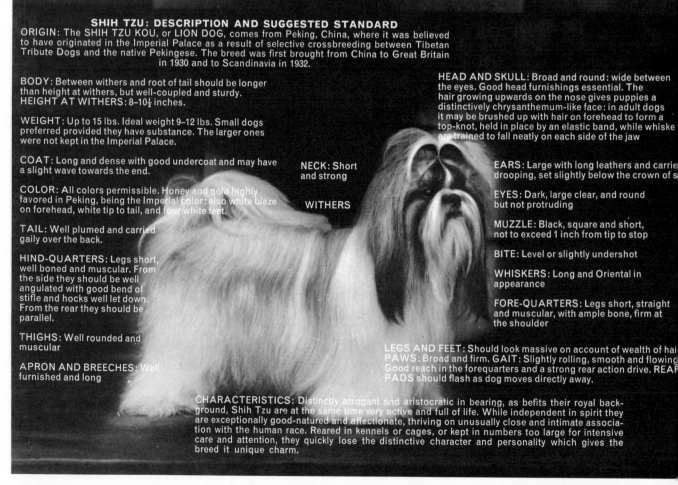

SHIH TZU: DESCRIPTION AND SUGGESTED STANDARD

ORIGIN: The SHIH TZU KOU, or LION DOG, comes from Peking, China, where it was believed to have originated in the Imperial Palace as a result of selective crossbreeding between Tibetan Tribute Dogs and the native Pekingese. The breed was first brought from China to Great Britain in 1930 and to Scandinavia in 1932.

BODY: Between withers and root of tail should be longer than height at withers, but well-coupled and sturdy.
HEIGHT AT WITHERS: 8–10½ inches.

WEIGHT: Up to 15 lbs. Ideal weight 9–12 lbs. Small dogs preferred provided they have substance. The larger ones were not kept in the Imperial Palace.

COAT: Long and dense with good undercoat and may have a slight wave towards the end.

COLOR: All colors permissible. Honey and gold highly favored in Peking, being the Imperial color: also white blaze on forehead, white tip to tail, and four white feet.

TAIL: Well plumed and carried gaily over the back.

HIND-QUARTERS: Legs short, well boned and muscular. From the side they should be well angulated with good bend of stifle and hocks well let down. From the rear they should be parallel.

THIGHS: Well rounded and muscular

APRON AND BREECHES: Well furnished and long

NECK: Short and strong

WITHERS

HEAD AND SKULL: Broad and round: wide between the eyes. Good head furnishings essential. The hair growing upwards on the nose gives puppies a distinctively chrysanthemum-like face: in adult dogs it may be brushed up with hair on forehead to form a top-knot, held in place by an elastic band, while whiske are trained to fall neatly on each side of the jaw

EARS: Large with long leathers and carrie drooping, set slightly below the crown of s

EYES: Dark, large clear, and round but not protruding

MUZZLE: Black, square and short, not to exceed 1 inch from tip to stop

BITE: Level or slightly undershot

WHISKERS: Long and Oriental in appearance

FORE-QUARTERS: Legs short, straight and muscular, with ample bone, firm at the shoulder

LEGS AND FEET: Should look massive on account of wealth of hai
PAWS: Broad and firm. GAIT: Slightly rolling, smooth and flowing Good reach in the forequarters and a strong rear action drive. REAR PADS should flash as dog moves directly away.

CHARACTERISTICS: Distinctly arrogant and aristocratic in bearing, as befits their royal background, Shih Tzu are at the same time very active and full of life. While independent in spirit they are exceptionally good-natured and affectionate, thriving on unusually close and intimate association with the human race. Reared in kennels or cages, or kept in numbers too large for intensive care and attention, they quickly lose the distinctive character and personality which gives the breed it unique charm.

Ch. Mar Del's Chia Jen of Copa is pictured winning at the 1972 Tidewater Kennel Club Show under judge Wilma Hunter. Everett Dean handled for owner Coni Nickerson of Richmond, Virginia. The sire was Ch. Mar Del's Chow Mein ex Ch. Mar Del's Samantha.

A darling photograph of a Shih Tzu mother and her puppy, owned by Gail Fletcher.

Ch. Dunklehaven Luv-Lee Ladee, bred by Elsie and James Dunkle and owned and shown by Carol Bogner. Ladee was later co-owned by J. Ray Johnson of Muncie, Indiana. Ladee is pictured here winning under judge Frances Thornton. She was whelped in September 1973.

The Carefree Kid pictured at 8 months of age. His sire was Ch. Char Nick's Foryo of Shirlynn out of Chumulari Ho Feng. Bred and owned by Nessa Gale of Phoenix, Arizona at her Ju I Kennels.

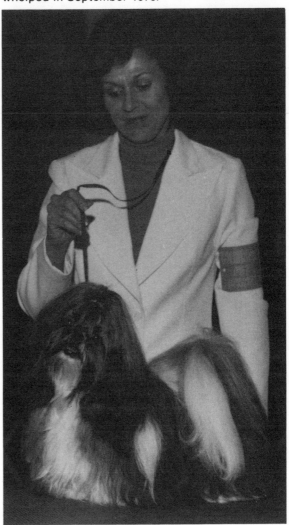

Zizi's Bombo-Tjimbo, bred by Ruth Laakso and owned by Mrs. Kirsti Wessel Dehlin of Fredrikstad, Norway. The sire was Norwegian Ch. Zizi's Law Hu, and the dam International, Swedish, Danish, Finnish and Norwegian Ch. Zizi's Lhamo. Photo by A. Laakso.

Chapter 6
COLOR AND APPEARANCE

Present-day standards prescribe no fixed color for the Shih Tzu, a position which may be explained by the varieties of coloring which have been seen in the breed since it first became known to the western world.

Interestingly enough, the first and second prize-winners at the Shanghai Kennel Club Show of May 30, 1930, probably among the first Shih Tzu ever to appear in a western-style show ring, were all black in color. Their photographs are to be seen in two consecutive issues of the *China Journal*, those of June and August, 1930.

Black and white was also frequently in evidence, so much so that the Countess d'Anjou somewhat disparagingly described them as "striking," but "very ordinary and not as precious as the golden." She made this observation in a letter from Juan-Les-Pins in France, dated May, 1955, which was reprinted in the American *Shih Tzu News*, March, 1967.

At the court golden-yellow, sometimes described as honey, was the "favorite" or "proper" color, and it has been claimed that these were the only ones kept in the palace. There may be some truth in this, but it is not clearly stated in the Countess' letter and Elsa and Ellic Howe assert that three of the Empress Dowager's "sleeve dogs" were greyish-white. We may be reasonably sure that these were not Shih Tzu Kou, however, as the "Tibetans" normally did not quite fit into the "sleeve" category, or so we are led to believe by Colonel Valentine Burkhardt.

Fuller details regarding Chinese views on color will be found in *The Lhassa Lion Dog* by Madame Lu, who makes the interesting point that "the yellow color of Lhassa Lion Dogs is more like that of a camel. If it is a bright and glossy yellow, the dog is not of a pure breed type."

Yellow has been the imperial color, of course, a fact not easily forgotten by anyone who has seen the golden-yellow tiled roofs of the Peking Palace. Yellow dogs are also more lion-like in appearance and it must not be overlooked that the word "Shih Tzu" means "Lion" in Chinese, the little dogs having been bred to resemble that animal as the Chinese conceived it. Although it is highly unlikely that many of them had ever seen a real one, the lion not being indigenous to China, they had a long-standing familiarity with "the fancy conventionalized types of lions introduced into China from India with Buddhism." This quotation is from Berthold Laufer's *Chinese Pottery of the Han Dynasty* which describes in detail how the lion motif made an enduring impression in old China as "its numerous connections with the legends woven around Buddha and the saints deeply appealed to the popular mind."

Faced with the existence by that time of a variety of coat colors, but anxious to do justice to the facts of history, the 1938 Peking Kennel Club Standard for the Shih Tzu runs, "all colors permissible, single and mixed. Tawny or honey-colored highly favored."

From this the 1958 British standard selects only, "all colors permissible," but adds the words, "a white blaze on the forehead and a white tip on the tail are highly prized." Also permitting any color, the French Standard of the mid-1950's comments, "honey-colored and white are rare and much appreciated."

The mention of white in the latter Standard reflects the fact that a leading French breeder in Peking—not the Countess d'Anjou—had a large number of all-white Shih Tzu, but it must be questioned whether the "appreciation" shown for them did not come more from westerners than from the natives of the city. Some six hundred years previously the Mongol, or Yuan, Dynasty did not share Chinese feelings on the subject, according to V.W.F. Collier's *Dogs of China and Japan in Nature and Art*, but in general there seems little doubt that "a dog of pure white, it being the color of mourning, was not an asset, as the Chinese hate to be reminded of death."

Apparently this aversion did not apply to white markings in the appropriate places, which were highly prized. The fullest reference to them in modern standards, although lacking in detail, appears to be in the "Breed Classification" for the Shih Tzu, handed by the American Kennel Club to judges while judging them in the Miscellaneous Class, which ran "all colors are allowable but in general the darker shades predominate. The white blaze, collar, socks and tail-tip combine

Peter of Jaxbo, 5-month-old puppy bred by Mrs. Julius Brown and owned by Mrs. James Davis of Jackson, Mississippi. The sire was Ch. Taramont Wang Chi ex General's Brown Sugar Nyu Chi.

One of Shirley Peerson's Shih Tzu. The Peerson Shih Tzu kennels are located in Pontiac, Michigan.

to create a highly prized ensemble.

Since the Chinese regarded the yellow-colored Shih Tzu as especially precious, it is understandable that is should have been particularly hard for westerners to lay hands on them, the Countess d'Anjou being very greatly privileged in this regard for the reason already stated. We are told, in *The Lion Dog Through the Looking Glass*, that it was the black and white, and grey and white, which first were found on the market at street fairs in China, and even in their case, exportation was at first forbidden.

When it did come become possible to export specimens of the breed, naturally it would appear that the least favored colors were the most easily obtainable. As a result, some years later we find it stated that in the show ring in Great Britain, "the dominant colors are black-and-white, grey-and-white and shades of brindle-and-white, with a few solid blacks. Goldens are seen less often, which is a pity." The words are those of Mrs. L.G. Widdrington, president of the Manchu Shih Tzu Society, in one of the society's newsletters.

It would seem certain that this scarcity of goldens accounts for the highly surprising omissions of any special preference for that color in the British standard, which appears to have been based on the situation prevailing at the time in England rather than on the Chinese ideal for the breed.

In the endeavor to secure a position of priority for the imperial color, a leading part has been taken by Mrs. Audrey Fowler, who—without doubt bitterly regretting that her original two little 12-pound imports left no issue—has stressed that, according to the Countess d'Anjou, honey, golden and gold-and-white were the most highly prized in China. Examples of this will be found in the British Magazine, *Our Dogs*, December, 1961, page 41; the British *Shih Tzu News*, February, 1966, page 17; and the American *Shih Tzu News*, June, 1966, inside back cover.

Not only in color but also in appearance the Shih Tzu is supposed to resemble a lion, albeit a lion as pictured by the Chinese who may never have set eyes on the real animal.

Stolidly Anglo-Saxon in appearance, too many Shih Tzu bear a much closer resemblance to the Cheshire cat as portrayed in children's editions of Lewis Carroll's *Alice in Wonderland*. In such cases, only the most strictly selective breeding can restore to succeeding generations the oriental look. After passing through the "chrysanthemum" stage, for a time a Shih Tzu puppy can legitimately resemble a very cuddlesome Australian koala bear, but an adult should be distinctively and unmistakably Chinese in appearance.

RELATIONSHIP TO THE PEKINGESE

Although some western scholars have question-

Ch. Lau Rin Destiny of Shang T'kow, owned by Laura Riney of Louisville, Kentucky. Breeder was Eleanore Eldredge.

ed it, as we have seen it was quite certainly believed in China that the Shih Tzu were, at least in part, Tibetan in origin. While such strongly established and widely held opinions may not be accurate sources of information regarding details, they are rarely without some foundation in fact.

For this reason I find myself personally unconvinced by Berthold Laufer's assertion that, after having "specially hunted for this purpose" through the available records, he could not "find, in fact, any instance in Chinese history of dogs having been exported from Tibet into China."

In any event, the Shih Tzu's Tibetan heritage is surely demonstrated by its appearance and by its close similarity—in certain respects—to the Lhasa Apso, which undoubtedly hails from that country.

Vigorously challenged by some western breeders, but firmly believed by those in China who were in a better position to know, is the fact that the Shih Tzu from Tibet were on occasion interbred with the native Pekingese. For example, Volume III of Colonel Valentine Burkhardt's *Chinese Creeds and Customs* mentions this, distinguishing the Shih Tzu from the imperial lap dogs but pointing out that they were interbred. Parallel statements are to be found in V.W.F. Collier's *Dogs of China in Nature and Art*, on pages 164 and 186, as well as in *The Lhassa Lion Dog*, on pages 6 and 7, where Madame Lu takes the fact of cross-breeding for granted.

Ch. Rockee-Vollee Kim-Ko of Luv-Tzu, pictured winning at a 1976 show on the way to championship. Owned by Rockee-Vollee Kennels of Forest Lake, Minnesota.

Hadda Shu van de Oranje Manege, bred in Holland by Eta Pauptit and imported by owner Eleanore Eldredge. She was the dam of Best in Show dog, Int. Ch. Freya Shu van de Oranje Manege and many other American champions. Hadda was also the dam of the first West Coast Shih Tzu champion.

Chumulari Erh-Tzu-Ying, 20 month old gold and white dog with black tippings, owned by Mrs. Glae S. Bickford of Nevada.

At ease! Ch. Lansu Magnolia Time, owned by Diana Henry of Columbus, Ohio. The sire was Lansu Eastertime of Elfanzo ex English Ch. Golden Summertime of Elfann. Breeder was Tom Hoyle.

Ch. Largyn Forget-Me-Not of Nanjo. "Munchkin" is owned by Largyn Shih Tzu, Virginia Smigley, Phoenixville, Pennsylvania.

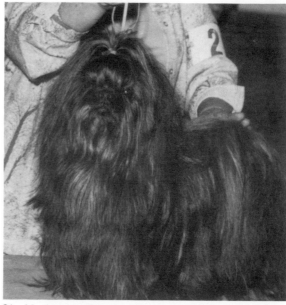

Ch. Maricam's Tiki Tiki Tembo, whelped in August 1971, has numerous Breed and Group Placements. The sire was Ch. Fluff and Stuff of Paisley ex Ki X Lin of Chasmu. Bred and owned by Camille Beranti and Marie Beranti of Bethpage, New York.

If this thought seems strange to western fanciers, it must be remembered that the Chinese did not breed by pedigree; rather, they aimed to produce a type as close as possible to a picture before them.

Thus, cross-breeding was apparently done sometimes to reduce the size of the Shih Tzu (Burkhardt), sometimes to improve the coat of the Pekingese (Collier), while Madame Lu suggests that it was also done to produce different types and colors.

This last might possibly explain the Princess Der Ling's reference to vain efforts by the Empress Dowager to reproduce a dog which "seemed sort of outcast. His coloring was yellow and black, and his measurements were perfect. Her Majesty had spent much time to try and find a mate for him with the same markings, but during my time at court she did not succeed. It was one of her few failures."

It is also possible that the cross-breeding was designed to change the shape of the Tibetan dog's skull and to flatten the forehead, making it more lion-like in Chinese eyes. We refer to the article by Miss S.M. Lampson, entitled *Lion Dog of the Manchu Emperors*, in the British magazine *Country Life*, June 14, 1962, on page 1413. There Miss Lampson shares our view that "the Shih Tzu of China are unquestionably very close relations of the Apsos of Tibet."

Since the eunuchs vied with one another in the production of exquisite little gems for the ladies of the imperial court, it may well be that their "trade" secret was the occasional introduction of Pekingese blood. As has been suggested to us by a student of the subject, it is perfectly possible that little or nothing of this secret was known outside the servants' quarters.

Whether or not this last point is true, for one reason or another it seems undeniably true that Pekingese blood was on occasion introduced into the palace "Tibetans" or Shih Tzu Kou.

This is the justification for the "Peke cross," introduced on one occasion in England in 1952 with the specific purpose of eliminating "certain faults in the breed." This was done under the strictest possible controls, and with the full knowledge of the British Kennel Club and of the officials of the breed club at the time.

In fairness to all concerned, it must be remembered that there were very special reasons why it seemed necessary in England at that time to introduce the cross to produce "a new bloodline to be bred back to the original strain." The words are those of Mrs. Thelma Morgan, a founder member of the Manchu Shih Tzu Society and an enthusiastic supporter of the breed.

"If a World War, and a clamping down of trade afterwards had not prevented more stock being obtained," Mrs. Morgan recalled in 1966, "then I doubt whether a cross would have been either contemplated or allowed by the English Kennel Club." While this provides the immediate reason for the action taken at that time, very much more important is the fact that it can be amply explained and defended in the light of the background and history of the Shih Tzu.

The cross was made under the meticulous supervision of Miss E.M. Evans, a distinguished and highly successful breeder of Pekingese, whose growing love for the Shih Tzu led her to the conviction that this courageous step was necessary for the betterment of the breed in England. In defense of her action, she explained that the Shih Tzu in her homeland were too large, too high on leg, too long of muzzle with very bad pigmentation and too closely inbred.

For this reason, Miss Evans bred a Shih Tzu bitch, Elfann Fenling of Yram, with a beautifully coated black-and-white Pekingese, Philadelphus Suti T'Sun of Elfann "with perfect pigment, large dark eyes, whose only fault was *straight* legs."

The offspring of this one and only outcross were bred back to purebred Shih Tzu, only one from each generation being selected for this purpose, and the successive breedings were fully recorded with the British Kennel Club in the crossbred register. With the fourth generation, containing only one-sixteenth Pekingese ancestry, the dogs were recognized by the British Kennel Club as purebred Shih Tzu and were registered and shown as such.

Published fourteen years after, the *Manchu Shih Tzu Society News Letter,* March, 1966, on pages 5, 6 and 7, contains a clear summation by Miss Evans who writes that, by that time, British breeders "with the cross are greatly in the majority and their owners appear to be quite happy with

The Pekingese Cross of 1952 was introduced as follows:

Tee-ni Tim of Michelcombe
(dog)

        Sire: Fu Chuan of Elfann
        (Shih Tzu)

Shih Wei Tzu   *Sire:* Ch. Choo-ling (Shih Tzu)
of Elfann (bitch)

        Dam: Yu Honey of Elfann

                                       Sire: Philadelphus Suti
                                       T'Sun of Elfann
                                       (Pekingese)
Mu-Ho (bitch)   *Dam:* Yu Sunny of Elfann
                                       Dam: Elfann Fenling of
                                         Yram (Shih Tzu)

Third Cross   Second Cross   First Cross

Except for Ch. Choo-ling, who belonged to Lady Brownrigg, all the dogs concerned belong to Miss Evans.

After the third cross, all subsequent generations were given a Class I Certificate by the Kennel Club (England) and accepted as purebred Shih Tzu. The American Kennel Club required three or more generations. A great-grandson of Tee-ne Tim of Michelcombe, Fu-ling of Clystevale—imported into Sweden in 1958—was six generations from the original cross (1/64th Pekingese)—one generation short of the very stringent requirement of the American Kennel Club.

International and Scandinavian Ch. Dralhas Fei-Ying. She was the top-winning bitch in Sweden for 1976. Bred by Mrs. Inger Fallberg, she is owned by Mrs. Ulla-Britt Wifalk of Taby, Sweden. The sire was Duc Tzu av Willehard ex Formaregardens Pi-Nhette.

Tai-Chi's Aimee, born in March, 1972, and pictured at 3 months of age. Aimee is breeder owned by Rita Ravn and Christian Ravn, Kennel Ta-Chi, Viborg, Denmark. The sire was Int. and Scan. Ch. Bjorneholm's Hsiao-Ping ex Ah-Kamas Rebecca.

Norwegian Ch. Khublai-Khan van de Blauwe Mammouth, whelped October 1969. Bred by Baronesse van Panthaleon van Eck-Klasing, at her Kennel de Blauwe Mammouth in the Netherlands, Kubi is owned by Ruth Laakso of Drammen, Norway. The sire was Rockafella of Bracewell ex Emma of Myarlune. Kubi is grandfather of the top-winning Shih Tzu in Sweden for 1975 and 1976. Photo by A. Laakso.

their dogs, and there are now 15 champions with the cross. Certain improved characteristics have been claimed—especially pigmentation and the correct shorter leg."

There can be little doubt that the majority of informed Shih Tzu breeders, both in Great Britain and elsewhere, would now agree that this very carefully controlled cross was good for the breed and had ample historical justification.

According to the *Manchu Shih Tzu Society News Letter* of May/June, 1968, something of the "Peke Cross" was introduced into the Scandinavian line ten years before this with the importation into Sweden of the English-bred Fu-Ling of Clystvale. This stud was exchanged for the Swedish-bred Jungfaltets Jung Ming, an exchange of bloodlines which is said to have done much to improve both Scandinavian and English stock.

Mrs. Erma Jungefeldt has written an interesting account of their visit to England in 1958 when she and her husband attended championship shows at Blackpool and Windsor, looking for "a small Shih Tzu as a stud dog for our own kennel and the Shih Tzu breed in Sweden."

"The Shih Tzu were mostly terribly big, near 18 pounds in weight," Mrs. Jungefeldt recalls. "Suddenly we found a small black-and-white youth by the name of Fu-Ling of Clystvale, owned by Mrs. Longden. We saw Fu-Ling at both shows. He was a little bit bashful and not a real shower, but of real good size, low on legs, a wonderfully strong chest and with a weight of about nine and a half pounds, the smallest one we had seen in England."

Fu-Ling proved an outstanding success in the Scandinavian show ring, not only by his own successes but also by those of his offspring. Quickly winning his Swedish championship with very favorable comments from the judges, he eventually sired "more than 23 champions and challenge certificate winners, many Best In Show and Group winners, and his sons and daughters have won in several countries of Europe and also in the United States."

At the age of eleven, this famous sire was described as "still going strong and admired for his low weight and small type." Clearly, Fu-Ling of Clystvale's distant relationship to Miss Evan's Pekingese had done him no harm, to say the least!

In a statement issued by the Manchu Shih Tzu Society, Shih Tzu imported to America from England should be at least seven generations removed from the original cross, which means that the three generation export pedigree should not carry the name of any dog registered with the British Kennel Club as a cross breed.

Int., Dan., Fin., Swed., and Nor. Ch. Zizi's Lhamo, owned and bred by Ruth Laakso, Drammen, Norway. A top-producer and well-known in her native land, her sire was Ho-Thi-Bi Fan ex Dan. and Nor. Ch. Marinas Dog-Rose.

Swedish and Finnish Champion Zizi's Lingschi-Tang, shown at 8 months. "Tangen" is the sire of the top-winning Shih Tzu in Sweden for 1975 and 1976. Int. Nor. Ch. In-Cheng. He is also sire of Mrs. Else Grum's dog Ting-Mo in Norway. Bred by Ruth Laakso, he is owned by Rose Akersten of Stockholm, Sweden. The sire was Nor. Ch. Khublai-Khan van de Blauwe Mammouth ex Int. Scan. and Dan. Ch. Zizi's Lhamo.

Handsome trio featuring Mi Ti Fli N Mouse of La Ke, C.D., on top, and owned by Geni Johnson. Lower left, Ch. Jocliff Hi N Mi Ti of La Ke owned by Elizabeth A. Rovillo and Kati Busby, owners of Mi Ti Pum Kin Boi of La Ke, featured on the right. Photo by Jim Oates.

Mrs. Else Grum with Tsing-Tze, owned by Ruth Laakso, Norway, shown in a photo taken during the summer of 1971.

Similarly, the three-generation export pedigree should not list the name of any import, so that Shih Tzu coming from Europe to the United States should be at least four generations removed from those brought out of China.

This clarification by the Manchu Shih Tzu Society is borne out by a letter from Mr. John Brownell, Assistant to the Executive Vice-President of the American Kennel Club, addressed to Miss Olga Dakan and dated June 14, 1963. As the years go by, however, these questions should become matters of purely academic interest.

Defending the Pekingese cross made by Miss Evans in 1952 to improve the quality of the Shih Tzu in England, other fanciers on both sides of the Atlantic have been quick to point out that there are "many breeds which, to improve type, have had another breed introduced to them." One asserts that the Cavalier King Charles Spaniel had two breeds crossed into the strain in its early days. Another maintains that the Affenpinscher and Standard Schnauzer together produced the Miniature Schnauzer, the Australian and Yorkshire Terriers, the Silky Terrier, while "in England the Bearded Collie was crossed into the Old English Sheepdog to reduce the size of the latter," and Cocker Spaniel blood was apparently

Yingsu Brendee Lee of Gralee is pictured winning Winners Bitch at a 1976 Canadian Specialty Show for a 3-point major. Brendee is pictured here at 10 months of age finishing her championship in August 1976. Brendee is owned by Leslie Sherratt of Ontario, Canada.

introduced to save the Sussex Spaniel from the threat of extinction.

On such matters, every Shih Tzu fancier is entitled to express his own point of view. Those who claim to have "pure" stock "without Pekingese blood," however, as is occasionally advertised, somehow give the impression that they believe the Shih Tzu to have dropped straight from heaven in its present form! Certainly no one who has ever lived in China would make the mistake of assuming that court breeding practices were similar to those rigidly enforced by a modern European or North American Kennel Club.

THE SHIH TZU TIBETAN HERITAGE

If the views just expressed seem controversial, it cannot be too strongly emphasized that they represent a relatively mild echo of opinions expressed by at least one authority in China during the period when the Shih Tzu was first becoming known to the western world. Mr. A. Sowerby, editor of the *China Journal* of Shanghai and an obviously knowledgeable dog-lover, wrote in the February, 1933, issue on page 12:

"It is in our opinion that the Tibetan Lion Dog is the result of a cross between the Lhassa Terrier and the Pekingese, which has arisen out of the mixing of the two breeds both in Tibet and China, since the dogs of each country have been taken to the other from time to time by tribute envoys and officials. The cross in Tibet, that has been taken out of that country by way of India, has been called the Apso, while the cross in Peking has been called the Tibetan Poodle or Lion Dog. Doubtless, the Tibetan cross has more of the Lhassa Terrier in it, while the Chinese cross has more of the Pekingese."

Finally, in June, 1937, after reading a book called *Pure Bred Dogs,* published in the United States, Mr. Sowerby commented in his periodical on page 365:

"A picture of a Lhassa Terrier is given that helps clear up for us in China the difficulty surrounding the identities of so-called 'Tibetans.' This apparently is the 'Apso' of English fanciers, and it may at once be distinguished from the Tibetan Lion Dog which we get in Peiping by its much longer and straighter legs."

"Old China Hands" will have no difficulty in understanding Mr. Sowerby's approach to the problem and will agree that he is probably right in his conclusions.

As has already been noted, when first imported into England in 1930, the Shih Tzu were classified as Apsos, the two breeds not being distinguished until 1934. Noting the existence of "con-

Nor. Swed. and Fin. Champion Zizi's Tara, the top-winning bitch in Scandinavia. She has been Best in Show and has 10 C.A.C.I.B. certificates from nine different judges. Sire was Int. Scan. Ch. Marinas Muff-Lung-Fang ex Int. Scan. Danish Ch. Zizi's Lhamo. Owned by Ruth Laakso, Drammen, Norway.

Danish Consul Kaj Grum with Ting-Tze at Huk in Oslofjord, Norway during the winter of 1973.

siderable confusion," and obviously concerned that any "said to be" Chinese Lion Dog should challenge the longer established Pekingese, a commentator was quick to point out that the newcomers were very definitely not lion-like in looks. This criticism might still have been levelled at some English Shih Tzu in the several years that followed since their appearance did much to create confusion with the Lhasa Apso.

In this respect, the Shih Tzu of Scandinavian

background were in a different category. We have never heard of any dogs of their lines being mistaken for Lhasa Apso, even after importation into the United States. Their distinctive appearance was such that there was no likelihood of confusion.

As far as the United States is concerned, the aforementioned seven early imports from England are said to have been registered as Apsos between 1942 and 1952. Steps were taken to prevent further mistakes of this nature, once the error was known. The British Shih Tzu Club expressed their fear of potentially "disastrous" cross-breedings in the United States and agreed to encourage future American purchasers to do everything possible "to avoid any further confusion between the Shih Tzu and Lhasa Apso in the U.S.A."

Although the two breeds have been kept completely separate for many years now, on April 7, 1966, it was reported in the *New York Times* that "one obstacle (in the way of recognition) was that the Shih Tzu strongly resembles the Lhasa Apso, also a Tibetan breed that already was in the American Kennel Club's official family of purebreds. The American Kennel Club needs assurance that the two are separate breeds."

The situation was not helped by the photograph accompanying the article, presumably supplied by a well-meaning fancier, showing a dog which bore a striking resemblance to a Lhasa Apso. By a strange coincidence, apart from a difference in position and color and a slightly different combing of the head furnishings, it was virtually identical to a Lhasa Apso which had been pictured in the same newspaper almost exactly one year previously, on April 8, 1965. As long as fanciers continue to give prominence to Shih Tzu of this type, apparently believing that the breed need only be shaggy and without any distinctive Chinese characteristics, confusion with the Apso seems inevitable.

In this regard, there is much wisdom in the advice of Mrs. Irene Booth, editor of the *Manchu Shih Tzu Society News Letter*, who wrote in the December, 1965, issue: "We help by always showing the Shih Tzu with the long sweep of hair on the top of the head tied with a rubber band into a top knot, the hair above the head then fanning out into a 'palm tree.' The Apso, on the other hand, has its long hair of the head parted in the center, then mingling with the ear featherings."

An illuminating discussion of the relationship between the two breeds is to be found in the Shih Tzu column in *Popular Dogs* of October and November, 1968, where the guest columnist was

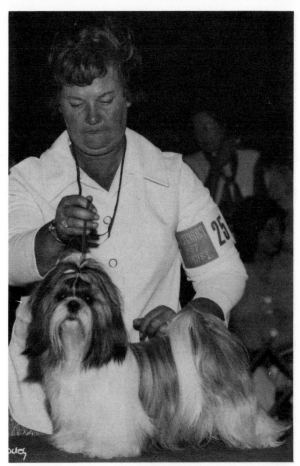

Ch. Aja Shu van de Oranje Manege, Dutch import owned by Ellen M. Keenan of Phoenix, Arizona, is pictured winning Best of Winners on the way to championship at a 1973 show under judge Heywood Hartley. Judy Webb is handling for the owner.

an English fancier who has made an extensive study of Tibetan-Chinese breeds. An Apso breeder of international repute, this lady has belonged to the British Tibetan Apso Club, of which she is a listed judge. So important are her observations that we repeat them at length:

"Shih Tzu people even now meet the question, 'Is it a Tibetan?' Apso breeders are asked, 'It's a Shih Tzu, isn't it?' That confusion still exists about the two breeds poses some questions. Are we careful enough to emphasize the distinctions of the two breeds' types? Do we really appreciate the subtleties of the different characteristics of Chinese Shih Tzu and Tibetan Apso?

"In those indications of their countries of origin lies the key to it. That both Shih Tzu and Apso have common ancestry is highly probable; that they have become two quite distinct breeds is certainly the result of selectivity by man, and, even more important, the different climates and environments of the lands in which they developed.

"There is good reason to suppose that the cult of the 'Lion Dog' began in Tibet around Lhasa,

Three Shih Tzu owned by Colonel and Mrs. David Langdon of Washington, D.C. Left to right are Ko Ko of Shu Lin, and Pia Mia of Shu Lin, both bred by Dr. and Mrs. Sidney Bashore of Colorado. In the center is their daughter, Ta Kao Josephine of Ssu-Chi.

American and Bermudian Champion Mar Del's Chow Mein. Bred by Ingrid Colwell, the owner is Margaret Edel MacIntosh of Millerstown, Maryland. The sire was Jungfaltets Wu Po ex Si-Kians Mi-Tzi.

Seven month old Chumulari Huo-Chi, owned by Mrs. Clara Bothe of Maryland.

Ch. Marco Polo di Visconti was used to represent the Shih Tzu Standard in *Dog World* Magazine in 1978. His litter brother Kublai Khan was the representative in 1976. Marco is owned by Jon C. Ferrante of Waldorf, Maryland.

American and Canadian Ch. Chumulari Ying-Ying was photographed by Alton Anderson on his 11th birthday for owners Rev. and Mrs. D. Allan Easton of Gardiner, New York.

Canadian Ch. Elfann Golden Adonis, owned by Del and Connie Smart, Conwynn Shih Tzu, Akron, Ohio.

and preceded the similar cult in China by several centuries.

"The earliest 'Lion Dog' in Tibet were probably long-haired and small and somewhat similar to the Maltese in type. As the cultural and religious ties between Tibet and China ebbed and flowed over the centuries, the exchange of dogs no doubt became a two-way affair. The Chinese most certainly interbred their small dogs, of which there were many varieties, with the long-haired Tibetans, and something similar no doubt occured in Tibet.

"The outcome of this interbreeding were the Shih Tzu—which the Chinese are said to call the 'Tibetan Lion Dog'—and the Apso which the Tibetans refer to as *Apso Seng Kyi* or 'Apso Lion Dog'.

"The Chinese would undoubtedly try to retain the characteristics they admired—the unnaturally short face and broad head, the wide barrel-like chest, the low-to-the-ground look.

"The Tibetans, on the other hand, would not be able to hold these characteristics, because of the climate and environment of the land itself. Tibet is an area of high altitudes, and Lhasa, the real home of the Apso, is high. The very short face, with its restricted nasal development, and the heavy body and short legs, would be at a disadvantage in these conditions, and could not survive as fixed characteristics of a breed. They

would adapt, naturally, to the environment, so that Tibetans would produce a dog slightly modified from the Chinese dog of a similar ancestry.

"If one views the Chinese and Tibetan dogs on a scale of progression from the natural dog to the most unnatural, the importance of these distinctions can be appreciated more readily.

"The Tibetan Terrier is probably the nearest to the basic canine, a long-headed type, compact but natural in conformation.

"Then comes the Apso, which shows the influence of some 'foreign type.' This influence results in a small dog, shorter in the leg than its terrier relative, shorter in the nose—approximately 1½ inches, with proportions of one third to two thirds of the whole head, as against the terrier's two inch nose and half-and-half proportions. The teeth and jaw formation reveal the shortening of the face, the lower incisors being set in a straight line, and not in a curve as in the basic dog. The eyes are not oblique, though not globular, and are more frontally placed. The skull is a concession to the Tibetan environment and is narrow, though not as narrow as that of the terrier.

"Compare this with the Shih Tzu, in which the 'foreign' characteristics are more emphasized than

Pictured here at three months of age is future American and Canadian Ch. Raina's Moonglow, owned by Lorraine Parasiliti of Binghamton, New York.

Noble's J-Son is pictured winning the Toy Group under judge William Kenrick at the 1973 Dog Fanciers Association of Oregon show. Bred and owned by Orpha Noble, J-Son is handled by Gloria Busselman. The sire was Maril-jac De End ex Noble's Ma-ling Si-Sing.

in the Apso, and reveal its Chinese origin. The chest is wider, the leg is shorter still, and although it must appear straight, the foreleg can have a slight bow to the upper part (provided feet do not turn out and the elbows in). The nose is further reduced, to approximately an inch, or about one-fourth to three-fourths of the whole head. The skull is broad and the whole appearance of the head is short and broad. The movement is strong and free, but more arrogant and not as floating and agile as the Apso.

"The Chinese characteristics in the Shih Tzu, however, are not nearly as exaggerated as in the Pekingese, in which they become the furthest removed of all from the basic, natural dog."

Smallness must have been fashionable and something of a status symbol in both Apso and Shih Tzu, the column continues, provided the essential characteristics and type were maintain-ed. In this regard, the Chinese breeding program

was more effective than the Tibetan, being less casual, although in both breeds, in that writer's opinion, "you get true miniatures."

After the publication of this article, there was a challenge about whether the *original* Tibetan Lion Dog, bred by monks in the monasteries many centuries ago, was probably extinct, the present Apso being a modification of it with some Chinese blood.

According to his comments in the February, 1933, issue of the *China Journal* of Shanghai, quoted earlier, Mr. Sowerby would have endorsed this suggestion wholeheartedly, and the views of such an authority on Oriental breeds are not to be taken lightly.

Although I have not seen it personally, I am reliably informed that strong support for the above suggestion will be found in a letter by Mr. Brian Vesey-Fitzgerald, which appeared under the Tibetan Breed notes in the British magazine

Lainee X-Tra Exciting, bred and owned by Elaine Meltzer of New York City and co-owned by Patricia Wells. In limited showing Exciting has won both majors including a Best of Breed win from the classes. He was whelped May 20, 1975.

Bill Feigert is pictured with his award-winning photograph of Mary Marxen's Shih Tzu named "Doc." 856 photographs were submitted for the 22nd Annual Convention of Professional Photographers of Ohio. Bill is the owner of the Feigert Studios.

Jane Fitts with the 6-month-old Encore A I Jen at her Encore Kennels in Solvang, California.

Our Dogs, of July, 17, 1953. According to an informant in whom I have the utmost confidence, this letter ran:

"Such information as I have came from Kusho Chang Fa (Ringang), one of the old ruling caste of Tibet and a former minister, who was educated at Rugby, (a well known English boarding school), and was a great friend of mine.

"As I understand it, Apso means dog, no more than that. Once it used to mean Temple dog, and in that connection came to mean Lion Dog (a temple synonym), but that was a long time ago. I have always understood that it was about 1650 that three temple dogs, holy dogs, were sent to China and that from these three came the Shih Tzu. About 100 years later, so I have always understood, the then-Dalai Lama (and up to that time the temple dog had been his special property), gave some away to distinguished visitors, who were Russians. These dogs were stolen before they had reached the border, and about the same time, during a civil upheaval, a good many more disappeared from the Dalai Lama's monastery and reappeared in various parts of the country. That was the end of the Temple or Lion Dog, the Apso. From then on, all sorts of small dogs bearing some resemblance, however vague, to the Apso of old became known as Apso. It was the end of the temple dog, but it was the start of the Monastery dog and also the caravan dog."

Ch. Hodari Tam Lin of Moon Ling, pictured at 15 months of age. Co-owned by Laurie Battey and Helen McClarnon of Torrance, California.

Hwang-Han V.D. Blauwe Mammouth, gold and white dog, pictured here at 5 months of age, bred in the Netherlands by the Baronesse van Panthaleon van Eck and presented to the Rev. and Mrs. D. Allan Easton in recognition of their services to the breed.

Ch. Taramont General Su Wu, pictured going Winners Dog under judge Louis Murr at the 1973 Tallahassee Kennel Club Show with his handler John Murdock. Owned by Mrs. Julius Brown and the late Dr. Brown of Jackson, Mississippi.

American, Bermudian, and Canadian Champion Mai Ling of Mountainside, owned by Mrs. Dorothea Breganti of Newton, New Jersey. She is the first American female in the breed to win a championship in all three of these countries, and receive a *Dog World* Magazine certificate to commemorate the accomplishment. She is a "Pif" daughter out of Mariljac Su Ling of Montnside.

The contents of this letter may not be wholly accurate, not only because the English writer could have been confused regarding detail, but even more because most of the information must have been passed down from one generation to another for some two centuries. For example, it is questionable whether "Apso" does mean only "dog," there being some reason to believe that it means also "goat-like" or "shaggy."

However, none of the parties concerned could have had the slightest reason to fabricate the story regarding the extinction of the original Holy Dog, least of all the Tibetans, who would have been much more likely to conceal the fact that there had been any break in the direct line of succession. In our opinion, the highly unexpected nature of the story is itself convincing evidence of its truth.

If this is correct, neither the present day Apso nor the Shih Tzu can be regarded as "pure" representatives of the historic Tibetan Holy Dog,

both being the products of interbreeding in various degrees. In any event, the two are clearly historically related, the Apso having developed along distinctively Tibetan lines, while the Shih Tzu, through climate, environment and human planning, has become essentially Chinese.

In Reverend Easton's December, 1965, Shih Tzu column in *Popular Dogs* magazine he wrote, "Closely related in the distant past, for centuries the two breeds have developed along totally different lines. While the Apso remained in the remote vastness of Tibet, from which it came to us recently by way of India, long years ago the Shih Tzu was taken eastward to share in the life of the Chinese court.

"In Scandinavia, where it was brought directly from Peking 33 years ago, the Shih Tzu is classified and shown as a Toy. Undoubtedly, this is a correct interpretation of the Chinese ideal. How else can we explain the careful introduction of the Pekingese strain, except that it was design-

Best in Show Ch. Char Nick's Be-Wit-Ching of Copa. Owned by Carole S. Davis of Richmond, Virginia. The sire was Ch. Char Nick's I Gotcha ex Ch. Char Nick's Sesame of Sam Chu. Breeders Mr. and Mrs. Louis Sanfillippo. The Witch was Best of Breed at the 1974 American Shih Tzu Club Specialty Show.

Wix Oliver Tu of Toi-Lan, owned by Glenda Wicks of Kansas City, Kansas.

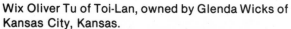

Char Nick's My Sin pictured winning at the 1972 Trenton Kennel Club show under judge Anna Katherine Nicholas. Handler was Mr. Sanfilippo.

Ch. Ca Pi of Dreghorn, whelped in 1965, finished for championship in 1970, handled by Richard Vaughn for owner Mrs. T. W. Ruggie of Ft. Lauderdale, Florida. This Scottish import was bred by Mrs. V. G. Knox of Midlothian, Scotland, and is pictured finishing under judge Cass.

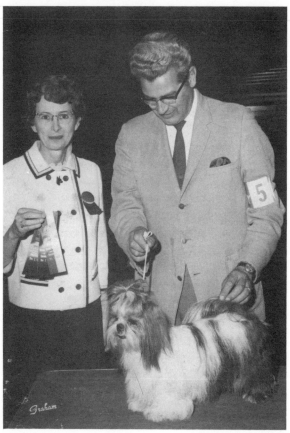

ed to make the larger mountain watchdog more suitable for the imperial drawing room? This is part of the breed's unique heritage, of which we have no cause to be ashamed.

"For all his lion-hearted courage, the ideal Shih Tzu is essentially a small dog.

"Both physically and in temperament, there is an unmistakable difference between the cautious guard dog from the hidden Himalayas and his gaily topknotted little relative, who comes as a household pet from the more-sophisticated palaces of Peking."

It should be noted that the traffic appears to have operated in both directions, Pekingese and other palace dogs being on occasion taken, or sent as gifts, to Tibet where they were interbred with the native variety. Although it is improbable that the process was as carefully controlled as at the imperial court, there is some evidence that it did lead to the appearance of dogs with strong similarities in character to the Peking Shih Tzu.

In the year 1900 at the hill station of Muree in India there was shown for the first time as a separate breed a variety known as the Lhassa or Bhutan Terriers, sometimes called Lhassa Spaniels, their place of origin presumably indicated by their name. Of these dogs it is written that "they are most lovable little fellows, clever as performing dogs, devoted companions, exceedingly quaint, and with a charm of their own.

They are described as natural beggers, so much so that the Princess of Wales, later to become Queen Alexandra, remarked on seeing one on exhibit in England, "That little dog is begging to leave the show." In fact, nothing could have been further from the truth, the little performer being in his element!

Regarding this breed, Mrs. McLaren Morrison, an early importer and authority, wrote in 1904, "I would like to see much more attention paid to size, to which the natives of the country they come from attach the greatest importance. There really should be two classes for them, over and under a certain weight."

No such division was made at that time, in spite of Mrs. McLaren Morrison's urging, but the question of size was to arise 62 years later with the comments that the breed in England, by then known as Tibetan Spaniels, was "not dainty enough," being "heavier" and "bigger all over." At about the same time, another English writer suggested that there was a "strong resemblance" between the Tibetan Spaniel and "some Apso." Reference to this will be found in the English *Dog World* of February 11 and May 27, 1966.

In a discussion of the background of the

Tibetan Spaniel, to be found in *About Our Dogs* by A. Croxton Smith, we are told that Mrs. McLaren Morrison regarded it as "ancestor of the Pekingese. Others say it owes its origin to the Chinese dogs, which were taken into Tibet and crossed with the Lhassa Terriers. He is a small toy, standing on short legs and having a rather long body. The legs are straighter than those of the Pekingese and the jaws are of a natural state."

Describing the breed in the 1930s, after "over thirty years experience of judging Tibetan Spaniels," the Honorary Secretary of the Kennel Club of India wrote in *Hutchinson's Dog Encyclopaedia:*

"The Standard might be put into a few words, viz. 'A Pekingese gone wrong,'—the face is not flat, and the muzzle is as prominent as in any ordinary breed; the skull, instead of being flat, is more rounded. The body is long for the dog's height, the coat like a Pekingese, the plume not so full as the Peke but the tail lighter feathered and curled over the back; legs short, but the forelegs quite straight; chest not wide like the Peke, the

Ch. Dashi's Chin-Tan pictured winning with handler Wendell Sammet for owner and breeder Catherine Pouliot of Manchester, Connecticut.

Jennifer Murphy with Hsi Jenni Tu as a puppy. Tina was sired by Ch. Mariljac Ta-Kuai ex Mariljac Thumbelina.

Foxhall Floydian Slip, pictured with her handler Terry Hubbs. Owned and bred by Peter and Marie von Brockmann of Pescadero, California, she was sired by Ch. Parquins Pretty Boy Floyd ex Aruna von Tschomo Lungma. This lovely gold and white bitch is, as of this writing, on her way to completing her championship.

body much the same from the chest to the loin, which of course is quite different from the Peke."

"Surely that is a Pekingese gone wrong!" is accepted by another writer in the Enclyclopaedia as "the very natural mistake most people make when they see (a Tibetan Spaniel) for the first time." Clearly there must be some relationship to the palace dogs although the full facts are hard to find.

In the English *Dog World* of December 24, 1965, some illuminating comments on the subject will be found, based on a conversation with Mrs. Annie Foy, an 89 year old woman who spent her youth in Sikkim and Bhutan on the borders of India and Tibet. Describing the Tibetan Spaniels which Mrs. Foy saw in Bhutan, the article states: "There were long-nosed and long-coated types and also some short-muzzled ones, but these were, even so, longer in muzzle than a Pekingese—but the different types were in different monasteries, and the shorter muzzles came from nearest to the Chinese borders."

As was pointed out in an authoritative article in the British *Kennel Gazette* in August, 1934, the influence of the Chinese dogs brought to Tibet was affected by the fact that there were no standardiz-

ed types in that country. "This results in unnatural dogs being bred there, or, as one might say, dogs that weren't very specialized.

In other words, in the more crude conditions prevailing in Tibet, the Shih Tzu type of dogs tended to lose their refined man-made characteristics and to become larger, coarse and more terrier-like in appearance. Keeping the Palace Lion Dogs small in size and short in features, two characteristics which distinguish them from the Apso, requires the most strictly selective and careful breeding. This is as true in England or America today as it was in old China and Tibet.

As a surprising footnote, it was reported in 1935 that the late Dalai Lama has possesed "a Pekingese (of a sort)." Strangely enough, his favorite pet was a Dachshund!

That there were also Shih Tzu-like dogs in Tibet during this period is confirmed by the evidence of the Venerable Akong Rimpoche, Abbot of Lhakang and later of the Tibetan Monastic Center in Dumfriesshire, Scotland. On seeing an English-bred Shih Tzu of 18- 20 pounds, the Abbot commented that he had seen similar dogs in the hands of Tibetan noble families, but they were much smaller with coats sweeping the ground.

Marya Winds Chaisa Geisha is pictured winning under judge Al Treen at a 1976 show. The sire was Mariljac Mari-Pet ex Town Hall's Floria Gloria. Kay Gress handled for owner Martha Coalina of Valpariso, Indiana.

An impressive portrait of Quang-Te van de Blauwe Mammouth, the most titled dog in the history of the Shih Tzu breed. The Eastons just achieved the finishing of Quang-Te's American championship.

Ch. Gambrel's Far Fair Suzuki, golden and white bitch whelped in June 1970. Sire was Ch. Chumulari Ying Ying ex Chumulari Mei-Mei. Breeders were Kathleen Kilbert and Frank Sterling of Bethlehem, Connecticut. Mei-Mei is pictured here winning on the way to her championship under judge Anne Cowie with her owner-handler Frank Sterling.

Ch. Char Nick's Swing Erh of Copa captured in pen and ink by artist Paul Nickerson of Richmond, Virginia.

Artist Paul Nickerson's rendition of an 11 inch porcelain incense burner featuring the Shih Tzu-type Foo dog on top. It is from the Chien Lung period, 1736-1795.

Another of Annette Mellinger's water colors depicting a Shih Tzu in a native oriental setting. Mrs. Mellinger owns the World-Vu Kennels in Matawan, New Jersey.

Ch. Chumulari Trari is pictured in an oil painting by Geoffrey Dali, nephew of famous artist Salvador Dali. The original painting is in the possession of the Eastons, Trari's owners.

Artist Paul Nickerson's painting of a pair of typical Foo dogs. Foo dogs are said to represent the various breeds of small "lion dogs" in China, one of which is the Shih Tzu.

Australian Champion Tsuyung So Sweet Sum Wun, Australia's record-breaking Shih Tzu. One of the first of her breed to win a major award at a Royal show, she was further honored to have won it under Finnish judge Hans Lehtinen in 1973. She finished her title at eight months of age with multiple Group and Best in Show wins. Owned by John L. Sheppard of New South Wales, Australia.

Chapter 7
SHIH TZU SIZE

Throughout the entire period of development of the Shih Tzu breed in this country, no other subject of discussion has been more hotly contested than Shih Tzu size. Eventually a standard was approved and published, and supposedly all Shih Tzu fanciers settled down to serious breeding according to that standard. It was hoped that this would be the end of the controversy. But such was not the case. Even today, long after the Shih Tzu has reached a very substantial place in the dog world, a controversy still rages about what size the Shih Tzu should be. These differences of opinion cannot be dismissed as a mere "tempest in a teapot," for we know that there are definite reasons behind each opinion whether they are right or wrong. The fact remains that the breed is in the Toy Group; they should therefore be "Toy" in size.

In 1978, almost a decade after the Shih Tzu was recognized by the American Kennel Club, there is still much discussion about size. Since the publication of our first book, *This Is The Shih Tzu,* almost a decade ago, the die-hards are still trying to push their case. In the breed's early days in this country, there were several reasons for the controversy over size in addition to mere personal preferences.

During Joan Brearley's five year tenure as editor of *Popular Dogs* magazine 1967-1972, the Shih Tzu breed was striving for recognition and much material and arguments crossed her desk regarding their size. There was much correspondence, about the cross-breeding of Shih Tzu to Lhasa Apso to achieve what was believed to be the desired size once the standard was established. There was also a substantial amount of mail revealing that cross-breeding to reduce the size of the British imports had been practiced. Many confused people bred small Lhasa Apso to undersized or small Shih Tzu to try to get what they wanted. Fortunately, this did not become a trend or reach a large portion of the breeders, for this was not the way to create the ideally sized Shih Tzu.

Needless to say, there were times in the history of the Shih Tzu when using other breeds was necessary. In our first book, we made quite a point of presenting the long history of establishing the Shih Tzu as an individual breed and what had to be done to achieve this. We have had no reason in the intervening years between that book and this to change our emphasis on this important point. On the question of size, here are some historical facts, presented in our first book that still hold true and bear repeating.

As has already been noted, according to Colonel Burkhardt, the imperial Shih Tzu were occasionally interbred with the Pekingese "to reduce the size." The Colonel wrote from first hand experience of Peking Palace life not long after the 1912 revolution, and before rising nationalistic feelings made the presence of foreign military officers unwelcome.

Published some time later, the preface to Madam Lu's booklet expresses a similar opinion, apparently written by someone connected with the newly formed Peking Kennel Club. The *Peiping Chronicle* of May, 17, 1936 describes the translator of the booklet as Mr. C.S.K. Chou, but unfortunately does not identify the writer of the preface. Referring to the "Lhassa Lion Dogs," the passage runs: "There is also every evidence to show that these dogs have been bred down from a larger-sized breed and this theory is supported by the great variety of size and weight which is found in this class of dogs."

Although we are told that the Empress Dowager discouraged the use of "cruel practices" to stunt the growth of the dogs, the two above quotations would seem to imply that the imperial eunuchs tried to keep the Shih Tzu small by strictly selective breeding. Such selective breeding met with the approval of the Empress, according to Mrs. Dixey, but it is clear that it was not always successful as far as the production of uniform size was concerned.

This appears to have been especially true in the years immediately following the 1912 revolution, during which Colonel Burkhardt tells us that "the mating was rather haphazard." Not surprisingly, some 20 years later we find the complaint in Madame Lu's booklet regarding "the great variety of size and weight." The same could have been said of the imperial goldfish which must have

Floridonna's American Dream, owned by K. Coffee, Minot, North Dakota.

Their willingness to learn tricks is another of the endearing characteristics of the Shih Tzu. Here we see one of Donna Ellis's Shih Tzu doing it very nicely. The Ellises are from Clearwater Beach, Florida.

started to increase in size with the breakdown of controlled breeding.

Strong support for this viewpoint is to be found in the *China Weekly Chronicle* of June 10, 1934. Reporting Peiping's First International Dog Show, held on June 7 of the same year, the paper states that the Lhassa Lion Dogs were, "on the whole, disappointing in spite of their numbers, showing too much deviation from the standard, especially in size, suggesting the necessity of careful breeding to the standard in future." Since the Peking Kennel Club's official standard did not come until four years later it is uncertain what standard is referred to at this earlier date. Presumably it was a tentative one, based on what was known of the lion dog's background at that time.

We have since received from a Norwegian fancier a copy of a highly important article which we have been trying to trace for more than two years. Although the author's name is not given, almost certainly it was written by Dr. Walter Young, author of *Some Canine Breeds of Asia.*

Published in Peiping shortly before the first Peking Kennel Club Show, the article begins, "at least as common as good Pekingese in Peiping are the Tibetans, the shock-headed long-coated little dogs which came to China during the Manchu dynasty as gifts from the grand lamas at Lhasa."

It is a "novel little breed," the writer continues, complaining that at that time, "no effort is made to distinguish what is quite evidently two distinct types, one considerably larger and higher on the leg than the other."

"They are commonly bred by Chinese fanciers who, to be sure, have not publicized the fact. And although there are no commercial kennels of a respectable character which breed these dogs, specimens of mixed merit, both of the large and the small varieties, may occasionally be seen at the disappointing dog markets at Lung Fu Ssu and Hu Kuo Ssu on fair days, either 'bred by exhibitor', or otherwise acquired."

At that date the writer was prepared to accept the placing of the breed in the non-sporting group, but it must be remembered that this was almost eighteen months before the return of the Princess Der Ling to Peking. Until she came on the scene and shared her knowledge with the Countess d'Anjou, fanciers in the city had no means of finding out the full truth about the palace dogs of old. Indeed, the writer of this article admits that at the time there was much confusion about the breed.

"Probably not one in ten persons owning specimens of such dogs in Peiping," he acknowledges frankly, "is able to give its correct breed name, or even to distinguish it from the popular Pekingese."

The writer himself goes so far as to assert that the Empress Dowager "seems to have been unsuccessful in breeding these Tibetans." This

Zizi's Pu Yi and Zizi's Phi-Phi, two five week old puppies, take a look at their owner's oriental art treasures in their home in Drammen, Norway. This charming photograph by A. Laakso was the centerfold photo in the Norwegian Magazine, *Alt om Hunden,* in November, 1976. Pu Yi is now owned by Mrs. Kirsten Kauffman and Phi-Phi is owned by Mrs. Laila Brendengen, bred by Ruth Laakso.

statement, which we now know to be wholly incorrect, betrays a complete lack of accurate information at that time regarding the imperial dogs.

What is important is that the article fully confirms our theory regarding the existence of two types of Shih Tzu in Peking, at least as far as the 1930's are concerned, one "of the very small variety, in size more or less similar to the Pekingese," the other larger and apparently closely resembling what we now call the Apso, although "smaller, and with shorter legs."

It should be noted that the writer was also aware of "many cases of crossing" of Shih Tzu and Pekingese.

Said to be "sometimes indiscriminately called Lhassa Terriers or Apsos," the Lhassa Lion dogs formed "the largest breed class in the show." Few details are given other than that "the dog class was won by a pure-bred Lhassa whose two half sisters also won the puppy class." The breed does not appear to have been put into any group, but there is some indication that it was in a measure associated with "the Novelty Class, including

Asiatic breeds for which the western official standards are either wanting or inadequate." Regarding this, the evidence is confused.

Since very few names are given in the report, it is impossible to say whether or not the Countess d'Anjou's Shih Tzu appeared at this first Peking Show, but it seems unlikely. Certainly if she had been recognized at that date as an authority on the breed, it is probable that some mention would have been made of the fact. We do know that her friendship with the Princess Der Ling must have originated considerably later, as the Princess only returned to Peking on October 3, 1935, "after an absence of nearly ten years." Prior to that date it seems clear that the Countess had no special source of information about the breed.

At the next Peiping International Dog Show, held on June 8, 1935, several Shih Tzu dogs, bitches and puppies were exhibited. On this occasion the *China Weekly Chronicle* reported enthusiastically that "one of the most sensational entries was a Lhassa Terrier, an excellent, small, black-and-white bitch, owned by Mrs. Kun Chin,

101

Four gorgeous Lhakangs Shih Tzu relax on the grounds of Newton Hall, Sheriff and Mrs. Widdrington's home in the North of England. Mrs. Widdrington is known world-wide for her dogs.

which took an amazing number of blue ribbons and cups."

Named "Shiao Ya," which could mean "Little Duck" or "Little Bud," this bitch won the cup for Best bitch in Show presented by the British Minister to China, His Excellency Sir Alexander Cadogan. Shiao Ya also won ribbons for being Best Lhassa Lion Dog bitch and Best of Breed, and cups for being the best Chinese-owned entry in the Show and the Best Non-Sporting bitch—there is no mention of any class for "Toys" or "Small Dogs."

A large, enthusiastic crowd attended the day-long show at which a panel of eleven judges officiated, all apparently European or American, and including the Count d'Anjou.

The Lhassas of Madame Wilden, wife of the French Minister to China, are also described as being "exceptionally beautiful dogs, from the layman's standpoint." A dog of Madame Wilden's was second to one owned by Madame Lu, almost certainly the author of the "Lhassa Lion Dog," while a bitch owned by the Count d'Anjou came second to Mrs. Kun Chin's outstanding specimen.

It may be significant that the bitch which is unidentified was registered in the Count d'Anjou's name and that it is he who appears most active in Peking Kennel Club affairs at this time. Although the Countess must also have been interested, is it too much to suggest that her full involvement dates from the time that she learned the full details of the Shih Tzu's fascinating history from the Princess who came to Peking almost exactly four months after the 1935 show? We shall never know the answer, but there are some indications that this may be so.

Reporting the 1936 Peking International Dog Show, which took place on May 16, the *Peiping Chronicle* by a strange mistake described it as the "Second" of its kind. "Exceptionally good were the Lhassa Lion dogs," the paper announced; "some excellent specimens were exhibited. This class was judged by Madame Lu, an expert and breeder of long standing and author of the book on Lhassa Lion dogs."

At this show, which was attended by the mayor of the city and by the United States Ambassador to China, Mr. Nelson T. Johnson, "Mayflower Gaston," a dog owned by an American, Mrs. Paul Jernigan, "copped the blue ribbon for this class (the Lhassa) while "Biscotte," owned by the Countess d'Anjou was judged the best Lhassa Lion bitch in the show."

With a Chinese judge, for the first time on record Shih Tzu owned by foreigners were given top placings, which was either an exercise in international courtesy or a mark of increasingly responsible western involvement in the breed. There was, in fact, no mention of any Lhasa shown by a Chinese. For the first time, also, the Countess d'Anjou is mentioned as an exhibitor, and a highly successful one, interestingly just seven months after the arrival in Peking of the romantic Chinese Princess from whom she learned so much about the palace dogs.

102

Champion Bjorneholms Leidza, a bitch, bred by Miss Jeppesen of Denmark in 1964. She is owned by Mrs. Birgitta Sabats of Sweden.

Although her lion dogs had been highly praised at the show of June, 1935, no mention of Madame Wilden's name occurs in connection with that of 1936. This is understandable, as her husband had died suddenly of a heart attack on September 23, 1935, just ten days before the return to Peking of the Princess Der Ling.

By the fourth annual show in 1937 the Countess d'Anjou had clearly emerged as the leading Shih Tzu breeder in Peking, her successes being recorded in the *North China Star* of Tientsin on May 17, 1937. This show is the last we have been able to trace and was quite possibly the last to be held. The Countess' Lhasa Lions "Nuisance" and "Hutze" took first and second places in the breed, while her "Lhassa Lion" was Best Non-Sporting bitch. At the same time her brace, "Shih Tse" and "Nuisance" were placed second in the "Small Breeds," apparently the nearest equivalent to a Toy Group. Shih Tse was also best bitch in the show.

Looking over the details of the four Peking shows, it is clear that the lack of effective control over the previous 20 years had led to some confusion regarding the breed in the 1930's. Some Peking fanciers were obviously doing their best to restore to the Shih Tzu something of the imperial grandeur which had been its birthright in happier days, and the Countess d'Anjou—advised by the Princess Der Ling—was increasingly becoming the leader of this group. Unfortunately, the Japanese occupation of Peking in early summer of 1937, to be followed by the attack on Pearl Har-

bor 4½ years later, brought a speedy end to their short-lived hopes and dreams.

A HIGHLY IMPORTANT DOCUMENT

Some exceptionally valuable information regarding Shih Tzu size and weight comes to us in the form of a personal letter, dated May, 1955, written by the Countess d'Anjou to Mrs. L.G. Widdrington, leading English fancier and widely recognized authority on palace lion dog history. Written by the Countess on her return to France after a visit to England, this highly important document has not yet received the attention it deserves. The contents of the letter, in entirety, will be found in the American *Shih Tzu News* of March, 1967.

The Countess begins, "I am enclosing the Standard we have made out for France." This standard set weight limits for the Shih Tzu of 11-22 pounds, 11-15 pounds being declared preferable (*"de 5 a 10 kilogs mais de preference de 5 a 7 kilogs,"* is the exact wording), and is said to have been very carefully prepared, *"Minutieusement etabli,"* by the Count and Countess d'Anjou.

The whole standard is also said to have met with the complete approval of two other French fanciers from pre-Pearl Harbor Peking, although it is highly unlikely that either of them knew nearly as much about the breed's history as the Countess. The available evidence regarding both suggest strongly that their experience of Shih Tzu dates from the confused period *before* the Princess Der Ling arrived in Peking to bring to light the

Two Shih Tzu "on the rocks!" Chumulari Phola and Willows Golden Amber were photographed in their backyard in 1970. Owned by Florence Sheldon.

Am. and Can. Ch. Li Ming's Ping Kan, pictured winning on the way to championship under judge Howard Tyler in 1976. Sire was Ch. Lou Wan Casinova ex Tienchao's San Se Chin. Dawn Tendler, who co-owns with Bob Tendler of Ridgefield, Connecticut, is shown handling.

Chin Yu Oriole is co-owned by William C. Roxby, Jr. and Kathleen V. Wisser, Wyncote, Pennsylvania. The sire was Ch. Chumulari Sheng-Li Che and the dam was Chin Yu Black Eye Su.

Jaisu Ling-ho Chinese Junk, handled during his show career by Faye Wine and owned by Donna Fritts of Nashville, Tennesee.

German Import, Nodis Khan's Ty Noh, imported by Mr. and Mrs. Joseph Edwards of Bloomington, Illinois. He was purchased in 1972.

Champion Li Ming's Po Lo Mi is bred and owned by Dawn Perretz Tendler of Ridgefield, Connecticut and handled by Dee Shepard. The sire was Ch. Lou Wan Casinova ex Tienchao's San Se Chin.

Lakoya's Sugar 'N Spice, bred by Ruth Ragle and owned by Eleanore Eldredge of Shang T'ou Kennels, Easton, Washington.

Canadian Ch. Belair The Candyman, owned and shown by Mrs. Marilyn Szalay of Ontario, Canada.

Three bitches owned by Mrs. Ewa Bergman of Savar, Sweden. At left is Kickan, pictured at 4½ years of age. In the middle is Zizi's Wei, 3 years old. On the right is Jungfaltets Shi-Ka, 8 months old.

full truth about the imperial lion dogs as she had known them in the palace.

Making no reference to the new French standard she was enclosing, other than the eleven words just quoted, the Countess went on in her letter to make it quite clear that she was far from happy about the weight limits permitted. Apparently, she had accepted them against her better judgement, perhaps persuaded by her husband that they were the best possible under the conditions then prevailing in France, but very obviously she did not regard such a weight range as historically correct or even as desirable.

The Countess's letter to Mrs. Widdrington reads, "Yes, I did think the Shih Tzu too big in England. They really should be under 12 pounds. In fact, we had two classes in Peking, up to 12 pounds and over 12 pounds were judged separately. They never had the big ones in the Imperial Palace . . ."

Contrasting sharply with the much higher weight range in the standard she was enclosing, these emphatic words, in her own handwriting, must surely be taken as expressing the Countess' true feelings on the subject. It must not be forgotten that her information came from the Princess Der Ling who, as a lady-in-waiting at court, had been in a unique position to know what the palace dogs were like. The Countess may well have been the only westerner to whom the facts of Shih Tzu history were made known.

The reference to two classes in Peking can only refer to a practice which must have been established by the Peking Kennel Club which initiated dog shows in 1934 and set up a standard for the Shih Tzu in 1938. With a weight range of 10-15

pounds, this standard makes no mention of a division at 12 pounds, so we are fortunate to have this clearly documented evidence from the Countess that such a division into two weight classes was made in Peking. This may explain why the "Small Breeds" at the 1937 Peking Kennel Club Show, "Lhassa Lion" in the one, "Shih Tse" and "Nuisance" in the other.

It is regrettable that the Countess' letter gives no indication what happened to the larger Shih Tzu which must have appeared, at least occasionally, even during the days of carefully controlled court breeding. Quite possibly the Princess Der Ling was unaware of their fate and may not even have known of their existence, such matters having, in all probability, been kept to themselves by the eunuchs.

An interesting suggestion is that they may have been used as fighting dogs to provide back-kitchen "sport" for the imperial servants, unknown to their royal masters and mistresses. Commuting daily to the palace, with a strong sense of obligation towards their little charges, these eunuchs must have had ample opportunity to smuggle out puppies to become dearly loved family pets.

Alternatively, they may have been smuggled out of the palace for sale elsewhere. Although the

Int., German and Swiss Champion Tang La v Tschomo-Lungma, bred and owned by Mrs. Geusendam of Germany. Tang La is a litter sister of Swiss, Czech. and Can. Ch. Tangra v Tschomo-Lungma, owned by the Eastons, and dam of the famous Am. and Can. Ch. Chumulari Ying Ying.

Zizi's Bijou-Carre, golden and white bitch from the best litter Kennel Zizi ever produced. The sire was Norwegian Ch. Zizi's Law Hu ex Int., Scan., Finnish, Norwegian, and Danish Ch., Zizi's Lhamo. Bred and owned by Ruth Laakso, Drammen, Norway. Photo by A. Laakso, 1971.

punishment for this is said to have been drastic, undoubtedly the wily eunuchs had their own ways of avoiding detection.

Stealing by the eunuchs seemed to have been "taken for granted," according to Sir Reginald Johnston, and was by no means always punished on detection. Since it would have involved acknowledgment of the theft, such punishment would have meant "loss of face" for the master or mistress of the unfaithful servant. For that reason many offenses were overlooked.

Writing about his experiences in Peking in 1923, Harry A. Franke affirms that for many decades past—not least during the days of imperial rule—there had been very little effective control over the activities of the eunuchs who were virtually a law unto themselves. We may be quite sure that they did their best to profit from all dogs of their breeding, even if it meant illicitly permitting oversized specimens to pass into the hands of the general public. This would readily explain why, when looking for Shih Tzu in Peking, the first English importers found that "some were very large."

What the Countess d'Anjou's important letter does make clear is her conviction that only the smaller Shih Tzu were kept in the Imperial Palace, and her pride in the fact that some

measure of priority was given to them at Peking Kennel Club Shows—an arrangement which she would very obviously have liked to see continued in Europe. In this regard the documentary evidence is beyond dispute, and it is worth recalling that the Countess was widely accepted as the leading western authority on the breed.

MORE RECENT DEVELOPMENTS IN EUROPE

As the curtain falls dramatically on Shih Tzu history in China, the scene shifts to Europe where, as we have seen, specimens of the breed were taken to the British Isles and to Scandinavia in the early 1930's.

In Scandinavia the Shih Tzu has always been recognized as a small dog, with nine to eleven pounds being regarded the desirable weight. This information comes from Mr. Carl Olof Junge-feldt, member of the board of the Swedish Kennel Club and of the Special Club for Non-Sporting Dogs and Toys, whose success in breeding high quality Shih Tzu has been marked by the award of the important Hamilton Trophy by the Swedish Kennel Club.

Pointing out that the breed has always been placed in the Toy Group in Scandinavia, although the Standard makes no mention of weight, Mr.

International and Scandinavian Champion Beldams Fu-Ma-Thing, bred in 1958 at Mrs. Marianne Berg's Beldams Kennels in Sweden. Fu-Ma-Thing was the first Swedish born international champion in the breed and the dam of seven champions, including two international champions and one Best in Show winner. Her sire was the English import Ch. Ful-Ling of Clystvale, and her dam Swedish and Finnish Champion Ting-e-Ling av Brogyllen whose ancestors go back to early Shih Tzu in Norway.

Jungefeldt emphasizes in his letters to Reverend Easton that all Swedish Shih Tzu which have won Best In Show at major events have weighed about ten pounds.

Expressing a somewhat similar point of view, leading Dutch fancier Eta Pauptit, in the June, 1966, issue of the *Manchu Shih Tzu Society News Letter,* stressed that in five years of breeding she "has never had a puppy go over twelve pounds, adult weight."

In England, a different situation developed as the Shih Tzu put on weight after importation in 1930, each generation tending to grow larger than the one before. "Climactic conditions" have been suggested as a reason for this, but such an explanation fails to account for the fact that the Scandinavian imports and their successors appear to have remained more or less stable in size. It is

much more likely that the growth in size of the English dogs reflects the fact that they were descended from larger Shih Tzu, sold by the eunuchs outside the palace.

The growth in size became more and more difficult to counteract, although stress was placed on the need to keep the breed small, since shortage of numbers means that "in these days it was necessary to breed every bitch we had, to keep the breed going." Details regarding this dilemma, which was to have such far-reaching effects on the future of the Shih Tzu in England, will be found in *The Manchu Shih Tzu Society, Selected Items from 1960-1963, News Letters Nos. IX-XXIV.*

Little guidance was available from China at this time; as there was still uncertainty in both Peking and Shanghai regarding the desirable size for the breed. As we have seen, it was not until October,

1935, that the Princess Der Ling arrived in Peking and was able to clarify the situation. Even so, it was only in 1938 that the Peking Kennel Club standard for the Shih Tzu was declared officially.

Some assistance might have been obtained from Scandinavia, but it does not seem to have occurred to English fanciers of the 1930's to look in that direction for more knowledge of the Shih Tzu. Even today it is highly questionable whether they realize the importance of Mr. Henrik Kauffman's imports.

In the resulting confusion the first British standard of 1934 initially did not specify either size or weight, merely stating "considerable variation permissible, provided other proportions are correct and true to type." Not until later were the weight limits set at 14-19 pounds, based on the size of the Shih Tzu appearing in the English rings at the time, not, as in Peking, on a study of the breed's background and history. These weight limits, determined solely by the size of the few Shih Tzu then in Great Britain, remained in force until 1958.

Thus, for over 20 years British Shih Tzu breeders worked with a *minimum* weight which was two pounds heavier than the *maximum* said by the Countess to have been regarded as desirable for palace dogs. They had no means of knowing this, of course, as the facts of the breed's history must have been seriously hampered by the Japanese advance of 1937 and the subsequent harassment of westerners in North China.

In the trying war years that soon followed, Shih Tzu fanciers everywhere had more serious matters to occupy their attention than the setting of the correct standard for the breed. Not surprisingly, it seems to have been a very considerable time before English breeders fully realized that the Peking Kennel Club had set a standard with weight limits very different from their own.

Perhaps even more disconcerting must have been the fact that, "on numerous occasions visitors from China who came to see us at the shows would tell us: 'Your dogs are very lovely, but far too big!'" Hearing such criticism repeatedly from those who obviously knew what they were talking about, it is little wonder that conscientious fanciers found themselves compelled to recognize that "things were not really right with the breed."

Not long after the Countess d'Anjou's letter to Mrs. Widdrington had made the position clear, Mr. K.B. Rawlings, chairman of the British Shih Tzu Club, explained at the club's annual general meeting that some change in weight range must be made. "Over the years the breed has been getting far too large," Mr. Rawlings admitted when questioned.

An illuminating hindsight on this situation is found in the cautionary phrase in the present British standard, "type and breed characteristics are of the utmost importance and on no account are they to be sacrificed to size alone." While no one will quarrel with such a praiseworthy expression of opinion, it is highly significant that nothing of this nature appears in the Peking Kennel Club Standard. Strongly defensive in tone, these words would appear to have been inserted by British breeders to explain and justify their use of larger dogs when they had no other choice.

Much of the same might be said of the often-quoted assertion from the British standard that the Shih Tzu is "neither a terrier nor a toy," an essentially negative and defensive statement to which I have as yet found no parallel in Peking Kennel Club writings and with which Scandinavian breeders could hardly be expected to agree.

It is certainly not true in the United States, where the American Kennel Club has placed the Shih Tzu in the Toy Group, a decision which was strongly resisted by a few breeders but which the vast majority have accepted gladly.

In the movement to lower the weight limits set by the first British standard, a leading part was taken by Mrs. L.G. Widdrington, President of the Manchu Shih Tzu Society, who has done much for the betterment of the breed in Great Britain and beyond.

"As regards my own breeding operations, although I had bred Shih Tzu upwards of fifteen years, and many had become champions, they were all bigger than they should be, and there seemed nowhere to turn to stop a continuous upward trend," Mrs. Widdrington writes, recalling her early frustrations. "I often used to think 'How gorgeous this or that one would be if only half the size' but there seemed at the time little hope of establishing the breed in the size it should be, under 12 pounds. Even by using the smallest good dog available, the offspring were often larger than either parent."

In these early days, Mrs. Widdrington recalls regretfully, an Anglo-Chinese woman living in England, booked two bitch puppies from her before seeing any English Shih Tzu. Visiting a major English show before taking delivery, she promptly cancelled the order, disappointed at the size of those exhibited and insisting that the true Shih Tzu should be "small and jewel-like."

In 1954 it was discovered, by happy chance, that the union of certain bloodlines made it possible to reduce the size of the British strain. This

Above:
Mother and son ... on the left is the dog, Basse, whelped in 1963 and Lhe-Ming, his dam, who was whelped in 1961. Basse is bred and owned by Mrs. Ragnhild Dyrdal of Norway.

Left, top:
Miss Kathrine Sondergaard of Asaa, Denmark and her Shih Tzu Zizi's Aidzo. The sire was Norwegian Ch. Zizi's Ching C'Hoo ex Nord, and Swed. Ch. Kwan-Jin van de Blauwe Mammouth.

Left, bottom:
Norwegian Champion and 1976 Best in Show winner Zizi's Law Hu. This gold and white dog was owner-bred by Ruth Laakso, Drammen, Norway. The sire was Nor. Ch. Ching Ming ex Scan. Ch. Zizi's Tara.

Below:
Norwegian Ch. Ban-Zai, bred by Mrs. A.S. Seger, Sweden and owned by Miss Randi Windjusveen, Oslo, Norway. The sire was Int. Nor. Ch. Lyckobringarens Kwan-Do ex Duchess Soraya.

Above:
Maudee's Isa, whelped in 1965 and bred by Mrs. Ingrid Bakkane of Oslo, Norway. The sire was Maudee's Ling-Ling ex Maudee's Mira. Owned by Mr. Finn Eriksen, Oslo, Norway. Mrs. Bakkane was one of Norway's leading Shih Tzu breeders from 1955 to 1965. Photo by A. Laakso.

Right, top:
Swedish, Norwegian and Finnish Ch. Zizi's Tara pictured winning a Best in Show. This win put her over the three win mark needed for the Gold Dog award in 1970. Tara has 10 C.A.C.I.B. certificates and is pictured here with her breeder-owner-handler, Ruth Laakso. Photo by Per Henriksen. The sire was Int., Nor. Ch. Marinas Muff-Lung-Feng, ex Int., Scan., and Dan. Ch. Zizi's Lhamo.

Right, bottom:
Swedish and Norwegian Ch. Kwan-Jin van de Blauwe Mammouth. Whelped in 1969, she was bred by the Baronesse van Panthaleon van Eck-Klasing, Kennel de Blauwe Mammouth, Holland. The sire was Rockafella of Bracewell ex Emma of Myarlune. Owned by Ruth Laakso and photographed by A. Laakso.

Below:
Zizi's Pu Yi, photographed at 13 months of age, was bred by Ruth Laakso and owned by Mrs. Kirsten Kauffmann of Stavanger, Norway. The sire was Nor. Ch. Zizi's Law Hu, a Best in Show winner, ex Scan. Ch. Zizi's Tara, also a Best in Show winner. Photo by A. Laakso.

111

Miss Eta Pauptit of Holland and two of her van de Oranje Manege Shih Tzu. Miss Pauptit is also known around the world for her famous line of Afghan hounds.

"She looked over my little Min Yuenne and Tien Memashib very carefully, both black-and-white and not more than 10 pounds, and pronounced them identical in size and coloring to the ones she had owned in China."

While in Peking, General Sir Douglas Brownrigg had been Assistant Adjutant and Quartermaster General to the British Army's North China Command. Some years after his return to England he was appointed an aide-de-camp to King George V, a position which he occupied from 1933 to 1934. During these early years he and Lady Brownrigg took a leading part in introducing the new breed to the English public.

We are told that Lady Brownrigg was very particular about keeping the noses short and that she would go round the benches at shows, measuring each exhibit with the end joint of her thumb to make sure that none were over an inch in length. "She also constantly warned against letting the breed get too big," recalls Mrs. Widdrington in the April, 1969 *Manchu Shih Tzu Society News Letter,* "a tendency which the English climate seemed to encourage. Then some of the later imports,

led to the formation of the Manchu Shih Tzu Society, originally founded "to promote and protect the interests of the smaller Shih Tzu (12 pounds and under) as bred in the Imperial Palace, Peking." Now by far the larger of the two clubs in Great Britain devoted to the Shih Tzu, in 1968 the Manchu Shih Tzu Society had 283 members, the British Shih Tzu Club 166.

Encouraging the appearance of smaller Shih Tzu in the show ring, the Manchu Shih Tzu Society founders drew renewed public attention to the breed. So popular did they become that within a short space of time it was estimated that at least half of those registered with the British Kennel Club were of the smaller type.

"Since the smaller dogs have appeared at shows, people who knew the breed in China have hailed them as being more correct in size and type, and judges who remember the original dogs have put them up," Mrs. Widdrington recalls.

"In 1957, after dining at the Palace Hotel, Paignton, after the show, some of us were strolling around the gardens with our dogs, when a distinguished-looking elderly woman came running breathlessly after us, explaining that she had owned similar dogs in China. Her husband came running from the car and both were thrilled and filled with nostalgic memories to come across the breed over here." Mrs. Widdrington continues,

Mrs. L. G. Widdrington, leading English authority on the breed, and president of the Manchu Shih Tzu Society. The society was founded in 1954 to promote and protect the interest of the smaller Shih Tzu (12 pounds and under) as bred at the Imperial Palace in Peking.

although bringing in much new blood, were inclined to throw a proportion of offspring rangier and longer-nosed than was typical."

Mrs. Widdrington gives a vivid account of her own introduction to the Shih Tzu in 1939:

"My first glimpse of the breed was in Thurloe Square Gardens, London, when Mrs. Doig, the Brownrigg's cook, was exercising about eight or ten of them on leashes, and I though I had never seen such amazing creatures—part lions, part Chinese dragons, part gargoyles, and I felt I *must* own one!

"I called on the Brownriggs at 48 Thurloe Square and met Mona (Lady Brownrigg) looking very charming in her Red Cross uniform. The house seemed a fitting background for these oriental dogs, being full of Chinese antiques and pictures.

"I was told that there was one puppy bitch left which I could have quite reasonably as it was rather big, and Lady Brownrigg was so busy just now with her Red Cross work. But I could only have her on condition that I bred and showed her. Neither had entered my mind. However, it was a promise made, and whole new worlds opened for me in the keeping of it."

The confusion of these years, made much worse by wartime difficulties, are colorfully illustrated by Mrs. Widdrington's description of a visit she and Lady Brownrigg paid to a lady in the Isle of Wight:

"A beautiful small golden 'Shih Tzu' with black tips ran joyfully to greet us, and we both pronounced it a beautiful specimen in every way. Imagine Mona's consternation when told by the owner that it wasn't a Shih Tzu at all—not a drop—but a cross between a Maltese and a Pekingese!"

Lady Brownrigg died in April, 1969, just two days after hearing the good news of the breed's acceptance by the American Kennel Club. A devoted lover of the Shih Tzu and one of the breed's most enthusiastic supporters, Lady Brownrigg always felt that the breed needed to be kept as house pets with plenty of human companionship. She hated to think of anyone breeding them for purely commercial reasons.

British breeders finally agreed to compromise, four years after the foundation of the Manchu

Murray's Chin Te Nu Shen poses with her first litter of two—Murray's Dee Dee, the female on the left, and Murray's Buffy Muise, the male on the right. The sire was Chumulari Hai Yang Wang, also owned by Tom and Leah Murray of Arcadia, Nova Scotia.

Int., Nor., Dan., and Finnish Ch. Marinas Muff-Lung-Feng, Best in Show winner in Norway, pictured here at 12½ years of age. Feng is owned by Ruth Laakso and was sired by Int., Scan. Ch. Marinas Muff-Chang-Tzu ex Int., Scan. Ch. Beldams Fu-Maeo-Thing. The breeder was Mrs. Marianne Berg, Kennel Marina, Gothenorg, Sweden.

Shih Tzu Society, making provision for fanciers of both large and small types. The weight limits found in the 1958 British standard were altered to include all sizes from 9 to 18 pounds. At the same time, the hope was expressed that "in a few years" the upper limit might be reduced to 16 pounds—and in time the whole weight range perhaps narrowed to 10-15 pounds, as in the Peking Kennel Club standard.

Overleaf:
Top: Ch. Moonling's Wu Tai Shan, bred by Sara Weinberg and Janine Zervoulis and Ch. Lakoya Momotaro Asian Peach, bred by Jean Gadberry. Owners: Jan and Bill Zervoulis. Photo by Bill Zervoulis. **Bottom:** The great Ch. Greenmoss Golden Talon of Elfan, owned by Daniece Greggans' Kathways Shih Tzu Kennels. Photo by Missy Yuhl.

114

Swedish and Norwegian Ch. Luckobringarens Mr. Magoo, who won Best in Show in Norway in May 1976, and in Sweden in September. He was also Best in Show at the Swedish Shih Tzu Specialty Show in Hallstahammer in 1975. Mr. Magoo, bred and owned by Margrethe Svendsen of Sandared, Sweden, is sired by Int. and Scan. Ch. Tempelgardens Chi-Co-Tzu ex Bey-The-Wang. His ancestry can be traced directly back to the three original imports to Scandinavia from China in 1932.

The late Lady Brownrigg pictured in 1949 with Pu-Yi of Taishan. A stickler for short noses, Lady Brownrigg insisted on this in her own "Taishans."

Chumulari Hai Yang Jung Chu, a brood bitch owned by Tom and Leah Murray, Arcadia, Nova Scotia.

Overleaf:
Top left: Ch. Paisley Ping Pong, owned by Joan Cowie, pictured here with handler Barbara Alderman. **Top right:** Ch. Hapiours Swing on a Star O'Copa pictured winning Best of Breed under judge Ken Miller. Shown exclusively by Barbara Alderman for co-owners/breeders Patsy Williams and Coni Nickerson. **Bottom left:** Ch. Rondelay Shang Po at the Puritan Shih Tzu Club Match show in Marlborough, Mass. in 1976. Judge was Margaret Easton; owner is Jo Ann Webster. **Bottom right:** Ch. Link's Bamboo Too Too, owned by Pat Deering and co-owned and bred by P. Link. Cathie Phillips handling.

These changes have not yet been made, and the British standard remains, "Up to 18 pounds. Ideal weight 9-16 pounds," the 16 pounds "ideal" maximum being stressed in the hope of getting, in the words of Mr. Rawlings, " a much better compact dog."

SOME CRITICS OF THE BRITISH STANDARD

Aimed at satisfying breeders with widely different ideas of ideal Shih Tzu size, the 1958 British standard was a compromise. As such, it has not been universally accepted as the proper solution to the complex situation arising from the course of the breed's history in that country.

Unwilling to accept even a division into two weight classes, which "merely suggests that there are two types and the judge can choose whichever he likes," the late Mr. Leo Wilson, distinguished editor of the British *Dog World*, and an all-around judge, insisted that "the judge must be educated into realizing that the smaller Shih Tzu is the most typical."

"A Shih Tzu," he wrote, "should be small, yet solid, low to the ground with a short face. Grow him to outsize and he has only to fail a little in shortness of nose to be mistaken for a Lhasa Apso."

"Who wants a Shih Tzu—or any other toy breed for that matter—weighing over 14 pounds? Mr. Wilson added. "That is bigger than many terriers, and what need is there for such size? And don't point out to me that the breed is not a Toy. I know it is not classified as such by the Kennel Club, and that the Shih Tzu Club has gone out of its way to point out that it is not a Toy, but that does not alter the fact that originally the Shih Tzu was a pet, a lady's companion."

Mr. Wilson was understandably confused regarding the racial origin of the old-time Shih Tzu fanciers in the Peking Palace, which was Manchurian and not Tibetan, but that does not weaken the force of his contention that the imperial lion dogs were small. While it may be debated whether or not they should be regarded as lap dogs, their smallness of size has been demonstrated beyond doubt. Mr. Wilson urged English fanciers to recognize such facts in order to avoid "a path towards a confusion which can be the downfall of a breed."

Pointing out that the smaller Shih Tzu had been proven by that time to be in the majority in England, the well-known editor and judge suggested that it was not fair that they should be shown along with the large ones, which did not require the same carefully selective breeding.

"It is, of course, easier to breed a good big one than a good little one in any small or medium breed," he wrote, "for with size often goes coat, bone, substance of body and skull and so forth, but one might as well give Championship Certificates to Shetland Sheepdogs of 20 inches in height because they have big coats or long heads." The above quotations are from the British *Dog World* of July 26, 1957, page 1216.

A week later Mr. Wilson returned to the subject

Norwegian Champion Zizi's Lhu-Lhe, whelped in 1975 and photographed by Arne Laakso at 3½ months old. The sire was Zizi's Bombo Tjimbo ex Swed. and Nor. Ch. Kwan-Jin van de Blauwe Mammouth. This little bitch grew up to be a Best in Show winner in Norway. Owned and bred by Ruth Laakso.

Overleaf:
Top left: Hai-Du's Hai-Di of Hsu Jih and Ch. Hai-Du's Honey Bear, owned at the time of this win at the 1973 Rio Grande Kennel Club show by Linda A. Miller and Susan Haiducek. **Top, right:** Dragonseed's Fu-Ke-Tu-U, owned and shown by John J. Marsh. **Bottom, left:** To Te Mei's Sundance, bred and owned by Irene Caty of Glendora, California, winning a 3-point major under judge Dorothy D. Nickles at the 1976 Pontiac Kennel Club show. **Bottom, right:** Ch. Nanjo Cinder-Ella of Largyn winning at the 1976 Erie Kennel Club show. Barbara Alderman handled for owner Virginia Smigley.

BEST
BRACE
IN SHOW

BEST OF
OPPOSITE SEX
ERIE
KENNEL CLUB, INC.
JUNE 13, 1976   KLEIN

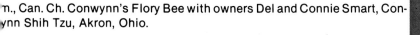

m., Can. Ch. Conwynn's Flory Bee with owners Del and Connie Smart, Conynn Shih Tzu, Akron, Ohio.

n. Rex Landor Di Visconti wins Best of Breed under judge Ken Miller with wner-handler Billy L. Baker, Washington, D.C. Bred by Jon C. Ferrante, Rex ished for his championship at 14 months of age with four major wins and ways owner-handled.

Ron D Vous Suki-Yaki, owned by Jean Johnson of Decatur, Illinois.

Three puppies from the Luv-Tzu Kennels of Mary Marxen. They are Mai-Sir-Jun, Mai Fystee Wun, and Tuffee.

Omar Play Boy, first U.D. titlist in the breed, and Canadian C.D. as well. Shown and trained by Mary Hollingsworth and owned by John F. Hollingsworth.

119

Chin Yutang of Flinthaug with his mother, Lindi Lu, and a friend. Lindi Lu was pure Scandinavian, Chin half English in breeding. Owned by Mrs. Marie Hynaas of Norway.

Agnes van Panthaleon, Baroness van Eck of the Netherlands, with her British Shih Tzu at the Brussels International Show in Belgium in May 1969. Left is Rockafella of Bracewell, 9 months of age to the day and the minimum age for showing in that country, and on the right, Emma of Myarlune at 13 months of age.

Debbie Inkpen caught in a tender moment with Janiric's Ruk-a-tatin' Roc-Kee, in Ontario, Canada.

on which he previously had strong feelings. "I think it ought to be made clear," he commented, "that in talking about Shih Tzu I am just as much against weeds as I am against out-size specimens. The ideal to aim at is, in my opinion, between 10 and 12 pounds, which is the happy medium." This comment appeared in the British *Dog World* issue of August 2, 1957.

Similarly strong views have been expressed by Mr. Leo Helbig, international judge and highly respected leader in German dog circles, who has asserted emphatically that "breeders should have stayed with the rules, set by the Royal Palace in Peking, to breed only with dogs under 12 English pounds or 5,400 grams. It would have saved a lot of headaches." The full text will be found in the German magazine *die Hundewelt* of April and May, 1965.

A FURTHER DISCUSSION OF SIZE

Even now that the facts regarding the breed's background and history are more fully known, it appears that there are some English breeders who still prefer to breed dogs of the larger type. We can well understand their feelings in this regard, since it is natural that they should have become attached to the dogs which they may have been permitted to breed in England for so many years.

For these reasons, I believe that it would be wholly wrong, at this late stage, to suggest that the British Standard be altered to deprive breeders of that country of their long-standing right to breed the larger type of Shih Tzu.

This also applies to the United States and other countries where it is essential that fair consideration should be given to those who, having at the time no means of knowing the full details of the breed's story, have in good faith imported, or bred, dogs of the larger type.

In addition, like the palace servants of old, every Shih Tzu breeder is liable at some time to find himself with one or two larger specimens in a litter that is otherwise small. While some—including the authors—would not wish such dogs of the

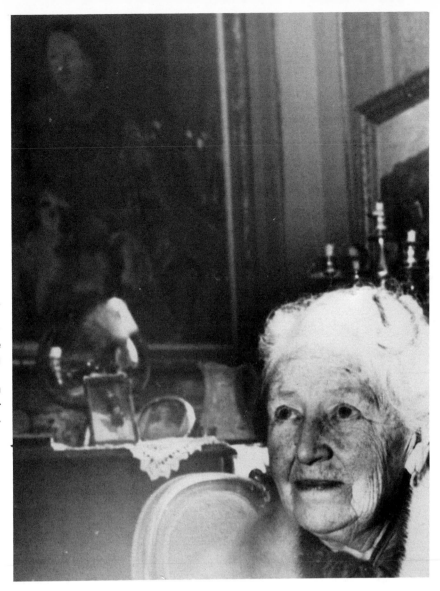

Mrs. Aasta Helliksen Finstad pictured here at 81 years of age, in 1972. She was one of the early famous fanciers in Norway and is pictured sitting in front of a painting of herself with some of her early Shih Tzu done by artist Gerda Knudsen. Active in the fancy in the 1930's, Mrs. Finstad now lives in a castle, where she spends her days weaving carpets. In pre-World War II days she used spun wool from her dogs for her carpet weaving. Photo by Arne Laakso.

Little Charlotte Bai with her grandmother's Ch. Zizi's Foo and Zizi's Chu Ko Liang, in Arendal, Norway.

Overleaf:
Top: Abacus' Chairman of the Board going Best of Winners at the American Shih Tzu Specialty show in 1976 under judge Erna Jungefeldt, a pioneer breeder in Sweden. **L. to r.:** Judge Jungefeldt, handler Sandy Cox, co-breeder (with R.C. Smith) J.D. Basil and owner Julia Pier. **Bottom:** A Bit of Flower Power, Am. and Bda. C.D., pictured with owner-handler Karolynne McAteer, Brooklyn Heights, New York, winning under judge Carlton Williams at the 1976 Pittsburgh show.

121

Kan Tu Wei Huo Shou Ling at 8 weeks of age has aspirations to become a fire chief. Owned by Edythe Kennedy of Barnstable, Massachusetts.

Left to right: Ch. LuvLees Wee Panda Bear and Ch. Seng Fu Luv Li Poo Bear, pose with their six week old offspring, Zalay Me-Cute Na-Tasha. All are owned by Marilyn Szalay of Windsor, Ontario, Canada.

Mrs. Helga Melleby of Oslo with her Swedish, Danish and Norwegian Champion Tai-Ping-Lhu. Whelped in 1961, the sire was Int., Nor. Ch. Ack-Lhe ex Wai-Lhu. The dog was one of the top winners in Norway before Mrs. Melleby's death in 1967. Tai-Ping had many C.A.C.I.B. certificates and group wins to his credit.

Ch. Balkaren Nan Kara Shan, who won his C.D. title in 1969 in three straight trials. He is the first C.D. titlist in the breed in Canada. The sire was Ch. Beldams Kanshung Ling and the dam Int. Ch. Isis Shu van de Oranje Manege, both imports. Owned by E. Joyce Harris, Alberta, Canada.

Overleaf:
Susan and Lance Barr of Salt Lake City, Utah, with San Yen Tinker Toi and Ch. Imperial Mikko Ling Chan Bear, in a beautiful sylvan setting.

Yingsu Paquerette of Jay Mar, owned by Doreen Madeley, Canada.

Janiric's Jamb-o-Laya and Janirics Chelsea Morn pictured winning at the Nipissing Kennel Club show under American judge Mel Downing. Handling are breeder-owners Janice and Richard Logie, Janiric Kennels, Ontario.

Yingsu Cherie and Yingsu Honey Bee photographed at 2½ months of age at their home in Ontario. Owned by Mrs. Marie Jameson.

Canadian Ch. Mir Hua Elegance of Yingin, owned by Sue Miller of Green, South Carolina.

Ch. Dynasty's Wind-up Toi pictured at 6 months of age. Bred and owned by Fredrick M. Alderman at his Dynasty Kennels in Mundelein, Illinois. The sire was Ch. Chumulari Ying Ying ex Jaisu Ling-Ho Pla-Toi O'Dynasty.

125

Rue Eckes

Christmas puppies at the House of Wu in Denver grew up to be (from l.) Ch. House of Wu Mimosa, Ch. House of Wu Tiz Tu, House of Wu Wa Pink and Ch. House of Wu Witches Brew. All bred and owned by Mrs. Charles Eckes.

House of Wu Wa Ping decorates a Christmas card for Mrs. Charles R. Eckles.

Chumulari Shen Shih photographed at 10 months of age. Shen's sire was Am. Can. Ch. Chumulari Ying Ying and his dam Ch. Chumulari Hih-Hih. Owned by Rev. and Mrs. D. Allan Easton.

Opposite:
Top: Ch. Mistybank Ouzo v Zervlistan, photographed before the "Garden" show where he went Winners Dog in 1974 under judge Tom Stevenson. Bred by M.E. Banga, he is owned by Janine R. Zervoulis. Photo by Bill Zervoulis. **Bottom:** House of Wu Wei Pink, bred and owned by Mrs. Charles R. Eckes of Denver. Photo by Rae Eckes.

larger size to appear in the show ring, it would be highly unrealistic to suggest that this feeling would be shared by more than a tiny minority of very strictly selective breeders. Nor is there any reason why it should be, since we do not recognize that there were larger specimens in Peking, although they were not kept in the palace.

The only fair solution, in our opinion, is that we should follow the example set by the Peking Kennel Club when it was discovered that, even in the breed's native city, a considerable variation in size had developed in the years following the breakdown of restricted court breeding. Such a solution involves a division which frankly recognizes the coexistence of two types of Shih Tzu, small and large, but—if the Countess d'Anjou is to be believed—gives a measure of priority to the smaller as representing the imperial ideal.

Some slight hint of this is to be found in an article by Mr. Will C. Mooney, long-time American fancier, who wrote in the American *Dog World* magazine in December, 1964:

"There are two distinct sizes of these dogs, the smaller dogs being from 8 to 10 pounds, the larger members of the breed scaling around 18 to 20 pounds. However, although two distinctly different sizes are recognized, the breed is not separated into different varieties, as are some breeds of dogs."

Some months later a leading English breeder, Mrs. Marion C. Boot, added: "If we are wanting to make changes why don't the two clubs (the Manchu Society and the Shih Tzu Club) iron out the problem of the two wide-apart sizes? There is no comparison at all between a nine pounder and an eighteen pounder." This was in the British *Dog World* of April 1, 1966, on page 614.

Attempts to establish such a division had been made before at a much earlier date by other well-known English fanciers. At the 1956 annual general meeting of the British Shih Tzu Club, Mrs. L.G. Widdrington, seconded by Mrs. Audrey Fowler, moved that "classes for Shih Tzu under 12 pounds weight (adult) be put on at two or more shows in 1956." When this motion was defeated by one vote (9-10, with 2 abstentions), Mrs. Widdrington and Mrs. Fowler went on to move and second that "a separate club be formed" to further the interests of those desirous of breeding the smaller type of Shih Tzu.

"Further discussion regarding the advisability of the Club altering its present policy in order to support the breeding and showing of two sizes in the breed ensued."

The motion to form a separate club was lost by four votes (7-11, with 3 abstentions).

(The above quotations are from the minutes of the annual general meeting of the Shih Tzu Club, March 27, 1956.)

At the Shih Tzu Club's annual general meeting the following year, Lady Brownrigg returned to the subject with the proposition that the breed be divided into two sizes, up to and over 12 pounds. Mrs. Bode spoke at some length on the question, saying that there were at that time three distinct sizes and that many of the dogs were far too big.

After much all around discussion, an amendment was proposed by Mr. Rawlings, and seconded by Mrs. Leslie, that "the Standard be altered to cater for the smaller Shih Tzu, i.e. the weight for the standard size be 12 pounds to 18 pounds and for the smaller dogs, 8 to 12 pounds." This amendment was carried unanimously.

At the same meeting, Mrs. Bode proposed that the Shih Tzu Club sponsor the Imperial Palace Shih Tzu Society (the name first given to the Manchu Shih Tzu Society). The motion was seconded by Mrs. Watts-Farmer. Citing the increased number of registrations in the past year, Mrs. Bode said that these were in no small measure due to the number of breeders who "now prefer the smaller size."

The motion to sponsor the formation of such a separate club, to protect and further the interests of the smaller palace-type Shih Tzu, was carried by 12 votes to 7, with 3 abstentions. Now known as the Manchu Shih Tzu Society, this younger club, as we have seen, now has substantially larger membership than the sponsoring body, demonstrating the widespread appeal of the palace-type of dog.

(The above quotations with regard to this are taken from the minutes of the annual general meeting of the Shih Tzu Club, held in London on March 29, 1957.)

In emphasizing the need for a division of the Shih Tzu into two classes, we derive immense encouragement from the fact that a precisely similar conclusion was unanimously reached by the members of the British Shih Tzu Club at the 1957 annual general meeting, to which we have just referred. This meeting appears to have been attended by the vast majority of those who are now leading breeders in that country, including the key figures in both the present club devoted to the breed, all of whom must have given their approval to the proposal.

Such a division would undoubtedly have been made, had not the British Kennel Club taken the attitude that the breed was not sufficiently numerous to be split into two classes and that fanciers would be wiser to go ahead on a broad over-all

Dutch and American Shih Tzu meet in Saudi Arabia! On the left, Netherlands and International Champion Lou Shu van der Oranje Manege, bred by Eta Pauptit. On the right, Chumulari Hoo T'ee, bred by Rev. and Mrs. D. Allan Easton.

Ch. Talifu Bobby Dazla at 11 years of age. This beautiful import is owned by Patte Link of Charlottesville, Virginia.

A trio of Canadian-bred puppies owned and bred by Marilyn Szalay of Ontario. The sire was Best in Show winner, American Ch. Sitsang Whiz Bang ex Ch. Seng Fu Me-Tu Suzi-Q. The puppies were photographed at 8 weeks.

Zizi's Bombo-Tjimbo, owned by Mrs. Kirsti Wessel Ochlin of Fredrikstad, Norway. Bred by Ruth Laakso, Bombo is the sire of Nor. Ch. Zizi's Lhu-Lhe.

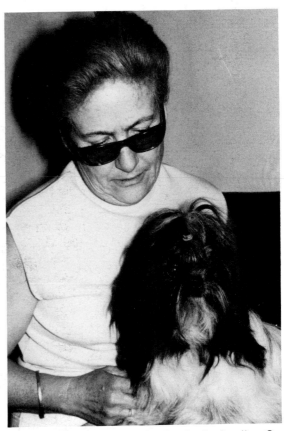

Mrs. Erika Geusendam of Lubeck, the leading German Shih Tzu breeder, with her youngest show winner, the 8 month-old bitch Naga v Tschomo-Lungma.

Overleaf:
Top: Ch. House of Wu Tiana, bred and owned by Mrs. Charles R. Eckes of Denver. **Bottom:** Ch. House of Wu Tiz Tu, also breeder-owned by Mrs. Charles R. Eckes.

129

HOUSE OF WU
SHIH TZU

WINNERS

ONONDAGA KENNEL
ASSOCIATION, INC.

NOV. 9, 1975   KLEIN

The Baroness Van Panthaleon Van Eck, Shih Tzu Columnist for the Dutch Magazine *De Hondenwereld,* and one of the leading European authorities on our breed.

Club were right in their original decision, the British Kennel Club very sadly mistaken in rejecting it. Had the club's unanimous recommendation of 1957 been accepted by the British Kennel Club, frank recognition being given to the fact that there are now two distinctly different types of Shih Tzu, the breed would be in a much less confused state today.

That this is true of Great Britain as well as of the United States is indicated by Mr. Marion Boot's letter, quoted earlier. Even as it is, apparently due to the pressure of obvious necessity, a division into two weight classes is being made at a number of British shows, the break being made at 12 or 14 pounds—the former, of course, following the pattern set by the Peking Kennel Club whose example is now only beginning to receive the attention it deserves.

As recently as April, 1969, the American magazine *Dog World* considered newsworthy the recognition by some breeders that "two distinct types of Shih Tzu exist—the larger, robust English Shih Tzu and the personable Scandinavian version," a very sweeping statement which completely overlooks the fact that not a few English breeders take special pride in producing the same exquisite little gems as were favored in the Imperial Palace.

Betraying no awareness of the historical facts which lie behind the existence of the two distinct sizes, and expressing no particular interest in find-

basis, 9-18 pounds being the figure finally decided with 16 pounds the "ideal" maximum.

Written by Mr. K.B. Rawlings, then and now chairman of the British Shih Tzu Club, an illuminating letter regarding this was published in the British *Dog World* on August 2, 1957. In the letter Mr. Rawlings explains that the Kennel Club was not prepared to accept the recommendations unanimously made by club members at the annual general meeting, either with regard to the two weight ranges or with regard to the formation of a new club to foster the smaller type of dog, and that for that reason no change could be made "until further decisions are taken by the Shih Tzu Club for submission to the Kennel Club."

In this regard it must very respectfully be suggested that the members of the British Shih Tzu

Bey-The-Wang, owned by Margrethe Svendsen and bred by Ulla-Britt Mouritzen, Sweden.

Overleaf:
Top: Ch. Lou Wan Casinova with four of his offspring, as he won Second Place in the Stud Dog Class at the 1976 American Shih Tzu Club Specialty Show under judge Erma Jungfeldt. Owned by Louis and Wanda Gec, Clifton, N.J. **Bottom:** Ch. Cresswood High Fashion going Winners Bitch and Best of Opposite Sex under judge Frank Oberstar. Handler Freeman Dickey. Breeder-owned by Mrs. Lucy M. Cress, Latrobe, Pa.

ing out what they were, the article indicated that such breeders planned to "combine" the best qualities of both types to produce "a new and, they hope, superior American Shih Tzu."

It was fervently hoped that most breeders would try to breed the best possible Chinese Shih Tzu rather than "improved" English or American versions. For this reason, breeding between the two size types should not be undertaken in a haphazard fashion but with the utmost discrimination and with a clear picture in mind of the Peking Palace prototype.

A POSSIBLE SOLUTION FROM HOLLAND

The wisdom of a weight division has been challenged on the grounds that dogs vary in weight from time to time, not to mention other practical difficulties. These have been clearly described by the British fancier Mrs. Thelma Morgan in the British *Dog World* of May 20, 1966. For this reason we might do well to consider whether there is not some other more effective way of distinguishing small Shih Tzu from large.

When the Countess d'Anjou wrote her letter to Mrs. Widdrington, it must be realized that her purpose was to make it clear that the palace dogs were smaller in size than those which she had just seen in England but which she was hardly likely to have weighed. Even more important, she was *not* affirming that the court in Peking had established a 12 pound limit. This becomes obvious when we recall that the avoirdupois weight system of pounds and ounces is an essentially western concept.

Thus, a 12 pound weight limit would have been quite meaningless to the palace eunuchs who most certainly did not use English or American-made scales to weigh their puppies! As any "old China hand" will readily appreciate, their overall objective was to produce the most compact dogs possible, exquisite little gems treasured for their neatness of size—not their lightness of weight.

As a careful reading of the Countess d'Anjou's letter will show, the reference to a 12 pound maximum occurs because the Peking Kennel Club

Aidzo, born in Peking in 1930 and imported by Charlotte Kauffmann of Oslo.

had decided that this was the best way to separate the large dogs from ths small, possibly through the influence of British or American members to whom such a measurement of weight would come naturally.

On this subject the opinion of the Peking Kennel Club deserves to be treated with the utmost respect, much more so than it has received to date in the English-speaking world. Such respect does not mean that we should follow their example blindly; however, if we can devise some better method of achieving the same objective—which, after all, is to distinguish the dainty palace-type Shih Tzu from the less compact ones which have become so frequently in evidence since the breakdown of the court breeding program—so much the better.

Concerning this we have received a suggestion from the Netherlands which we find of the greatest interest. Originally written to Reverend Easton personally, it has since appeared in the Christmas, 1968, issue of the Dutch magazine *De Honderwereld*. A most helpful and constructive criticism of the Peking Kennel Club's mode of division, it suggests a method which could both be simpler and more satisfactory.

"I agree that we should be breeding small dogs, as the Chinese undoubtedly did. However, a small

Overleaf:
Top: Can. Bda. Ch. Carrimount Ah-Ting-Ting winning Best in Show at the Purina Invitational Show of Shows, staged by the Ottawa Kennel Club in November, 1976. **L. to r.:** Dr. F. G. Walker, owner-handler, Mrs. A. Dickson, Mrs. A. Brown, president of the Ottawa Kennel Club and Mr. Webb, representing the Purina Company. **Bottom:** Chumulari Woo-Ya, owned by Madelyn Elliott of New York, is handled by Dawn Tendler, at the 1976 American Shih Tzu Club Show. Calaf is going strong here at 10 years of age winning the Veterans Class under judge Erna Jungefeldt.

BEST IN SHOW

THE OTTAWA KENNEL CLUB EST. 1900

PHOTO BY CLARK

dog could have bone and look less heavy than he actually weighs. What makes some Shih Tzu heavy is not only bone-structure, but width of chest and length of back, the latter even giving a large impression to an otherwise small dog. Then a dog with slightly bowed forelegs will be lower at withers than one with straight legs."

"To establish a fair method of size differentiation," continues our Netherlands correspondent, the Baroness Van Panthaleon Van Eck, wife of the Burgomaster of Emmeloord and Shih Tzu columnist for *De Hondenwereld,* "measure from one forefoot over withers to the other forefoot, following the legs closely. Add the length of the back from exactly between withers to beginning of tail. After some measuring I come to a maximum of 35 inches for the "small gems." But hundreds of dogs would have to be measured that way to fix the right size. Every judge could keep a string with a knot in it in his pocket to measure in the ring, if necessary."

Not nearly as subject to variability as weight, this highly ingenious Dutch suggestion is much less complicated than it seems on first reading. Since it makes provision for the fact that a sturdily boned and compact Shih Tzu can be surprisingly heavy, it may well provide the solution to our problem. At least it is worth the most serious consideration. I might mention that the Baroness is a devoted Shih Tzu fancier, breeding selectively with a few dearly loved house-pets of the smaller type.

THE IMPERIAL SHIH TZU

After the manuscript for our first book had been sent to the publisher, our continuing search for first-hand information brought to light a little-known essay by the Princess Der Ling which fully confirms the theory we have advanced regarding the development of two different types of Shih Tzu in old Peking.

Describing the royal kennels in this essay, which was published in the United States in 1933, the Princess gives some fascinating glimpses of the information which she received from the Empress Dowager about her beloved dogs.

Danish Consul Caj Grum and Mrs. Else Grum at their home in Oslo in the summer of 1975 with their Ting-Mo. Mr. and Mrs. Grum have been owners of Shih Tzu for over 43 years, which makes them the oldest Shih Tzu fanciers in the world! Photo by A. Laakso.

"Out of a litter of four," Her Majesty told me, "there are seldom more than two which are worth keeping. The others, even though they have the same father and mother, have something the matter with them—too-short legs, too-long bodies, or the wrong markings. They are inferior."

"Particular care must be taken with feeding," explained Her Majesty. "A *Harba Go* (Manchu words for this species of dog) must not be given too much water while he is growing, or he will become too large, which makes him ugly. The food must be as carefully selected as for a child . . ."

"If Her Majesty wished to examine one of the dogs closer she would indicate which one and the eunuch would hold the animal up for inspection. Then she would say, 'Its eyes are dirty; you must take better care of it,' or 'Its hind legs are not of the right length' or 'Its body is too long.' Whenever she commented thus on any dog, especially the puppies, it was a decree of exile—for it meant that the dog had to be taken away. Puppies were not killed," wrote the princess. "The eunuchs usually took discarded puppies out into the city and sold them, receiving good prices because the animals were from the imperial kennels."

Overleaf:
Top left: Amilou's Bragabout, owned by Gordon K. Kellogg of Stanton, California. **Top right:** Am., Can. Ch. Charing Cross Ching El Chang, multiple Best in Show winner with owner Lillian Phillips, Whispering Pines, North Carolina. Photograph by Troy Phillips. **Bottom left:** Ch. Bomshu Born Flee photographed by Bill Zervoulis during a visit to Santa Claus. This photograph was the December 1976 cover of the American Kennel Gazette. Owners: Jan and Bill Zervoulis. **Bottom right:** After the bath, or "I though she was going to drown me!" Ch. Mistybank Ouzo v Zervlistan gets ready for a show! Owned by Janine R. Zervoulis.

Clearly it was no secret that the palace eunuchs were able to find willing purchasers for the puppies which the Empress Dowager had rejected as inferior in quality. This would seem to have been accepted as the normal practice and to have been done on a considerable scale.

Being intensely fond of animals, doubtless the strong-willed old ruler was glad to see her puppies go to homes where they were valued, even though she regarded them as poor specimens of the breed. It may well have been her hope that they would be treated as pets, not used for breeding, but this was a matter over which she had no means of exercising effective control. Indeed it is questionable how much she knew of what went on outside the palace wall, as the life of the court was completely cut off from that of the ordinary citizens of Peking.

As a result, it is easy to see how two different types of Shih Tzu had developed in the Chinese capital by the time the breed became known to the outside world. On the one hand, hidden in the palace and beloved at court were the exquisitely dainty and well-proportioned little jewels, bred with the strictest selectivity and carefully screened to conform to the imperial ideal. On the other, accessible to the general public and bred by them with less discrimination were the coarser specimens, treasured by those who had long ago learned to be satisfied with something less than the best.

Shih Tzu of both types are to be seen in the show rings of England and North America today, though much less so in continental Europe where the neat but sturdy palace variety have always been recognized as the correct imperial dogs. Generally speaking, in the West the larger and coarser dogs have lost their Oriental appearance, while the more compact and daintier ones have retained a distinctively Chinese look. Although exaggerated, there is a measure of truth in the comment of a leading European authority—with an affection for both type—who wrote, "I regard them as, more or less, different breeds."

In fairness to the general public, which does have its rights in the matter, the two types of Shih Tzu should be clearly designated in a manner

International and Scandinavian Ch. Tempelgardens Chi-Co-Tzu and Bey-The-Wang with their four sons, Lyckobringarens Mo-Te, Mah-Di, Mah-Jong and Mr. Magoo and their owner Miss Margrethe Svendsen of Sweden.

The Baroness Van Panthaleon Van Eck with her stud dog, Giri Shu van de Oranje Manege, bred by Eta Pauptit, and winner of two international Championship prizes in France and two in Germany. The eight week old puppy she is holding is Zizi's Leidza, bred by Ruth Laakso. The puppy is named after her famous ancestor, Leidza, bred in the Peking Palace.

Overleaf:
Top: Mariljac Monsy Bonsy Colwell (center) whelped in 1964 and owned by Donna and Edgar Ellis, is shown with her daughters, Floridonna Monsy Bonsy Ellis and Floridonna Razzl Dazzl Ellis. Her son Chatterbox is a multiple Best in Show winner and her son Hajji Baba won the Open Dog class at the 1975 Westminster Kennel Club show. **Bottom:** A five-month-old Chumulari puppy sits proudly on an oriental rug brought home from Tibet by his breeders, Reverend and Mrs. D. Allan Easton of Gardiner, New York.

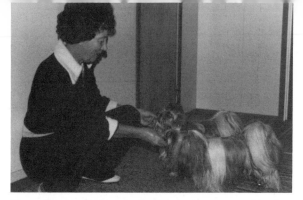

Mrs. Sonja Bail of Arendal, Norway with her Norwegian Ch. Zizi's Foo. Zizi's Chi-Ko Liang is in the background. Both dogs sired by Int., Nor., Ch. Marinas Muff-Lung-Feng ex Int., Nor., Danish Ch. Zizi's Lhamo, bred by Ruth Laakso.

Mrs. Grum with Toddie, Galloping and Ting-a-Ling in the garden of their home in Oslo, Norway.

Fus Shu van de Oranje Manege, a 9½ pound gold and white male bred in Holland by Eta Pauptit and owned by the Chumulari Kennels. Shown in Amsterdam in 1967, he was given a top rating as "excellent" by the judge. Fu Shu became a Canadian champion.

Danish and Norwegian Ch. Marinas Dog-Rose, whelped in 1963 and bred by Mrs. Marianne Berg, Kennel Marina, Gothenburg, Sweden. The sire was Bjorneholms Dhondup ex Swed. Ch. Marina's May-Be Shih. This was Kennel Zizi's first Shih Tzu and she lived to be 11½ years old. Photo by A. Laakso.

Overleaf:
Top: Willows Wizard pictured winning a 5-point major as Best of Winners at a recent Santa Barbara Kennel Club show under judge George Patton. Lois Frank handled for co-owners Consuelo Bolsaks and Louis Adams of Redding, California.
Bottom: Ch. Hodari Tam Lin of Moon Ling winning under judge Helen Lee James at a recent Santa Barbara Kennel Club show. Laurie Battey, who co-owns with Helen McClarnon of Torrance, California, is handling.

Father and sons . . . Kan Tu Wei Huo Shou Ling, Rondelay Mei Kan Tu Win and Ch. Rondelay Sheng Po. All three owned by Edythe Kennedy, Barnstable, Massachusetts.

which is historically accurate and in no way misleading. It had occurred to us that the larger could be known as the "English Shih Tzu," since it is in that country that most of them now seem to be bred, but such a title would obscure the fact that many English breeders prefer the smaller type. Perhaps the larger should just be known as "Shih Tzu," the smaller carrying the prefix "Imperial" to mark their special association with the Peking Palace.

It remains only to add that the Imperial Shih Tzu cannot be bred in any way other than on a very small scale and in a highly personal fashion. Reared with the greatest individual care and attention by the court eunuchs, the breed has derived its unique character from its close association with the human race.

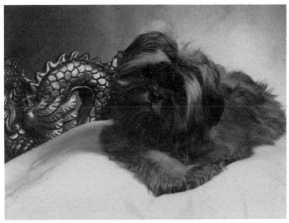

Wix Toi Lan Klasi Khasi, owned by K. Coffee of Minot, North Dakota.

Those who think in terms of large scale breeding in kennels, with an impressive listing of studs and bitches, would be well advised to confine their attention to the size our present day Standard requires. The very small ones could therefore be left strictly to the fancier with a darling house pet in mind.

None of us can offer the Imperial Shih Tzu the pomp and glory of palace life, but given plenty of affection and an honored place in our homes, they will be more than happy to attach themselves to the humblest family circle and to bring to it something of the splendor and dignity which is their heritage as a royal breed.

Swedish, Norwegian and Finnish Ch. ZiZi's Tara, gold and white bitch that is the top-winning bitch in Norway. Bred and owned by Ruth Laakso, Drammen, Norway, photo by A. Laakso.

Marya Winds Fortune Cookie photographed at 9 months of age. "Cookie's" sire was Ch. Dragonwyck The Great Gatsby ex Ch. Mariljac Marilyn of Chusanho. Owner is Martha Coalina of Valparaiso, Indiana.

San Yen Tami Shih O'Tani, owned by Susan Barr, Salt Lake City, Utah.

Overleaf:
Top left: Highlands Frosty Friday with owner Jackie Peterson. **Top right:** Marcy Barr and San Yen Tisha Wong Tong Bear, owned by Susan Barr, San Yen Shih Tzu. **Bottom left:** Norwegian Best in Show Winner, Ch. Zizi's Lhu-Lhe, whelped in 1975 and owned and bred by Ruth Laakso, Drammen, Norway. **Bottom right:** Mrs. Asta Hellisen Finstad, depicted in an oil painting with her Bijou, whelped in 1934.

Chapter 8
BUYING YOUR SHIH TZU PUPPY

There are several paths that will lead you to a litter of puppies where you can find the puppy of your choice. Write to the parent club and ask for the names and addresses of members who have puppies for sale. The addresses of breed clubs can be obtained by writing the American Kennel Club, 51 Madison Avenue, New York, N.Y. 10010. They keep an accurate, up-to-date list of reputable breeders from whom you can seek information on obtaining a good, healthy puppy. You might also check listings in the classified ads of major newspapers. The various dog magazines also carry listings and usually a column each month which features information and news on the breed.

It is to your advantage to attend a few local dog shows where purebred dogs of just about every breed are being exhibited in the show ring. Even if you do not wish to buy a show dog, you should be familiar with what the better specimens look like so that you may at least get a decent-looking representative of the breed for your money. You will learn a lot by observing the dogs in action in the show ring, or in a public place where their personalities come to the fore. The dog show catalogue will list the dogs and their owners with local names and breeders whom you can visit to see the types and colors they are breeding and winning at the shows. Exhibitors at these shows are usually delighted to talk to people about their dogs and the specific characteristics of their particular breed.

Once you've chosen the Shih Tzu as your breed because you admire its exceptional beauty, intelligence and personality, and because you feel the Shih Tzu will fit in with your family's way of life, it is wise to read as much literature as possible on the breed. Any library, workshop or pet shop can get hold of this information for you. When you have gone over this background material, it is time to start writing letters and making phone calls and appointments to see puppies.

A word of caution: don't let your choice of a kennel be determined by its nearness to your home, and then buy the first "cute" puppy that romps across your instep or licks the end of your nose. All pups are cute, and naturally you'll have a preference among those you see. But don't let preferences sway you. If you are buying your Shih Tzu as a family pet, preferences are permissible. But if you are looking for a quality puppy with show prospects, you must think clearly, choose wisely, and make the best possible choice. You will learn to love your Shih Tzu, whichever one you choose, whereas a case of "love at first sight" can be disappointing later on.

To get the broadest possible concept of what puppies are for sale and the current market prices, it is recommended that you visit as many kennels as possible in your area and write to others farther away. With today's safe and rapid air cargo flights on the major airlines, it is possible to secure dogs from far-off places at nominal costs. While it is always safest and wisest to see the dog you are buying, there are enough reputable breeders and kennels to be found for you to take this step with a minimum of risk. It can be well worth your while to obtain the exact dog or bloodline you desire.

It is customary for the purchaser to pay the shipping charges, and the airlines are most willing to supply flight information and prices upon request. Rental of the shipping crate, if the owner does not provide one for the dog, is nominal. While unfortunate incidents have occurred on the airlines in the transporting of animals by air, the major airlines are making improvements in safety measures and have reached the point of reasonable safety and cost. Barring unforeseen circumstances, the safe arrival of a dog you might buy can pretty much be assured if both seller and purchaser adhere to and follow up on even the most minute details from both ends.

Opposite:
Chumulari Trari, photographed by the famous dog photographer Tauskey, when she was 10 months old. This great gold bitch with black mask and tippings was a very important foundation bitch at the Eastons' Chumulari Kennels. Trari's sire was Si-Kians Tashi ex Wei Honey of Elfann. Tashi came from Swedish and French championship stock, while Honey was from English championship stock.

WHAT TO LOOK FOR IN A SHIH TZU PUPPY

Let us assume you want to enjoy all the cute antics of a young puppy and decide to buy an eight-week-old puppy. This is about the age when a puppy is weaned, wormed and ready to go out into the world with a responsible new owner. It is better not to buy a puppy under six weeks of age; it simply is not yet ready to leave the mother or the security of the other puppies. At eight to twelve weeks of age you will be able to notice much about the appearance and the behavior. Puppies, as they are recalled in our fondest childhood memories, are gay, active, and bouncy, as well they should be! The normal puppy should be interested, alert, and curious, especially about a stranger. If a puppy acts a little reserved or distant, however, such action need not be misconstrued as shyness or fear. It merely indicates he hasn't made up his mind whether he likes you as yet! By the same token, he should not be fearful or terrified of a stranger—and especially should not show any fear towards his owner!

In direct contrast, the puppy should not be ridiculously over-active either. The puppy that frantically bounds around the room and is never still is not especially desirable. And beware of the "spinners!" Spinners are the puppies or dogs that have become neurotic from being kept in cramped quarters or in crates. They behave in an emotionally unstable manner when let loose in adequate space; when let out they run in circles and seemingly "go wild". Puppies with this kind of traumatic background seldom ever regain full composure or adjust to the outside world. The puppy which has had the proper exercise and appropriate living quarters will have a normal, though spirited, outlook on life and will do his utmost to

win you over without having to go into a tailspin.

If the general behavior and appearance of the dog thus far appeal to you, it is time for you to observe him more closely for additional physical requirements. First of all, you cannot expect to find on the puppy all the coat he will bear upon maturity. That will come with time and good food, and will be additionally enhanced by the many wonderful grooming aids which can be found on the market today. Needless to say, the healthy puppy's coat should have a nice shine to it, and the more dense at this age, the better the coat will be when the dog reaches adulthood.

Look for clear, dark, sparkling eyes, free of discharge. Dark eye rims or lids are the most desirable and should be small and almond shaped. From the time the puppy's eyes open until the puppy is about three months old, the eyes might have a slightly bluish cast to them. The darker the blue the better the chances are for a good dark eye in the adult dog.

Check the bite. Even though the puppy will get another complete set of teeth somewhere between four and seven months of age, there will be some indication of their final position. You don't want too much of an overshot bite (top teeth too far out over the bottom teeth) or a badly undershot jaw (bottom teeth too far out under the top teeth). The gums should be pink in color, and the teeth should be a clear, clean white.

Puppies take anything and almost everything into their mouths to chew on, and a lot of diseases and infections start or are introduced in the mouth area. Brown-stained teeth, for instance, may indicate a past or present case of distemper, and they will stay that way. This must be reckoned with if you have a show puppy in mind. The puppy's breath should not be sour or unpleasant.

146

This can be a result of a poor mixture of food in the diet, or too low quality of meat, especially if fed raw. Some say the healthy puppy's breath has a faint odor vaguely reminiscent of garlic. At any rate, a puppy should never be fed just table scraps, but should have a well-balanced diet containing a good dry puppy chow and a good grade of fresh meat. Poor meat and too much cereal or fillers tend to make the puppy too fat. We like puppies to be in good flesh, but not fat from the wrong kind of food.

Needless to say, the puppy should be clean. The breeder that shows a dirty puppy is one to steer away from! Look closely at the skin. Make sure it is not covered with insect bites or red, blotchy sores or dry scales. The vent area about the tail should not show evidences of diarrhea or inflammation. By the same token, the puppy's fur should not be matted with excretion or smell strongly of urine.

True enough, you can wipe dirty eyes, clean dirty ears and give the puppy a bath when you get it home, but these things are all indications of how the puppy has been cared for during the important formative months of its life, and can vital-

Puppy love at its best! This adorable picture of a little girl and her dog submitted by Bill Kennedy, Barnstable, Massachusetts.

Three peas in a pod! A family of look-alike Shih Tzu taking the honors at the Calgary Kennel and Obedience Club in May, 1976. Left to right: Ch. Chumulari Li Jen, Best of Opposite Sex to her grandson in the middle, Ch. Nancarrow's Ki-Ki, who won the Breed and Group Third, and on the right Ki's daughter, Maui's Mai Jen, winning her second Best Puppy in Breed win. Mai Jen was bred and is owned by Mrs. Jan Shouldice of Calgary, Canada. The others are owned by E. Joyce Harris, Alberta.

Top, right:
Yinsu's French Connection, bred and owned by Marie and James Janeson, Ontario, Canada.
Top, left:
Chumulari Liu Mang, a gold and white dog pictured at 18 months of age. Owned by Mr. Joseph Hochrein of New York.
Left:
Carol Moorland Marshall's figurine of a Shih Tzu which was based on the Shih Tzu Chumulari Tai Tai, owned by co-author Joan Brearley.
Bottom, left:
Ch. Char Nick S'wing Erh of Copa won Best of Breed at the 1975 Raleigh, North Carolina Show under judge Anna Cowie. Jean Lade handled for owner Coni Nickerson of Richmond, Virginia.
Bottom, right:
International Champion Freya Shu van de Oranje Manege, Best in Show winner at the Zuidlaren International show in 1969. She is a daughter of Hadda VDOM and litter sister to the Eastons' import, Fu Shu van de Oranje Manege. Bred by Eta Pauptit in Holland, and owned by Eleanore Eldredge, Shang T'ou Kennels in Easton, Washington.

Top, left:
Ch. Capa's Golden Pandora of BoRu is owned by Charles and Anna Ballard of Camden, Ohio. The sire was Cresswood Tzu Tzu of Capa ex Accetta's More Fun. F. C. Dickey was handler for this win under judge Mrs. Heywood Hartley. The breeders were Paul and Carol Arcuragi.

Top, right:
American and Canadian Ch. Hidden Coves Golden Pendant, pictured winning Best of Opposite Sex under judge Iris Bueno at the 1974 Carroll County Kennel Club show. Owned by Barbara Ward of Revere, Massachusetts.

Right:
Willows Oh So Love pictured winning at a Match Show under judge Mrs. Stern. Handled by Lois Frank of Chico, California, for owner Consuelo Bolsaks. The sire was Starfell Solitaire ex Chumulari Phola.

Bottom, right:
Tarramont Golden Fu Chen pictured winning at a recent Lexington Kennel Club show with his handler Clint Harris. Owned by Mr. and Mrs. William Rhodes, Baltimore, Maryland.

Bottom, left:
Ch. Marya Winds Mariljac Marilyn of Chusanho is pictured winning under judge Kenneth E. Miller. The sire was Mariljac Maripet ex Ch. Mariljac Tattletail. Barbara Hussin handled for owner Martha Coalina of Valpariso, Indiana.

ly influence its future health and development. There are many reputable breeders raising healthy puppies that have been reared in proper places and under the proper conditions in clean housing, so why take a chance on a series of veterinary bills and a questionable constitution?

MALE OR FEMALE?

The choice of sex in your puppy is also something that must be given serious thought before you buy. For the pet owner, the sex that would best suit the family life you enjoy would be the paramount choice to consider. For the breeder or exhibitor, there are other vital considerations. If you are looking for a stud to establish a kennel, it is essential that you select a dog with both testicles evident, even at a tender age, and verified by a veterinarian before the sale is finalized if there is any doubt.

The visibility of only one testicle, known as monorchidism, automatically disqualifies the dog from the show ring or from a breeding program, though monorchids are capable of siring. Additionally, it must be noted that monorchids frequently sire dogs with the same deficiency, and to introduce this into a bloodline knowingly is an unwritten sin in the fancy. Also, a monorchid can sire dogs that are completely sterile. Such dogs are referred to as cryptorchids and have no testicles.

An additional consideration in the male versus female decision for the private owners is that with males there might be the problem of leg-lifting and with females there is the inconvenience while they are in season. However, this need not be the problem it used to be—pet shops sell "pants" for both sexes, which help control the situation.

THE PLANNED PARENTHOOD BEHIND YOUR PUPPY

Never be afraid to ask pertinent questions about the puppy, as well as questions about the sire and dam. Feel free to ask the breeder if you might see the dam, the purpose of your visit to determine her general health and her appearance as a representative of the breed. Ask also to see the sire, if the breeder is the owner. Ask what the puppy has been fed and should be fed after weaning. Ask to see the pedigree, and inquire if the litter or the individual puppies have been registered with the American Kennel Club, how many of the temporary and/or permanent inoculations the puppy has had, when and if the puppy has been wormed and whether it has had any illness, disease, or infection.

You need not ask if the puppy is housebroken—it won't mean much. He may have gotten

Luv-Tzu Han-sum Hubbee, owned by Mary Marxen, Luv-Tzu Kennels, Van Wert, Ohio.

the idea as to where "the place" is where he lives now, but he will need new training to learn where "the place" is in his new home! You can't really expect too much from puppies at this age anyway. Housebreaking is entirely up to the new owner. We know puppies always eliminate when they first awaken and sometimes dribble when they get excited. If friends and relatives are coming over to see the new puppy, make sure he is walked just before he greets them at the door. This will help.

The normal time period for puppies around three months of age to eliminate is about every two or three hours. As the time draws near, either take the puppy out or indicate the newspapers for the same purpose. Housebreaking is never easy, but anticipation is about 90 per cent of solving the problem. The schools that offer to housebreak your dog are virtually useless. Here again the puppy will learn the "place" at the schoolhouse, but coming home he will need special training for the new location.

A reputable breeder will welcome any and all questions you might ask and will voluntarily offer additional information, if only to brag about the tedious and loving care he has given to the litter. He will also sell a puppy on a 24-hour veterinary approval. This means you have a full day to get the puppy to a veterinarian of your choice to get his opinion on the general health of the puppy before you make a final decision. There should be veterinary certificates and full particulars on the dates and types of inoculations the puppy has been given up to that time.

PUPPIES AND WORMS

Let us give further attention to the unhappy and very unpleasant subject of worms. Generally speaking, mostly all puppies—even those raised in clean quarters—come into contact with worms early in life. The worms can be passed down from the mother before birth or picked up during the puppies' first encounters with the earth or their kennel facilities. To say that you must not buy a puppy because of an infestation of worms is nonsensical. You might be passing up a fine animal that can be freed of worms in one short treatment, although a heavy infestation of worms of any kind in a young dog is dangerous and debilitating.

The extent of the infection can be readily determined by a veterinarian, and you might take his word as to whether the future health and conformation of the dog has been damaged. He can prescribe the dosage and supply the medication at the time and you will already have one of your problems solved. The kinds and varieties of worms and how to detect them is described elsewhere in this book and we advise you to check the matter out further if there is any doubt in your mind as to the problems of worms in dogs.

VETERINARY EXAMINATION

While your veterinarian is going over the puppy you have selected to purchase, you might just as well ask him for his opinion of it as a breed as well as the facts about its general health. While few veterinarians can claim to be breed conformation experts, they usually have a good eye for a worthy specimen and can advise you where to go for further information. Perhaps your veterinarian could also recommend other breeders if you should want another opinion. The veterinarian can point out structural faults or organic problems that affect all breeds and can usually judge whether an animal has been abused or mishandled and whether it is oversized or undersized.

We would like to emphasize here that it is only through this type of close cooperation between owners and veterinarians that we can expect to reap the harvest of modern research in the veterinary field. Most reliable veterinarians are more than eager to learn about various breeds of purebred dogs, and we in turn must acknowledge and apply what they have proved through experience and research in their field. We can buy and breed the best dog in the world, but when disease strikes we are only as safe as our veterinarian is capable—so let's keep them informed breed by breed,

Encore Suki Lin and Encore Charlie Sun, owned and bred in the 1960's by Jane Fitts, Santa Barbara, California.

151

and dog by dog. The veterinarian represents the difference between life and death!

THE CONDITIONS OF SALE

While it is customary to pay for the puppy before you take it away with you, you should be able to give the breeder a deposit if there is any doubt about the puppy's health. You might also (depending on local laws) postdate a check to cover the 24-hour veterinary approval. If you decide to take the puppy, the breeder is required to supply you with a pedigree, along with the puppy's registration paper. He is also obliged to supply you with complete information about the inoculations and American Kennel Club instructions on how to transfer ownership of the puppy into your name.

Some breeders will offer buyers time payment plans for convenience if the price on a show dog is very high or if deferred payments are the only way you can purchase the dog. However, any such terms must be worked out between buyer and breeder and should be put in writing to avoid later complications.

You will find most breeders cooperative if they believe you are sincere in your love for the puppy and that you will give it the proper home and show ring career it deserves (if it is sold as a show quality specimen of the breed). Remember, when buying a show dog, it is impossible to guarantee nature. A breeder can only tell you what he *believes* will develop into a show dog ... so be sure your breeder is an honest one.

Also, if you purchase a show prospect and promise to show the dog, you definitely should show it! It is a waste to have a beautiful dog that deserves recognition in the show ring sitting at home as a family pet, and it is unfair to the breeder. This is especially true if the breeder offered you a reduced price because of the advertising the kennel and bloodlines would receive by your showing the dog in the ring. If you want a pet, buy a pet. Be honest about it, and let the breeder decide on this basis which is the best dog for you. Your conscience will be clear and you'll both be doing a real service to the breed.

BUYING A SHOW PUPPY

If you are positive about breeding and showing your dog, make it clear that you intend to do so, so that the breeder will sell you the best possible puppy. If you are dealing with an established kennel, you will have to rely partially on their choice, since they know their bloodlines and what they can expect from the breeding. They know how their stock develops, and it would be foolish of

A trio of 4 month old puppies bred by Shirlee Rainey of Pensacola, Florida. Right to left, Raintree's Dr. K's Midnight Special, Raintree's Promised Gold and Raintree's Tar Baby.

them to sell you a puppy that could not stand up as a show specimen representing their stock in the ring.

However, you must also realize that the breeder may be keeping the best puppy in the litter to show and breed himself. If this is the case, you might be wise to select the best puppy of the opposite sex so that the dogs will not be competing against one another in the show rings for their championship title.

THE PURCHASE PRICE

Prices vary on all puppies, of course, but a good show prospect at six weeks to six months of age will sell for several hundred dollars. If the puppy is really outstanding, and the pedigree and parentage is also outstanding, the price will be even higher. Honest breeders, however, will be around the same figure, so price should not be a deciding factor in your choice. If there is any question as to the current price range, a few telephone calls to different kennels will give you a good average. Breeders will usually stand behind their puppies should something drastically wrong develop, such as hip dysplasia, etc. Their obligation to make an adjustment is usually honored; however, this must be agreed upon in writing at the time of purchase.

THE COST OF BUYING ADULT STOCK

Prices for adult dogs fluctuate greatly. Some grown dogs are offered free of charge to good homes; others are put out with owners on breeders' terms. But don't count on getting a "bargain" if it doesn't cost you anything! Good dogs are always in demand, and worthy studs or brood bitches are expensive. Prices for them can easily go up into the four-figure range. Take an expert with you if you intend to make this sort of investment. Just make sure the "expert" is free of professional jealousy and will offer an unprejudiced opinion. If you are reasonably familiar with the breed standard, and get the expert's opinion, between the two you can usually come up with a proper decision.

Buying grown stock does remove some of the risk if you are planning a kennel. You will know exactly what you are getting for your foundation stock and will also save time on getting your kennel started.

CHECKLIST OF FAULTS TO BEWARE OF WHEN BUYING YOUR SHIH TZU PUPPY

Along with a copy of the breed Standard—which you should read carefully—take this checklist along with you!

DON'T choose a puppy with an obvious lack of animation or that doesn't want to play.

DON'T choose a puppy with a narrow skull, or narrow jaw.

DON'T choose a puppy whose eyes are set too close together.

DON'T choose a puppy if there is white showing in the corners of the eyes, especially the inside. This haw detracts from the true Shih Tzu appearance.

DON'T choose a puppy with small, beady eyes.

DON'T choose a puppy with an overshot bite, or too severe an undershot bite.

DON'T choose a puppy with a wrinkled muzzle like a Pekingese!

DON'T choose a puppy with broken pigmentation on the muzzle.

DON'T choose a puppy with inadequate head furnishings.

DON'T choose a puppy that appears to be too long in back.

DON'T choose a puppy with hindquarters lower than the forequarters, or vice versa. The more level the back the better.

DON'T choose a puppy that appears too high on its legs.

DON'T choose a puppy that is cow-hocked or bandy-legged.

DON'T choose a puppy with too-little coat, or a curly one.

DON'T choose a puppy that doesn't carry its tail proudly over its back. Even at a young age the gay tail indicates a happy, healthy puppy.

DON'T BUY a puppy under eight weeks of age. The best time is from eight to twelve weeks of age, and beware of the breeder that will sell you one before he is ready to go.

A charming trio . . . Ch. Luv-Tzu Shazam, Luv-Tzu Sing-Song of Ding-A-Ling, and Luv-Tzu Doc Alot of Ding-A-Ling owned by Mary Marxen, Luv-Tzu Kennels, Van Wert, Ohio.

Typical Shih Tzu puppies at play. These two 3-month-olds were owner-bred by Judith Goldberg of North Tonawanda, New York. The sire was Ch. Paisley Ping Pong out of Astrids Shih Ling.

Wild Meadows Shanghai Baby, owned by Ginny Mills, Honeoye Falls, New York.

Mary Marxen and some of her puppies bred at Luv-Tzu Kennels.

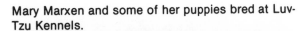

Tuckaway's Chin Te Fo, or "Pippin" as he is called by Jean Porter of Texarkana, Texas. He is 6 months old in this photograph.

Sim Sun's Sweet Sum Wun of Jaxbo, bred by Mrs. Julius Brown and owned by Mrs. P.B. Simpson of Pine Bluff, Arkansas. Pictured here at 5-months of age, at the time of this writing she was almost a champion!

Nancarrow's Wan Chi with her St. Bernard friend. Wan Chi is owned by Mrs. Phyllis Hodges, well-known Saint breeder, and was bred by E. Joyce Harris of Alberta, Canada.

Loo Mang of Myarlune. "Mopsy" was an import from England and is owned by Olive Ryan of Provincetown, Massachusetts. Pictured here "practicing Chopin," Mopsy is now 12½ years young.

Two 1-month-old puppies that grew up to be Ch. Dashi's Chin Tan and Dashi's Willie, bred and owned by Catherine F. Pouliot of Manchester, Connecticut.

Ch. Bosang Merrybelle Lee is a Best in Show-winning bitch owned by Lillian Phillips of Whispering Pines, North Carolina. The sire was Ch. Charing Cross Ching El Chang ex Bojang Satin Doll. Jean Lade handled for this win under Mrs. James Edward Clark.

Mexican Champion Mei-Lei's Pao Ting Fu, owned by Bernice Clark, Bernetts Shih Tzu.

Ch. Emperor's Something Else, a multiple Group winner, was handled by John M. Murdock for owner Sandra P. Adshead, of East Greenwich, Rhode Island. The sire was Ch. Emperor Ping Pong Partner ex Emperor's Delight of Delights. The judge pictured is Sue Kauffman.

Canadian Ch. Belair Infanta, photographed at 5 months of age, is owned and shown by Marilyn Szalay of Ontario, Canada.

Chumulari Ying Sheng, a Ying Ying son, pictured winning the breed at a recent Canadian show with his handler, Pat Tripp. Owned by the Eastons.

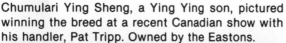

Chumulari Chumbi Tzu, photographed by Alton Anderson at 7 months of age. Chumbi is co-owned by Bernard Grizzaffi and Peggy Easton.

Lyckobringarens Geisha, owned and bred by Margrethe Svendsen, Sweden. This small black and white bitch is a granddaughter of the well-known English import, Swedish Ch. Fu-Ling of Clystvale.

Ch. Willow's Fancy Me, black and white bitch co-bred by Consuelo Bolsaks and Lois Frank. The sire was Ch. Hei Lein's Mr. Bo Jangles ex Willows Miss Muffit. Handled by Martin E. Gregory who co-owns with Bruce A. Allen.

Ch. Chasmu Solor, painted by artist Gladys Ray. The dog was bred by Audrey Fowler, Chasmu Kennels, London, and owned by Mary K. Frothingham of Sherban, Massachusetts.

The official insignia of the Chicagoland Shih Tzu Club.

Ch. Aagalynn Lion of Joppa, drawn in 1973 by the late artist Jean Gadberry, and used as the kennel logo for Gordon K. Kellogg's Joppa Kennel in Stanton, California.

Another kind of art form! This is a fancy oriental dog house for the Shih Tzu dogs owned by Ralph Zidanowicz of Bogota, New Jersey. Mr. Zidanowicz designed and made the dog house himself.

A Shih Tzu family portrait by Gladys Ray, of Betty R. Winters' Shih Tzu.

An original design by Marie K. Leeds for a needle-point tote bag. Four heads line the lid of the bag and her Maralee Kennel insignia is on the back of the bag. Mrs. Leed's kennels are in Des Plaines, Illinois.

Magnificent water color of a Shih Tzu done by Jennifer Winship of Greenville, Mississippi.

Arrows indicate the direction in which the Shih Tzu coat should be brushed: in layers in the direction in which it falls naturally. Start with the layers of the under coat first, holding the top layers out of the way with your hand. As one layer is finished let the next fall out of your hand, brushing it well in the same downward direction. A perfect part runs in a straight line down the middle of the back from the base of the skull to the root of the tail, with the hair falling on either side of the part. Then, the top knot hair is parted, half draping to one side, half to the other. Hair above the eyes should be caught up into a covered elastic band or something similar to form the top knot. Be careful not to pull the top knot too tight. The moustache and beard of the Shih Tzu should be treated in the same way as the body hair, being brushed layer by layer in a downward direction.

Chapter 9
GROOMING THE SHIH TZU

All dogs, especially the long-coated breeds such as the Shih Tzu, require regular, careful grooming. A beautifully-coated dog which proudly wears the thick, luxurious coat you've taken the time and trouble to cultivate, is a joy to behold, both in an out of the show ring. Once ruined or let go almost beyond repair, the coat takes endless time and energy to restore to its original natural luster and length. It is wise to take a little time each day to keep your dog in top condition, rather than to try to repair the damage that has been done by accumulated neglect. This is especially true if a dog is to be presented in the show ring.

To establish grooming as a common practice in the daily routine, you'll find matters simplified by choosing a particular spot for grooming your dog each time. You'll make it easier for yourself by placing the grooming table where the light is good and where the dog will have the least distractions. If you are grooming for the show ring it will be wise to set aside a time for grooming each and every day to keep the coat in top condition rather than let it go and then try to "catch up" as the show date rolls around. Eliminate temptations by keeping toys, dog biscuits, other dogs or family pets, etc., out of sight of the grooming area. Make the dog know there is work to be done and that you mean to do it. Be firm—but gentle—about it.

How you choose to position your dog for grooming is a matter of choice for your own convenience. Just remember that surface grooming is never enough. You must groom from skin to the ends of the hair if your efforts are to be effective. Just be sure that while the dog is on a grooming table that it is steady. Dog are always nervous about their footing and the table should be firmly planted on the floor. A ribbed rubber matting on the grooming table is best for the surface and is easy to clean.

There is no set amount of time recommended for grooming to produce the desired effect. Dogs that are more heavily coated will naturally require more time, but enough time should be allotted for going over the entire dog each time it is put on the grooming table. What you skip over one time would be twice as hard to remedy by the next time, and you always run the risk of pulling out twice as much hair when a certain spot has been allowed to get twice as tangled. These spots that you have missed will show up all too frequently, and this simply will not do for a show dog.

The correct brush for the Shih Tzu should have pin bristles; the coat should be brushed in layers from the skin out to the very ends of the hair. If your brush is gathering hair on one side only, you are not holding it properly. The coat should be brushed in the direction in which the coat is to fall. Use our visual diagram, with arrows indicating the direction in which hair should be brushed, as a guide. The top knot should be brushed up and a rubber band doubled over two fingers with the hair pulled through it, making sure that the hair is not pulled too tightly back over the eyes so as to pull the lids away from the eye sockets or make it difficult to blink their eyes. Be sure none of the hair you have gathered pulls the ears out of place.

The one exception to the grooming of the coat in the direction in which it is to fall is for puppies. Here, the method of brushing the coat "every which way" does the hair itself no actual harm and stimulates the skin and hair cells to encourage growth of the permanent coat. Also, the legs can be fluffed up before the last minute finishing touches.

Special attention should be given to the feet. The feet are usually the first part of the dog to get dirty. Therefore, they are also usually the first spots to get tangled and matted. The hocks and elbows should receive special attention, since bones are prominent in these areas and friction and wear can cause holes in the coat.

Should you find a bad tangle or mat, brush away the surrounding hair and take the mat in your hand. Take a little bit of mat at a time and shred it gently with your fingers, working it apart. Next, take a comb and carefully and gently work it out from the ends of the hair first until you get to the skin. Start at the bottom and work up toward the body. When the mat has all been separated, start brushing the broken hairs out gently until all the remaining hairs are free. Then you are ready to brush it back into the rest of the coat.

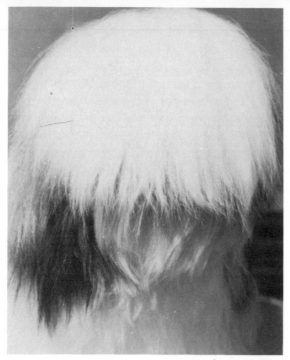

Grooming the top knot . . . Jan Zervoulis of the Zervlistan Kennels makes sure that all of her Ouzo's hair is combed out and thoroughly dry before putting it up in a band. Jan and Bill Zervoulis' kennel is in Basking Ridge, New Jersey.

Jubilation Can You Spare A Dime is co-owned by Linda A. Miller of Belton, Missouri. "Pan Handler" was bred by Garrett Crissman, who co-owns with handler Linda Miller. The sire was Ch. Hee Shee's Mr. Bullwinkle ex Jubilation White or Wong.

Floridonna Toki Boi Kan Du, owned by Jennifer Murphy of Jacksonville, Florida. The sire was Ch. Hajji Baba of Floridonna ex Hsi Jenni Tu. Photo by Gene Sukovich.

There are various kinds of grooming aids and coat conditioners that can help you keep your dog well groomed and smelling like a rose. They are on sale at all your pet shops and at the concession booths at all dog shows. Consult the breeder of the puppy you buy to learn which he or she has been most successful with and you will usually find that you have been given good advice. Naturally, if your dog has a tendency toward dry skin, you would prefer a dressing with an oil base. These are applied with an atomizer as you groom, and are brushed into the coat.

If your Shih Tzu is outdoors a great deal, or lives in a city where soot and excessive dirt plagues him, you will more than likely want to use one of the dry shampoos or lather dry baths between tub baths. Do not expect miracles from these man-made preparations. Only *you*, with proper grooming and proper feeding, will maintain the good health that will normally give your Shih Tzu the lustrous coat that it is meant to have.

GROOMING EQUIPMENT LIST

Steel pin brush
Wide and narrow width comb
2 or 3 spray bottles
Wrapping paper - rice, wax, porous paper or net material. Plastic wrap cut to size also can be used.
Baby powder
Corn starch
Tangle remover lotion
Shampoo - buy correct type for silky or coarse coat
Balsam creme rinse

Hair control spray (for outdoor shows)
Knitting needle (for making the part)
Rubber bands for top knot (or wrappings)
Nail clipper

GROOMING BEHAVIOR

If your Shih Tzu wiggles and squirms and backs off and fights you every bit of the way when grooming time rolls around, chances are you are being a little too rough. True enough, there are dogs that just never do get to like being groomed, and these dogs require extra patience and, quite possibly, extra work, since they will employ every scheme known to canines to put you off and hamper your progress. But more than likely, if you meet resistance it's because the dog is genuinely uncomfortable.

The main thing is to be gentle; be even more gentle in the sensitive areas such as the groin, the feet, under the tail, around the eyes, etc. The calmest of dogs will flinch when he sees the bristles of a brush or the shiny teeth of a steel comb flashing overhead. You can be pretty brisk on the body and chest, but such fervor in the tender regions can resemble the Chinese torture!

Since we are dealing with a long-coated breed, it will pay off later to get him to like being groomed from the time he is a puppy. Grooming will probably never seem easy, but it can be a gratifying experience for both dog and master if approached with common sense and patience. Let your dog see that you take a definite pride in taking care of him. He will appreciate this interest, gentleness and attention, and it will result in a closer communication between you and your dog through this personal relationship. He'll certainly look more beautiful with the right care!

GROOMING POSITIONS

There are several positions needed to make grooming easier that will be required throughout the dog's lifetime. One is a position on his back which allows you to trim nails, stomach hair and paw pads. Start this position at around four to six weeks and use it to cut his nails and to play. Rubbing his stomach to give him pleasure will encourage him to tolerate this position.

The second position that must be taught at a

Ch. Cresswood Breath of Spring, owned by Lucy M. Cress of Latrobe, Pennsylvania.

relatively early age is to get the puppy to lie on its side to groom the body coat. Almost all of the grooming can be done in this manner when he is young, but soon he must learn to maintain the third position which is the most important of all . . . standing on a grooming table. It may take a little time for him to get accustomed to the feel of the noose from the grooming arm.

The main thing to avoid with the grooming arm is that the puppy feels as if he is being "hanged" or strung up. Make sure there is enough slack in the noose to allow the puppy some freedom and to prevent choking. *Never* leave him alone when he is attached like this! If he should slip over the end of the table the dog might very well be hanged.

BATHING YOUR SHIH TZU

There are probably as many theories on how, and how often, to bathe a dog as there are dog owners. There is, however, no set rule on frequency or method, although it is certain that show dogs, or dogs that are outdoors a great deal in all kinds of weather and still spend time indoors with the family, will require a bath on occasion.

Once you've made up your mind that the time for the bath has come, the smartest thing to do is to put a drop or two of mineral oil in your dog's eyes to prevent burning from soap suds that might splash in, and you might also place small wads of cotton in the ears to prevent water from entering them. This will also soften the sound of the dryer while he is drying.

With dogs the size of the Shih Tzu you'll find a sink will make bathing easier. The drainage is ideal for the several rinsings that will be necessary, and a hand spray or length of hose can be attached to the faucet where there is adequate water pressure to speed the process.

The successful soaping that will clean your dog thoroughly can best be achieved if your dog is drenched well with warm water first. Start at the withers with the hose, after letting a little water run in the sink around his feet first, and then work from the withers backwards to the end of the tail. Save the head until very last. You will find the dog stays warmer and is less restless if he gets used to the feel of the water on his body before having the stream of water directed over his eyes.

Once the coat is thoroughly drenched with water, work up a thick lather with one of the richer shampoos. Make sure the soap is lathered in all the way to the skin all over the dog, and be just as sure that after you've lathered him for the second time that every last bit of shampoo is rinsed out of the coat. Place the stream of water from the hose as close to the skin as possible, separating the coat as you move along. The need to rinse every last bit of shampoo out of the coat cannot be stressed enough. Any soapy residue that is left behind will make the hair gummy, dull and lifeless, and will dry the skin as well. So, it is best to use a wide spray for the rinsing. Start at the head, rinsing down the neck, and over the body. Do not just dump a pail of water over the dog's head. Grasp the muzzle firmly in one hand, tilt the head up and back and let the water run down the head and neck from a point just behind the eyes. The foreface and chin should be done from underneath.

After the head and body are done, the feet and legs should get additional and particular attention, since some of the rinse water that remains in the bottom of the tub or doesn't run off quickly enough will cling to the feet. Rinse them once again until you are convinced the soap has been washed away completely. Then do it once again for good measure.

If you use any kind of conditioner or creme rinse on your dog, now is the time to apply it. After another rinse, let the dog drip dry for a minute or two before gathering him up in the towel for an initial drying. Try to avoid using a circular motion with the towel. Long-coated dogs tend to tangle from this and will pose a grooming problem later on. While you are drying with the towel it would be a good idea to start the dryer, not only to get the dog used to the sound of it, but it can be warming up to the desired temperature in the meantime.

When the dryer is ready, place the dog on the grooming table and with your brush, start brushing the dog dry, working within the current of warm air. Allow about a foot of space between the dryer and the brush and here again brush in layers in the direction in which the coat is to lie. Try to brush all over the dog so he dries evenly and not just in one spot while the rest is dripping wet. When brushing the feet and legs it is helpful to place the dog's feet at the edge of the table so that you can brush from the skin to the ends of the hair without hitting the table.

Your Shih Tzu should never be allowed to dry on the outside while remaining wet next to the skin; so don't bathe your dog unless you are fully prepared to finish the job properly once you've started it. Also, watch out for drafts or a room that is too cold.

BATHING THE PUPPY

Here again there are two schools of thought on the advisability of bathing the very young puppy.

Ch. House of Wu Mai Mai, whelped in January, 1975 and sired by Ch. Rosemar Very Bismark ex Ch. House of Wu Tiz Tu. Mai Mai is a Specialty Sweepstake winner, a Best in Show and Specialty BOS winner and a multiple Group winner. Owned by Ann Warner, Colorado Springs, Colorado.

If you are an advocate of the bath, the same technique can be used for the puppy that is advised for the grown dog. Drafts are very dangerous for puppies. Also, *never* leave a puppy only partially dry.

If you believe a bath exposes and endangers a puppy unnecessarily, it is wise to know about the dry shampoos mentioned earlier when a cleaning job seems advisable. These dry shampoos, plus regular brushings, will keep the puppy reasonably clean as well as stimulate the hair follicles and encourage the natural hair oils necessary for a good coat.

Bathing a dog is hard work at best, and if you don't know a few of the tricks of the trade, it can be a disaster with a long-haired dog, with everyone and everything ending up equally wet. We would suggest a rubber apron or an old, lightweight raincoat with the sleeves cut off at the elbows as proper attire because sooner or later your dog is going to shake himself!

SHIH TZU HAIRCUTS

Many people who love the breed and own Shih Tzu have neither the time nor the ability to keep their dogs groomed properly at all times. Even those of us who specialize in show dogs find that after a Shih Tzu is no longer being shown, with so many new dogs coming along for the show ring, there is less and less time available to keep all the "stay at homes" in top show condition.

Many of us have come to realize that there are alternatives which make their care quite simple and that still keep them close to looking like the show dogs they once were. The alternatives consist of several different kinds of "haircuts" which make grooming much easier without drastically changing the appearance or characteristic expression we have come to love in the Shih Tzu. These haircuts also allow pet owners, and those who can not find the time to groom their dogs as often as they should, the opportunity to own the breed

165

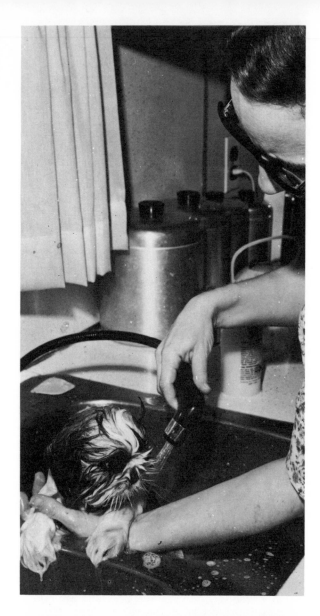

Above:
An electric hair dryer is a very useful piece of equipment to the Shih Tzu owner. A hair dryer enables the coat to be "fluff-dried," a process of brushing the damp coat while a stream of warm air is directed at the section being brushed. The finished result leaves the coat with a gossamer lightness very becoming to the wearer.

Right:
The coat should be thoroughly soaked before and after soaping. The purpose of a thorough rinsing after the shampoo is to make sure that no soap remains to dull the coat or to produce dandruff or mats.

Below:
Faro's Skal-Lee-Wag of Sanco, 6 months old owned by Sandi Cox, Sanco Shih Tzu, Lexington, Kentucky, is a well-groomed specimen.

Below, right:
A beautifully groomed Shih Tzu! This 11-month-old male, Mandarin Madrigal, is owned by Mrs. P. J. Harney, Pinafore Kennels, Woodinville, Washington. Madrigal is co-owned by Ruth di Nicola.

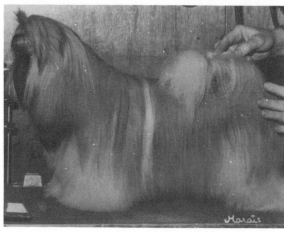

Ch. Pentara's Trinka, owned by the Happi Kennels, is a fine specimen who displays arrogance of carriage, one of the hallmarks of the breed.

with just a few minor adjustments with the coat pattern.

While the true breed advocates gasp at the shaved dog, with only fluffy ears, a top knot and feathery tail left after the visit to the grooming parlor, far too many Shih Tzu are seen that way because not all owners know about the various cuts that can be given the dogs to make them look more like they were intended to look. For instance, there is the cut that resembles the pattern used on Cocker Spaniels. The major portion of the body hair is stripped down and the legs thinned out and shortened. The ears are trimmed to just below the actual ear leather and the top knot is shortened to a length where a rubber band is not necessary to form a top knot.

Another cut, which resembles the Poodle kennel cut more than any other, is also seen a lot, especially on Shih Tzu that get groomed in Poodle parlors. However, the third, now becoming more and more popular, is the cut where the dog maintains his normal coat pattern but where the hair is cut and shaped to the conformation of the body at about one and a half to two inches in length. Here again the ears, top knot and tail can

be left in its natural length, or also cut to the two inches length to complete the Shih Tzu "puppy" appearance this cut gives the dog.

Of course, anyone who is handy with a pair of scissors can also create their own personal haircut that can make their dog look good, but the grooming parlors are also getting to know the various short cuts that make grooming so much easier, and if you tell them what you want they will very likely do a good job no matter which pattern you choose.

GROOMING THE WHISKERS

Even if you tie the side and bottom whiskers in rubber bands while your Shih Tzu eats, food will stick to the fur and a washing is necessary to prevent the hair from smelling foul. If you decide to let your dog eat "naturally" without the rubber bands, after he has finished you can rinse the whiskers in a small bowl of water, squeeze dry with paper towels, sprinkle with corn starch and brush dry, to keep them clean.

Even if you do tie the hair back with rubber bands, a careful check must be made to see that all food is removed and the whiskers cleaned and

167

Left:
Ch. Moon Ling's Wu Tai Shan pictured finishing for his championship under judge William Bergum at a 1974 show. Breeder was Frances Heller, handler Bill Zervoulis, who co-owns with Janine Zervoulis.

Elaine Mawson and Dhuti Vom Tschomo-Lungma, a West German import bred by Erica Guesendam. Dhuti is co-owned with the Eastons.

Imari Paint The Town Red, bred by W. F. Penn and Diana Henry (owner) of Columbus, Ohio. The sire was Ch. Copper Penny Bar-Na-Bi Jones ex Ch. Lansu Magnolia Time.

Ch. Nanjo Sunshine, sired by Ch. Lotos Panda Bear of Nanjo ex Van Emmells Duchess. Owner, Joan E. Cowie, Kimberton, Pennsylvania.

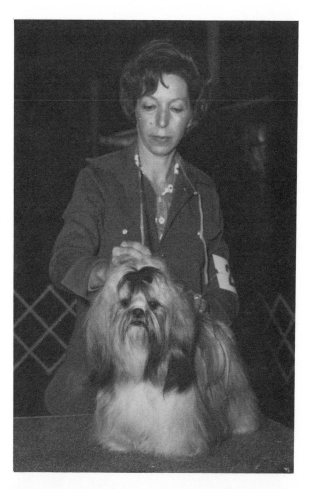

Highlands Frosty Friday, whelped in 1976 and owned by Carol Bogner of Wooster, Ohio. This 6½ pound dog stretches out on the garden wall in a typical Shih Tzu puppy position!

Ch. Nanjo Tiz Tu Pings, sired by Ch. Paisley Ping Pong out of De Vilbiss Wind Song pictured winning Best of Breed and Second in the Group under judge Ruth Turner at the 1975 Mispillion Show. Owned by Joan E. Cowie of Kimberton, Pennsylvania.

dried before they pick up dirt and get smelly. Also, you must be sure that when tying back the whiskers you in no way interfere with the dog's ability to eat. If his lips are pulled back too tightly he may not want to eat or be able to chew and swallow properly. If you use rubber bands, check to see that the mouth remains in a normal position for comfortable eating.

Whether or not you tie the whiskers, you should tie back the ears. The most effective method we have found is to pull back the upper lip whiskers and pull them with the ears into a top knot with a rubber band. However, be sure not to include the ear leather.

THE TOP KNOT

One of the most charming features of the Shih Tzu is the characteristic top knot, a gathering of the hair on top of the head secured with a rubber band, barrette or ribbon bow. Rubber bands will hold it adequately, but ribbons, being more decorative, are seen in the show ring, as well as in everyday use.

The small size rubber bands can be purchased at most five and ten cent stores, pet shops or concession booths at the dog shows. There is also a specially designed rubber band sold which does not risk pulling out as much hair as the regular rubber bands. These are especially recommended for show dogs where every hair must be preserved.

When learning to make the top knot, you will find you get the best results by observing and learning from the person from whom you buy your dog. A simple guide for putting up a top knot is to gather all the hair from the outside corners of the eyes and all over the top of the head between the ears, including a small semi-circle or small "V" slightly down the back of the head. When the hair is neatly and evenly gathered and brushed up together, place the rubber band around it securely. It may be necessary to double over the band to be sure it is tight enough to hold the hair in place.

Once the rubber band is secured in place, be certain that it is not so tight that it pulls the eyes or ears out of place, or that loose hairs not caught in it are pulling the skin. Move the band back and forth and around in place to be sure there is no pulling or the dog will scratch at it and break a lot of hair in the process. If there is any pulling or tightness, loosen the hair beneath the band until the tension is relieved.

Once you are certain it is comfortable, spread the hair above the band ever so slightly and gently toward the back of the head until it resembles a lit-

Carousel Foxy Lady pictured winning a 4-point major as Best of Winners under judge Harvey Berman at the 1976 Southshore Kennel Club Show. Owner, Sandra Lucchina, Torrington, Connecticut.

tle "palm tree". When you put the dog down on the floor watch for a moment to see that he is not going to scratch at it. If he does scratch or try to "rub it off" against the furniture, floor, or with his paws, remove the band gently and immediately, and start all over again until you get it right.

Practice makes perfect, and there is a knack to preparing a topknot properly. Once you learn, it quickly becomes second nature. It is suggested you practice on a wig, or on a doll, if possible. At any rate, you will soon become adept at making a top knot, or pien ji (pronounced been dye), as the Chinese call it.

WRAPPING THE COAT

Many owners, especially owners of show dogs, put up their dog's coat in "papers" between shows to prevent the ends of the hair from breaking off.

The art of putting dogs up in papers, netting, or any of the other things used for this purpose, is another "art" which requires observation, learning and lots of practice in order not to do more harm than good to the coat. *How* to wrap the hair, *where* to wrap the coat, *how long* to keep it wrapped and *what* is best to wrap the coat with are all very much a matter of individual preference and experience if you are to do it at all.

It is perfectly possible to have a show dog's coat be excellent without wrapping it. Rather than do it wrong, it is better to forget it if you don't learn from a good teacher. There are very definite ways to cut and fold the "wraps" and to apply the rubber bands to hold them in place. It must also be considered that a dog cannot be wrapped and left

Bombshu Mei Kou, whelped in May 1974, sired by T'en T'an's Hsing Fu ex Bomshu Val Glenka of Vanora. Bred by Jean W. Gadberry and Nora De Passe, she is owned by Janine Zervoulis. Photo by Bill Zervoulis.

Ch. House of Wu Mai Mai, bred by Mrs. Charles R. Eckes, owner Andy Warner. The House of Wu Kennels are in Denver, Colorado.

Mexican Ch. Pei Ho of Sang Chen, photographed in 1967. Sang Chen was handled and is owned by Daniece Greggans, Kathways Shih Tzu, LaVerne, California.

that way indefinitely. The wraps must be removed every couple of days and the dog given a complete grooming to assure the coat gets sufficient air and the skin proper stimulation. Wrapping should never be considered a substitute for grooming.

We will not, therefore, attempt to explain and teach how to do it in this book. Rather, we suggest that a professional handler, or the breeder of your dog, (if he shows dogs) would be the best source of knowledge if you feel your dog's coat requires extra care. With or without wrapping, if you are intending to show your dog, or merely want it to look as beautiful as a show dog, you must be sure that your dog is kept free of mats, groomed regularly, fed well, bathed frequently and checked for any debris that would damage its beautiful, flowing coat. That might not be easy, but it is well worth the extra time and care.

PREPARING THE SHOW DOG

If your Shih Tzu is to be a show dog, there are several additional phases which can be taken which will further enhance its coat and appearance in the ring. Sooner or later, every owner or handler comes up with what they consider the ideal way to prepare a Shih Tzu for the show ring, having achieved what they believe to be the perfect combination of sprays, creme rinses, oil baths, etc. This is not as simple as it may sound. All one has to do is pass a concessionaire's booth

Heavenly Dynasty's T'ai Tzu is breeder owned by Jo Ann White. "Fat Choy" is by Ch. Heavenly Dynasty's Yeh Shou ex Ch. Si-Kaing's I Ko Tien Shih, C.D., and has several group placements to his credit. He is also a sire of champions.

at a dog show and view the myriad of grooming aids and products on display to realize how long it takes to give all a fair trial before settling on the "perfect" way to prepare a dog.

With so many procedures and combinations available, the entire process is one of trial and error. Since all products, with rare exception, are of good quality, the selection can be said to be "to each his own" when purchasing the grooming products. It is for this reason that we recommend that the newcomer spend a great deal of time observing others until he can learn for himself how to handle grooming and bathing for the show ring.

Rather than working by "trial and error", let the professionals groom your dog until you have it down pat. This will avoid damage to the coat a few days before a show. Make certain that you observe a professional, or a breeder who really knows what he is doing. Attend a dog show, go to the handlers' tent and watch them preparing a dog. You will almost be able to pick out the winners in the grooming area by the outstanding way the dogs look while still up on the grooming tables.

Do not expect the owners and handlers to take time out to give you instructions during the frantic excitement before they go into the ring. Not only are they working on the dog and concentrating on the last minute touches to complete the process, but many people do not wish to reveal what they consider their personal secrets. On the other hand, there are others who are more than willing to help newcomers or those genuinely interested in learning about grooming.

Conwynns Forever Amber was sired by Ch. Elfann Golden Beau Brummel ex Ch. Elfann Golden Sunmaiden and owned by Jean Johnson of Decatur, Illinois.

The general consensus of opinion is that the very best place to learn and to ask questions is from the person that bred the dog, if he shows dogs as well. If he shows and wins, he is most likely familiar with the products and methods which work best with dogs that he has bred.

When one asks the proper way to prepare a dog for the show ring, we can guarantee that the same answer will never be given twice!

172

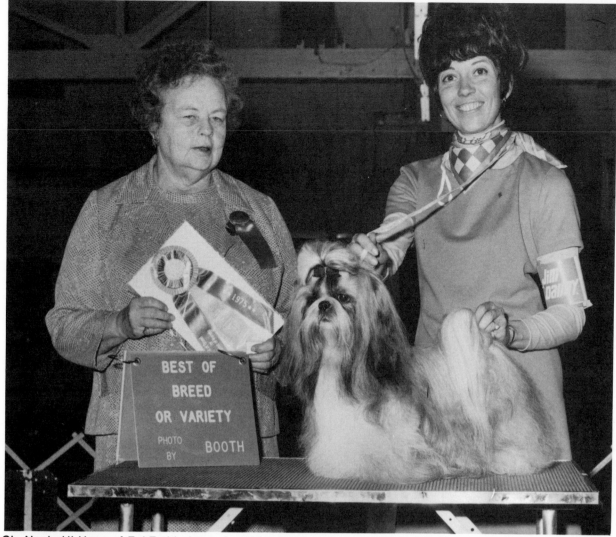

Ch. Nanjo Hi Hope of Ful-Fu-Li pictured winning the Breed at a 1975 Kennel Club Show with handler Barbara Alderman. The sire was Ch. Char Nick's I Gotcha ex Ch. Nanjo Ah So Sweet Sum Wun. Owner is Joan E. Cowie of Kimberton, Pennsylvania.

174

Chapter 10
THE DOG SHOW WORLD

Let us assume that after a few months of tender loving care, you realize your dog is developing beyond your wildest expectations and that the dog you selected is very definitely a show dog. Of course, every owner is prejudiced. But if you are sincerely interested in going to dog shows with your dog and making a champion of him, now is the time to start casting a critical eye on him from a judge's point of view.

There is no such thing as a perfect dog. Every dog has some faults, perhaps even a few serious ones. The best way to appraise your dog's degree of perfection is to compare him with the Standard for the breed, or before a judge in a show ring.

MATCH SHOWS

For the beginner there are "mock" dog shows, called match shows, where you and your dog go through many of the procedures of a regular dog show, but do not gain points toward championship. These shows are usually held by kennel clubs, annually or semiannually, and much ring poise and experience can be gained there. The age limit is usually reduced to two months at match shows to give puppies four months of training before they compete at the regular shows when they reach six months of age. Classes range from two to four months; four to six months; six to nine months; and nine to twelve months. Puppies compete with others of their own age for comparative purposes. Many breeders evaluate their litters in this manner, choosing which is the most outgoing, which is the most poised, the best showman, etc.

For those seriously interested in showing their dogs to full championship, these match shows provide important experience for both the dog and the owner. Class categories may vary slightly, according to a number of entries, but basically they include all the classes that are included at a regular point show. There is a nominal entry fee and, of course, ribbons and, usually, trophies are given for your efforts as well. Unlike the point shows, entries can be made on the day of the show right on the show grounds. They are unbenched and provide an informal, congenial atmosphere for the amateur, which helps to make the ordeal of one's first adventures in the show ring a little less nerve-wracking.

THE POINT SHOWS

It is not possible to show a puppy at an American Kennel Club sanctioned point show before the age of six months. When your dog reaches this eligible age, your local kennel club can provide you with the names and addresses of the show-giving superintendents in your area who will be staging the club's dog show for them, and where you must write for an entry form.

The forms are mailed in a pamphlet called a premium list. This also includes the names of the judges for each breed, a list of the prizes and trophies, the name and address of the show-giving club and where the show will be held, as well as rules and regulations set up by the American Kennel Club which must be abided by if you are to enter.

A booklet containing the complete set of show rules and regulations may be obtained by writing to the American Kennel Club, Inc., 51 Madison Avenue, New York, N.Y. 10010.

When you write to the dog show superintendent, request not only your premium list for this particular show, but ask that your name be added to their mailing list so that you will automatically receive all premium lists in the future. List your breed or breeds and they will see to it that you receive premium lists for Specialty shows as well.

Unlike the match shows where your dog will be judged on ring behavior, at the point shows he will be judged on conformation to the breed Standard. In addition to being at least six months of age (on the day of the show) he must be a purebred for a point show. This means that both he

Opposite:
A charming informal photograph of Ch. Dragonwick the Great Gatsby and his handler Peggy Hogg. Gatsby was top-winning Toy Group Winner for 1976, according to the Ken-L Ration Awards. Owner, Robert Koeppel of New York City.

and his parents are registered with the American Kennel Club. There must be no alterations or falsifications regarding his appearance. Females cannot have been spayed and males must have both testicles in evidence. No dyes or powders may be used to enhance the appearance, and any lameness or deformity or major deviation from the Standard for the breed constitutes a disqualification.

With all these things in mind, groom your dog to the best of your ability in the specified area for this purpose in the show hall and *exercise your dog before taking him into the ring.* Too many dog owners are guilty of making their dogs remain on their crates so they do not get dirty, and the first thing they do when they start to show is stop to relieve themselves. There is no excuse for this. All it takes is a walk *before* grooming. If your dog is clean, well groomed, *empty* and leash trained you should be able to enter the show ring with confidence and pride of ownership, ready for an appraisal of your dog by the judge.

The presiding judge on that day will allow each dog a certain amount of time and consideration before making his decisions. It is never permissible to consult the judge regarding either your dog or his decision while you are in the ring. An exhibitor never speaks unless spoken to, and then only to answer such questions as the judge may ask—the age of the dog, the dog's bite, or to ask you to move your dog around the ring once again.

However, before you reach the point where you are actually in the ring awaiting the final decisions of each judge, you will have had to decide in which of the five classes in each sex your dog should compete.

POINT SHOW CLASSES

The regular classes of the AKC are: Puppy, Novice, Bred-by-Exhibitor, American-Bred and Open. If your dog is undefeated in any of the regular classes (divided by sex) in which it is entered, he or she is *required* to enter the Winners Class. If your dog is placed second in the class to the dog which won Winners Dog or Winners Bitch, hold the dog or bitch in readiness as the judge must consider it for Reserve Winners.

PUPPY CLASSES shall be for dogs which are nine months of age and over but under twelve months, which were whelped in the U.S.A. or Canada, and which are not champions. Classes are often divided six and (under) nine, and nine and (under) 12 months. The age of a dog shall be calculated up to and inclusive of the first day of a show. For example, a dog whelped on January 1 is eligible to compete in a puppy class on July 1, and

Hi Jinks of Greenmoss, owned by Barbara Ward of Revere, Massachusetts. Jinks is pictured sitting in his victory bowl after winning Best in Match at the Puritan Shih Tzu Club Show.

Professional handler John Marsh of Long Island with 18-month-old Chumulari Yu-Lo, co-owned by him and Margaret Easton.

176

may continue to compete up to and including December 31 of the same year, but is not eligible to compete January 1 of the following year.

THE NOVICE CLASS shall be for dogs six months of age and over, whelped in the U.S.A. or Canada which have not, prior to the closing of entries, won three first prizes in the Novice Class, a first prize in Bred-by-Exhibitor, American-Bred or Open Class, nor one or more points toward a championship title.

THE BRED-BY-EXHIBITOR CLASS shall be for dogs whelped in the U.S.A. which are six months of age and over, which are not champions, and which are owned wholly or in part by the person or the spouse of the person who was the breeder or one of the breeders of record. Dogs entered in the BBE Class must be handled by an owner or by a member of the immediate family of an owner, i.e., the husband, wife, father, mother, son, daughter, brother or sister.

THE AMERICAN-BRED CLASS is for all dogs (except champions) six months of age or over, whelped in the U.S.A. by reason of a mating that took place in the U.S.A.

THE OPEN CLASS is for any dog six months of age or over, except in a member specialty club show held for only American-Bred dogs, in which case the class is for American-Bred dogs only.

WINNERS DOG and WINNERS BITCH: After the above classes have been judged, both for dogs and for bitches, the first place winners are then *required* to compete in the ring. The dog judged "Winners Dog" is awarded the points toward his championship title.

RESERVE WINNERS are selected immediately after the Winners Dog. In case of a disqualification of a win by the AKC, the Reserve Dog moves up to "Winners" and receives the points. After the male classes are judged, the bitch classes are called.

BEST OF BREED or BEST OF VARIETY COMPETITION is limited to Champions of Record or dogs (with newly acquired points, for a 90-day period prior to AKC confirmation) which have completed championship requirements, and the Winners Dog and Winners Bitch (or the dog awarded Winners if only one Winners prize has been awarded), together with any undefeated dogs which have been shown only in non-regular classes; all compete for Best of Breed or Best of Variety (if the breed is divided by size, color, texture or length of coat hair, etc.).

BEST OF WINNERS: if the WD or WB earns BOB or BOV, it automatically becomes BOW; otherwise they will be judged together for BOW (following BOB or BOV judging).

BEST OF OPPOSITE SEX is selected from the remaining dogs of the opposite sex to Best of Breed or Best of Variety.

Other classes may be approved by the AKC: STUD DOGS, BROOD BITCHES, BRACE CLASS, TEAM CLASS; classes consisting of local dogs and bitches may also be included in a show if approved by the AKC (special rules are included in the AKC Rule Book).

The MISCELLANEOUS CLASS shall be for purebred dogs of such breeds as may be designated by the AKC. No dog shall be eligible for entry in this class unless the owner has been granted an Indefinite Listing Privilege (ILP) and unless the ILP number is given on the entry form. Application for an ILP shall be made on a form provided by the AKC and when submitted must be accompanied by a fee set by the Board of Directors.

All Miscellaneous Breeds shall be shown together in a single class except that the class may be divided by sex if so specified in the premium list. There shall be *no* further competiton for dogs entered in this class. Ribbons for First, Second, Third and Fourth shall be rose, brown, light green and gray, respectively. This class is open to the following Miscellaneous dog breeds: Australian Cattle Dogs, Australian Kelpies, Border Collies, Cavalier King Charles Spaniels, Miniature Bull Terriers, Spinoni Italiani and Tibetan Spaniels.

IF YOUR DOG WINS A CLASS

Study the classes to make certain your dog is entered in a proper class for his or her qualifications. If your dog wins his class, the rule states: *You are required* to enter classes for Winners, Best of Breed and Best of Winners (no additional entry fees). The rule states: "No eligible dogs may be withheld from competition." It is not mandatory that you stay for group judging. *If your dog wins a group*, however, *you must stay for Best In Show competition.*

PRIZE RIBBONS
AND WHAT THEY STAND FOR

No matter how many entries there are in each class at a dog show, if you place first through fourth position you will receive a ribbon. These ribbons commemorate your win and can be impressive when collected and displayed to prospective buyers when and if you have puppies for sale, or if you intend to use your dog at public stud.

All ribbons from the American Kennel Club licensed dog shows will bear the American Kennel Club seal, the name of the show, the date and

Caralandra's Passing Fancy, sired by Ch. Dragonwyck the Great Gatsby ex Ch. Car-Lyn's Foxy Lady of Cambalu is pictured winning at the 1977 St. Joseph show under judge Kay Finch. Owner is Peggy Hogg.

Ch. Elfann Golden Beau Brummer, owned by Del and Connie Smart of Akron, Ohio. This darling Shih Tzu from their Conwynn Kennels sits on her crate for the signal to go into the show ring.

American, Canadian and Bermudian Ch. Winemakers Pla Boi, Best in Show winner in Canada and the U.S.A. The sire was Am. and Can. Ch. Greenmoss Gilligan, ex Mariljac Thumbelina. Owned by Carol McLister and Faye Wine of Clearwater, Florida.

BEST IN SHOW PHOTO BY *Graham*

the placement. In the classes the colors are blue for first, red for second, yellow for third, and white for fourth. Winners Dog or Winners Bitch ribbons are purple, while Reserve Dog and Reserve Bitch ribbons are purple and white. Best of Winners ribbons are blue and white; Best of Breed, purple and gold; and Best of Opposite Sex ribbons are red and white.

In the six groups, first prize is a blue rosette or ribbon, second placement is red, third yellow and fourth white. The Best In Show rosette is either red, white and blue, or incorporates the colors used in the show-giving club's emblem.

QUALIFYING FOR CHAMPIONSHIP

Championship points are given for Winners Dog and Winners Bitch in accordance with a scale of points established by the American Kennel Club based on the popularity of the breed in entries, and the number of dogs competing in the classes. This scale of points varies in different sections of the country, but the scale is published in the front of each dog show catalog. These points may differ between the dogs and the bitches at the same show. You may, however, win additional points by winning Best of Winners, if there are fewer dogs than bitches entered, or vice versa. Points never exceed five at any one show, and a total of fifteen points must be won to constitute a championship. These fifteen points must be won under at least three different judges, and you must acquire at least two major wins. Anything from a three to five point win is major, while one and two point wins are minor wins. Two major wins must be won under different judges to meet championship requirements.

OBEDIENCE TRIALS

Some shows also offer Obedience Trials, which are considered as separate events. They give the dogs a chance to compete and score on performing a prescribed set of exercises intended to display their training in doing useful work.

There are three obedience titles for which they may compete. First, the Companion Dog or C.D. title; second, the Companion Dog Excellent or C.D.X.; and third, the Utility Dog or U.D. Detailed information on these degrees is contained in a booklet entitled Official Obedience Regulations and may be obtained by writing to the American Kennel Club.

JUNIOR SHOWMANSHIP COMPETITION

Junior Showmanship competition is for boys and girls in different age groups handling their own dogs or one owned by their immediate family. There are four divisions: Novice A for 10 to 12 year olds, Novice B for those 13 to 16 years of age, (entrants in these two classes must have one or no previous junior showmanship wins) and Open A for 10 to 12 year olds (entrants must have earned two or more JS awards).

As Junior Showmanship at the dog shows increased in popularity, certain changes and improvements had to be made. As of April 1, 1971, the American Kennel Club issued a new booklet containing the regulations for Junior Showmanship which may be obtained by writing to the AKC at 51 Madison Avenue, New York, N.Y. 10010.

DOG SHOW PHOTOGRAPHERS

Every show has at least one official photographer who will be more than happy to take a photograph of your dog with the judge, ribbons and trophies, along with you or your handler. These make marvelous remembrances of your top show wins and are frequently framed along with the ribbons for display purposes. Photographers can be paged at the show over the public address system, if you wish to obtain this service. Prices vary, but you will probably find it costs little to capture these happy moments, and the photos can always be used in the various dog magazines to advertise your dog's wins.

TWO TYPES OF DOG SHOWS

There are two types of dog shows licensed by the American Kennel Club. One is the all-breed show which includes classes for all the recognized breeds, and groups of breeds; i.e., all terriers, all toys, etc. Then there are the specialty shows for one particular breed which also offer championship points.

BENCHED OR UNBENCHED DOG SHOWS

The show-giving clubs determine, usually on the basis of what facilities are offered by their chosen show site, whether their show will be benched or unbenched. A benched show is one where the dog show superintendent supplies benches (cages for toy dogs). Each bench is numbered and its corresponding number appears on your entry identification slip, which is sent to you prior to the show date. The number also appears in the show catalog. Upon entering the show, you should take your dog to the bench, where he should remain until it is time to groom him before entering the ring to be judged. After judging, he must be returned to the bench until the official time of dismissal from the show. At an unbenched show

Figurines of Chinese patron and patroness of the arts owned by Consuelo Bolsaks of Redding, California. You will notice that this very old set features an oriental foo dog on the centerpiece.

Two male puppies display their excellent profiles at 4½ weeks of age. Their sire was Ch. Royal White Tie and Tails and their dam Rondelay Wei Salli.

Canadian Ch. Hodari Shan Shuo, pictured winning Best in Show in Canada under Australian judge, Graham Head. The handler, Cathie Phillips, showed this 15-month-old for owners Laurie Battey and Helen McClarnon of Torrance, California. Sparkle finished for her championship in Canada undefeated and is a multiple Group winner.

180

Ch. Hil Ton's Rain Dragon, owned by Sylvia Hilton of Baltimore, Maryland.

Windsor Bumtar Tse Cho, bred and owned by Kathleen Kolbert of Oxford, Connecticut and pictured winning under judge Anne Rogers Clark at a 1973 show. The sire was Ch. Char Nick's I Gotcha ex Ch. Chumulari Mei Mei.

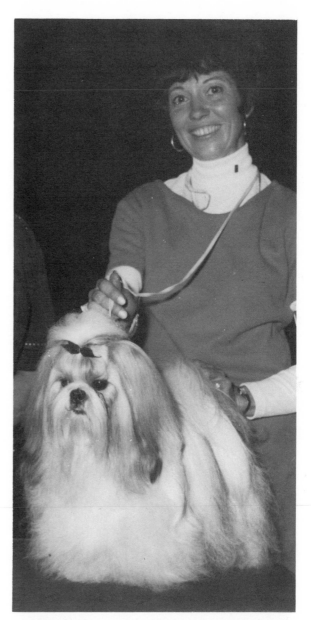

Ch. Paisley Pong of Davanik pictured finishing for championship under judge Baker. The sire was Mica Ching Ping Pong ex Den Lee Tee. Handled by Barbara Alderman for owners Davanik Shih Tzu in Runnemede, New Jersey.

Best in Show winner Ch. Gin-Doc's Suzy of Shanguish. Bred by Gini Evans, Suzy's sire was Ch. Winemakers Pla Boi ex Ch. Gin Doc's Suzy Wong. The judge was Herman Fellton at this 1976 Clermont County Kennel Club show.

the club makes no provision whatsoever for your dog other than an enormous tent (if an outdoor show) or an area in a show hall where all crates and grooming equipment must be kept.

Benched or unbenched, the moment you enter the show grounds you are expected to look after your dog and have it under complete control at all times. This means that short leads must be used in crowded aisles or getting out of cars. In the case of a benched show, a "bench chain" is needed. It should allow the dog to move around, but not get down off the bench. It is also not considered "cute" to have small tots leading enormous dogs around a dog show where the child might be dragged into the middle of a dog fight.

PROFESSIONAL HANDLERS

If you are new in the fancy and do not know how to handle your dog to his best advantage, or if you are too nervous or physically unable to show your dog, you can hire a licensed professional handler who will do it for a specified fee. The more successful or well-known handlers charge slightly higher rates, but generally speaking there

is a pretty uniform charge for this service. As the dog progresses with his wins in the show ring, the fee increases proportionately. Included in this service is professional advice on when and where to show your dog, grooming, a statement of your wins at each show, and all trophies that the dog accumulates. Any cash award is kept by the handler as a sort of "bonus".

When engaging a handler, it is advisable to select one that does not take more dogs to a show than he can properly and comfortably handle. You want your dog to receive his individual attention and not be rushed into the ring at the last moment because the handler has been busy with too many other dogs in other rings. Some handlers require that you deliver the dog to their establishment a few days ahead of the show so they have ample time to groom and train him. Other handlers will accept well-behaved and trained dogs that have been groomed from their owners at ringside, if they are familiar with the dog and the owner. This should be determined well in advance of the show date. Never expect a handler to accept a dog at ringside that is not groomed to perfection.

There are several sources for locating a professional handler. Dog magazines carry their classified advertising. A note or telephone call to the American Kennel Club will also put you in touch with several in your area. Usually, you will be billed after the day of the show.

DO YOU REALLY NEED A HANDLER?

The answer to that question is sometimes yes, sometimes no. However, the answer which must be determined first of all is, "But can I *afford* a professional handler?" or, "I want to show my dog myself. Does that mean my dog will never do any big winning?"

Do you *really* need a handler to win? If you are mishandling a good dog that should be winning and isn't, the answer may be yes, because it is made to look bad in the ring by its owner. If you don't know how to handle a dog properly, why make your dog look bad when a handler could show it to its best advantage?

Some owners simply cannot handle a dog well and still wonder why their dogs aren't winning in the ring, no matter how hard they try. Others are nervous and this nervousness travels down the leash to the dog and the dog behaves accordingly. Some people are extroverts by nature, and these are the people who usually make excellent handlers. Of course, the biggest winners at the shows usually have a lot of "show off" in their nature, too, and this helps a great deal.

THE COST OF CAMPAIGNING A DOG WITH A HANDLER

At present, many champions are shown an average of 25 times before completing a cham-

At a 1971 Shih Tzu match show, the late columnist and entrepreneur Francis X. Lohmann presented the Junior Showmanship prize to Debbie Levine. Debbie was also named Miss Kanine Korner, title of Mr. Lohmann's column in *Popular Dogs* magazine, and reigned as Queen of Mr. Lohmann's annual Dog Parade along Hollywood Boulevard. Debbie and her Shih Tzu were in good company; Lassie was canine Grand Marshal, and movie star Rudy Vallee the "human" Grand Marshal.

Cabrands Cara of Lou Wan is pictured winning Best Senior Puppy in Match at a recent Kennel Club of Northern New Jersey show. Owned by Cathy and Wanda Gec of Clifton, N.J.

Poetry in motion: Ch. Marga Winds Tie-Dye of Dynasty, bred by Martha Coalina and owned by Fredric M. Alderman, Dynasty Kennels, Mundelein, Illinois. The sire was Ch. Mariljac Maripet ex Town Halls Gloria Gloria. Photo by Pozen.

Westminster 1971 saw this charming brace of Shih Tzu as winners of the Toy Group. Am. and Can. Ch. Chumulari Ying Ying and his son, Chumulari Ho Ping won under judge Mrs. Yan Paul with their handler Roy Stevens. Both owned by the Eastons.

pionship. In entry fees at today's prices, that adds up to about $300. This does not include motel bills, travelling expenses or food. There have been dog champions finished in fewer shows, say five to ten shows, but this is the exception rather than the rule. When and where to show should be thought out carefully so that you can perhaps save money on entries. This is one of the services a professional handler provides that can mean a considerable saving. Hiring a handler can save money in the long run if you just wish to make a champion. If your dog has been winning reserves and not taking the points, a handler can finish him in five to ten shows, and you would be ahead financially. If your dog is not really top quality, the length of time it takes even a handler to finish it (depending upon competition in the area) could add up to a large amount of money.

Campaigning a show specimen that not only captures the wins in his breed, but wins Group and Best In Show awards, gets up into the big money. To cover the nations's major shows and rack up a record as one of the top dogs in the nation usually costs an owner between ten and fifteen thousand dollars a year. This includes not only the professional handler's fee for taking the dog into the ring, but the cost of conditioning and grooming, board, advertising in the dog magazines, photographs, etc.

There is a great satisfaction in winning with your own dog, especially if you have trained and cared for it by yourself. However, with today's enormous entries at the dog shows and so many worthy dogs competing for top wins, many owners who said "I'd rather do it myself!' and meant it became discouraged and eventually hired a handler anyway.

Still, if you really are in it just for the sport, you can and should handle your own dog if you want to. You can learn the tricks by attending training classes, and you can learn a lot by carefully observing the more successful professional handlers as they perform in the ring. Model yourself after the ones that command respect as being the leaders in their profession. But, if you find you'd really rather be at ringside looking on, then do get a handler so that your worthy dog gets his deserved recognition in the ring. To own a good dog and win with it is a thrill, so good luck, no matter how you do it.

Int. and Brazilian Ch. Chumulari Wu Lai, going Best in Show at Cayia Do Sul, Brazil, in November 1976. He is the winner of five Bests in Show under Brazilian and Argentinian judges, has 8 CACIB's and ten Group firsts. Owned by Murilo Leite, and bred by Margaret Easton.

Ch. Bojang Dixie Dewdrop was handled by Jean Lade to this win under Judge Morris Howard at a recent show. The sire was Ch. Charing Cross Ching El Chang ex. Ch. Taramount Samantha. Owner is Lillian Phillips of Whispering Pines, North Carolina.

Ch. Char Nick's High Time of Nanjo pictured winning Best of Breed at a 1973 show with Louis Sanfilippe handling for owner Virginia Smigley, Largyn Shih Tzu, Phoenixville, Pennsylvania.

Ch. Cinnabar's Golden Pirate, pictured with his owner Clarence Malone of Lexington, Kentucky. This black-masked golden was whelped in November, 1972.

Misty Isle Woo Mih of Willows pictured winning at a 1973 show under judge Russell Herman. The sire was Chumulari Yae Yin ex Sikians Firefly. Handled by Lois Frank for owner Consuelo Bolsaks of Redding, California.

Ch. Nanjo Good as Gold pictured winning Best of Opposite Sex under judge Ed Bracy at a 1974 show with handler Barbara Alderman. The Sire was Ch. Char Nicks I Gotcha ex Ch. Nanjo Ah So Sweet Sum Wun. Owned by Joan E. Cowie, Kimberton, Pennsylvania.

Ch. Cresswood Pir-Anha, handled by Freeman Dickey to this win under judge Mel Downing at a 1972 show. Owned by Mrs. Lucy M. Cress of Latrobe, Pennsylvania.

Willows Wizard pictured winning at the 1976 Sacramento Kennel Club Show under judge Dorothy Carson. Wizard just needed a major here to finish. The sire was Ch. Hei Lein's Mr. Bo Jangles ex Willows The Golden Sonnett. Lois Frank handled for owner Consuelo Bolsaks, Redding, California.

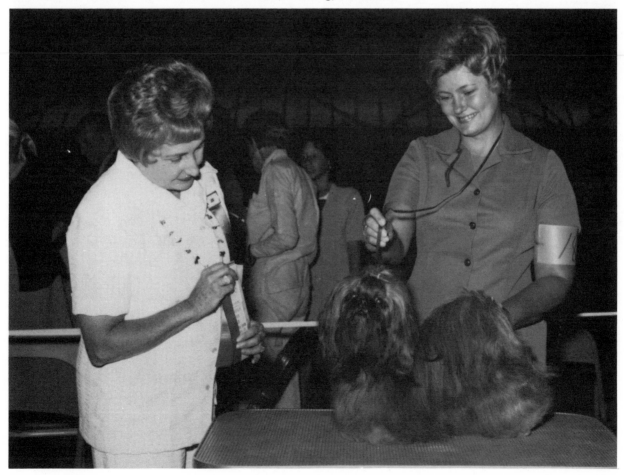

American and Bermudian Champion Witches Wood Yum Yum, a magnificent dog who has 41 Bests in Show in 3½ years of showing on his impressive record. Bred by Mrs. Judy Merrill, he is owned by Dr. and Mrs. J. Wesley Edel, and was handled during his illustrious show career by John and Georgia Murdoch.

Chapter 11
JUDGING AND SHOWING
THE SHIH TZU

Ever since Joan Brearley started judging dogs back in 1961, she has never entered a show ring to begin an assignment without thinking back to what the late, great judge, Alva Rosenberg told her when they discussed her apprenticing under him. His most significant observation she finds still holds true today: that a judge's first and lasting impression of a dog's temperament and bearing will be made the moment it walks into the ring.

Therefore, it has always been a source of amazement to her the way so many exhibitors ruin this important first impression of their dog. So many are guilty of carrying the dog into the ring and then dropping it down on the ground in place, not wanting to risk getting a hair out of place rather than letting the judge see the dog gait into the ring in all its glory! Others drag the dog along behind them, walking too fast, squeezing through the ringside crowds, snapping at people to get out of their way, arriving in the ring with the dog having had its feet stepped on by people pushing closer to the ringside as the classes are called. After the dog has been dragged that "last mile," he is suddenly expected to turn on the charm, fascinate the crowds, captivate the judge and bring home the silverware!

All this happens on a day that invariably is either too hot, too cold, or too rainy, and follows a couple of hours of standing rigidly on a crate being sprayed in the face and all over the body with a grooming substance that doesn't smell or taste too good. They have withstood being powdered into a fit of sneezing and brushed out to their handler's satisfaction—not to mention the hours in the bathtub and the grooming session the day before the show and the bumpy ride to the show grounds. Alva Rosenberg had a point: any dog that can strut into the ring after what they must regard as a 48 hour torture treatment *does* have to have an excellent disposition and a regal bearing.

GET ME TO THE RING ON TIME!

There is no reason why an exhibitor cannot allow sufficient time to get to ringside with a few minutes to spare, in order to wait calmly somewhere near the entrance to the ring until his number is called. They need only walk directly ahead of the dog, politely asking the people along the way to step aside with a simple statement to the effect that there is a "dog coming through." It works very well. Spectators promptly step aside, not only to oblige this simple request, but also to observe the beauty of the show dog going by.

The exhibitor making such a request not only clears a path in the aisle, but allows for the dog to follow behind in his steps without being pulled along or bumped. With enough time allowed to get to ringside before the class is actually called it is then possible to *walk* into the ring so the judge can get a look at the dog at its best.

The short waiting period at ringside also allows time for the dog to gain his footing and prospective and give the exhibitor time to get his arm band on securely so it won't drop down his arm and hit the dog on the head during their first sprint around the ring. These spare moments will allow the "nervousness" that travels down the leash to your dog to disappear, as the realization that you have arrived in your class on time occurs to you, and both you and the dog can relax.

ENTERING THE RING

When the ring steward calls out the numbers for your class, there is no need for you to try to be the first in the ring. There is no prize for being first! If you are new at the game you would do well to get behind a more experienced exhibitor or professional handler, where you can observe and perhaps learn something about ring behavior and procedures. The judge will be well aware of your presence in the ring when he makes a check mark next to your number in the judge's book. At the same time, they mark all absentees before starting to judge the class.

Enter the ring as quickly and calmly as possible with your dog on a loose lead, and at the first opportunity make sure you show your arm band to the judge so he can check you in. Then take a position in the line-up already forming in the ring (usually at the opposite side of the judge's table). This provides an opportunity for the judge to get the second important look at your dog. Set the dog up in the show pose, and when the judge has

The 1976 Shih Tzu Fanciers of Baltimore Match Show found judge Margaret Easton awarding Best in Match to Pat Neugarth and her dog. Ron Hoffman photo.

checked in all the dogs in the class, he will get an immediate impression of the outline of your dog in show stance.

The judge will then go up and down the line of dogs in order to compare one outline with another, while getting an idea of the symmetry and balance of each profile. This is the time when you should see that your dog maintains the show stance. Don't be nervously brushing, constantly adjusting feet, tilting the head, prompting the tail, etc. This all should have been done while the judge was walking down the line with his eyes on the other dogs.

By the time the judge gets to your dog it should be standing as still as a statue, with your hands *off* of it. Far too many exhibitors handle the show dogs as if they were marionettes. They are constantly pushing the dog into place, prodding it to the desired angle for the judge, placing its head, tail and feet according to their idea of perfection. More often than not, their fingers are covering the dog's muzzle or they are employing their thumbs to put a curl in the tail because there is not one there and they know there should be one. Repeatedly moving a dog's feet tends to make the judge believe the dog can't stand correctly by itself. If a dog is standing incorrectly, the judge might assume it just happened to be standing incorrectly at that moment and that the exhibitor couldn't imagine such a thing and therefore never noticed it.

Fussing over the dog only calls attention to the fact that the exhibitor has to do a lot to make the dog look good, or is a rank amateur and is nervously mishandling the dog. A free, natural stance, even when a little "off base," is still more appealing to the judge. All Shih Tzu are beautiful by themselves, and unnecessary handling can only be regarded as a distraction, not as an indulgence on the part of the exhibitor. Do not get the mistaken idea that if the judge thinks that a handler is working hard with his dog, he deserves to win!

MOVE THEM OUT!

Once the judge has compared the outlines, or profiles, of each dog, he will ask the exhibitors to move the dogs around the ring so that he may observe the dogs in action. This usually means two complete circles of the ring, depending upon the size of the ring and the numbers of dogs competing in it. This is the time when the judge must determine whether or not the dog is moving properly or if it is limping or lame. He checks the dog for proper gait, observing the dogs to see if they are gaiting according to the requirements for their breed. Hopefully, he can observe the dog moving freely on its own—not strung up on the end of a lead obeying a handler's demand to gait with head held high.

Two laps around the ring does not give the judge much of an opportunity to determine the true gait, especially if it is an outdoor show and the grass is high, or in the rain, when the water and/or mud splash against their stomachs. Good judges will allow for such "discomforts" and will also recognize a good gait when they see one. But such a disadvantage also means you must be that much more careful to see that the dog gaits on a loose lead, that you are pacing next to it at a safe

Champion Kalidan Sukee Cayenne, pictured finishing for championship with three consecutive majors at just 7½ months of age. Bred by Elaine Mawson, Sukee is owned by Ray Gaudet, and handled to this win under judge Eve Whitmore by Elaine MacDonald. The sire was Jaisu Playboy of Lingho ex Jaisu Ur-Chin of Filicia.

Sanco's Sebastian of Faro winning two points toward championship under judge Suzanne Rowe at the 1976 Little Rock show. This 8½ month old brindle and white dog is co-owned by Sandy Cox and Faith and Robert Brooks of Oakdale, Louisiana.

distance to the side so that the dog can move at its own best gait and that you are careful not to pull it off balance going around corners or while trying not to run into the judge's table on the next circling of the ring. You must also keep in mind not to get too close to the dog ahead of you and that you must keep far enough ahead of the dog behind you so that your dog doesn't get spooked—or that you don't break the other dog's gait.

Once the judge has had time to observe each of the dogs in motion, the signal will be given to one person to stop at a specific spot in the ring—usually where you were at the start of the class—and you all form a line-up for closer inspection of each dog by the judge. Starting with the first dog in the line, the judge will motion to you to place your dog up on the table provided, in show stance, so that he can go over your dog completely, evaluating it carefully in accordance with the Standard for the breed.

JUDGING THE HEAD

Once the judge has asked you to place your dog on the table, he approaches your dog to get the first close look at its expression. He wants to see the proper shape for the dark eyes, will check the length of the nose, the correct slightly-undershot bite, the shape of the top of the head, and will check to see that the hair pulled up in the top knot does not in any way alter the set and placement of the ears. A judge especially does not want to see any sign of fear (shrinking back or turning the head away) that would indicate shyness.

The judge will check the ear leather, perhaps raise the ears to check the length and thickness of the neck and to see how well placed it is on the shoulders. The angulation of the shoulders is traced with the hands and the placement of the front legs beneath the body is checked. When the distance between the front legs is ascertained, the judge may then lift the dog gently and let it down to observe how the dog lands on its feet. Many judges will also check the thickness of the pads of the feet as well, and how the dog puts its foot down when it is released.

JUDGING THE BODY

The judge will then run a hand along the topline, check out the brisket and rib cage and work his way back to the hindquarters. The judge will check to see that the dog is in good weight, not too thin or too fat. With today's nutritionally perfect food, it is not difficult to keep a dog in proper weight. If they are allowed sufficient exercise, freedom to move around, and to be an active member of your family, they should be in proper weight. If they are restricted in their activities or confined to cages for long periods of time they are liable to become lethargic and grow too fat. The healthiest and best conditioned dogs are the ones that are allowed to lead the normal "dog's life."

APPRAISING THE HINDQUARTERS

After a thorough examination of the body, the judge will move his hands down to the hindquarters. The tail will be checked to see if it is set properly, and carried over the body to the correct degree. The angulation of the hind legs is checked

Ch. Encore Flower Child, owned by Jane Fitts of Solvang, California, and handled for her here by Barbara Alderman. Flower Child was one of the top producing bitches for 1975, and was dam of four champions that finished for their titles during that year.

191

Ch. Bobbie's Brandy B-Bomb pictured winning under judge Joseph Faigel at the 1973 Council Bluffs Show. Brandy is handled by Lois Davis for owner Bobbie Franklin of Kansas City, Missouri.

Int. and World Ch. Quang-Te van de Blauwe Mammouth completes his Bermudian title at a 1978 show, adding a seventh national championship to his record. Judge Irving Diamond presents the award to handler Karolynne MacAteer. The Eastons are the owners. Quang-Te has since gone on to win an eighth championship, an American one, making him the most-titled dog in the breed's history.

Ch. De Amo Golden Fair, handled by Sylvia Kelly to this win under judge O.C. Harriman for owners Mr. and Mrs. G.W. Toliver, De Amo Kennels, Camarillo, California.

Ch. Johmar's Doodle Bug, pictured winning on the way to her championship under judge Louis Murr. Doodle Bug is the dam of three champions with many more pointed. Owner is Marion C. Potis, Reisterstown, Maryland.

Left:
Three-month-old Zalay O-Jay, bred and owned by Marilyn Szalay of Ontario, Canada.

Right:
Je Lee's Chinese Gem of Jaxbo, sired by Ch. Taramont Wang Chi ex Taramont Lu Fa Jen. Bred by Mrs. Julius Brown, and owned by Mrs. Je Lee Stout of Sugar Grove, Illinois.

Ch. Cresswood Tourmaline pictured winning under judge Thomas Gannon at a recent show. F.C. Dickey handled for owner Lucy M. Cress of Latrobe, Pennsylvania.

Ch. Encore Golden Suyen pictured winning Best of Opposite Sex under judge Dorothy Carson at a recent Lompoc Valley Kennel Club show. Madeline Thornton handled for owner Jane Fitts, Encore Shih Tzu, Solvang, California.

at this point, as well as a check made for the strength of the hindquarters. There should be no indication of weakness when the hocks are lightly "twanged" and no evidence of cow hocks. The hocks should show strength when moved gently back and forth. If it is a male dog, this is the point at which the judge will count testicles, and there must be two, or the dog will be disqualified. Some judges also place their hands on the rear end and gently apply pressure to see if the dog falters or moves its feet. Hopefully, it will stand firmly in place. A judge may then do the same at the shoulders to see if the dog can easily stand up under slight pressure without having to move its feet.

PROPER COAT TEXTURE

At some time during this examination, the dog can be checked for the proper coat texture. It should be lustrous, thanks to the availability of all the good food, remarkable grooming aids, and preparations available today. Good breeding also provides for a good coat and there is really no excuse for a Shih Tzu not being well put down. While a good coat is the product of both

hereditary and dietary factors, it can be additionally enhanced by grooming aids to present the ultimate in beauty by the time the dog is ready for the show ring. Be sure not to enter the ring with powder or chalk, or too much spray, or you will get yourself put out of the ring.

The Board of Directors of the American Kennel Club became so concerned with the increasing use of these aids that they ruled judges might not put up, or might even excuse, any handler from the ring found guilty of excessive use of foreign substances. Perhaps long-haired dogs should be shown soaking wet, with handlers forbidden to bring brushes and combs into the ring. We would miss the beauty of those flowing coats but a multitude of faults that escape many judges' eyes would not, and could not, be overlooked!

Once a judge has gone over the dog completely, he will usually step away from the dog and give it a final over-all side view look, keeping a complete picture in his mind before moving on to compare that image with the next dog to be put up on the table. This "last look" is one of the primary reasons for always having to keep your dog and yourself on your toes. You don't want the judge to suddenly take another look at your dog and find it sitting or chasing butterflies or lifting its leg on the number markers. On the contrary, this does not mean that every moment you have to have your dog strung up by the neck, or be grooming hairs individually, or constantly placing feet in position. That is a form of over-handling and can be a distraction to the judge and a nuisance to the dog. Surely during the time spent in the ring, the dog should be able to stand on its own, look alive and be ready for the next command that may be required during judging. If it isn't trained to this degree it is not ready for the ring. Training is done at home—*performance* is required at the show.

INDIVIDUAL GAITING

Once the judge has gone over each dog individually he will go to the end of the ring and ask each handler to gait his dog. It is important at this point to pay strict attention to the judge's instructions as to how he wants this done. Some judges require the "T" formation, others the half triangle. Further observations of your dog may bring a request for you to repeat the pattern, especially if your dog did not show well during the first trip. It is important that you hear whether the judge wants you to repeat the entire exercise or merely to gait your dog "down and back."

When each dog has been gaited, the judge will want a last look at all of them lined up together before making his final decisions. Usually, the procedure will be to once again present the left side of your dog with the judge then weaving in and out of the line to check once more the fronts or rears or other individual points of comparison. Some dogs may be asked to gait a third time, or to gait side by side with one of the other dogs should he want to "break a tie" on which dog moves best. Because such deciding factors can not be predicted or anticipated, it is necessary for the handler to always be ready to oblige once the request is given by the judge.

After the decisions are made, the judge will point to his four placements and those four will set their dogs up in front of the designated number markers on ths side of the ring. Be ready at this point to show the numbers on you arm bands

Dynasty's The Great Escape, a red and white male being shown to this win by breeder-owner Fredrick M. Alderman, Dynasty Kennels, Mundelein, Illinois. The sire was Ch. Dragonwyck The Great Gatsby ex Jaisu Ling-Ho Pla-Toi O'Dynasty.

so that the judge can mark the judge's book accordingly. The judge then presents the winners with the appropriate color ribbons and any trophies won, and you may leave the ring.

Contrary to popular opinion it is not necessary, or even correct, to thank the judge for the ribbon. It is to be assumed that the dog *deserved* the ribbon or the judge would not have awarded it. Handing you the ribbon is part of the procedure, and does not warrant a thank-you. The club, not the judge, is responsible for the donation of the trophies. If the win is significant enough so that you feel compelled to say *something*, a simple and not overly exuberant "I'm so pleased that you liked my dog," or something similar is still more than is necessary.

The "thank-you" for the ribbon has on some occasion become what some exhibitors like to think of as a "weapon." At ringside you can sometimes hear words to the effect that, "I didn't even thank him for that rotten red ribbon!" As if the judge had even noticed. However, it *is* expected that you take with you from the ring a ribbon of *any color*. To throw it on the ground or leave it behind in the ring so that the steward is obliged to call you back into the ring for the judge to hand it to you again is most unsportsman-like. You must play the game according to the rules. Your entry fee entitles you to obtain the opinion of your dog by the judge. You must take their opinion and behave accordingly. If you do not like it, do not give them another entry, but you owe the judge the courtesy of respect for their title.

After this judging procedure is followed in the five classes for dogs, and the Winners Dog and Reserve Winners Dog have been selected, the bitches are judged in the same sequence. After Winners Bitch and Reserve Winners Bitch awards have been made, the Best of Breed, Best of Winners and Best of Opposite Sex judging follows. (Class procedures are more thoroughly discussed in another chapter on showing your dog.) Once the judge has completed his assignment and signed the judge's book, it is permissible to request any photographs which you may wish to have taken of your wins.

At this time, it is also permissible to ask the judge his motives in his judging of *your* dog. If you do so, it should be done in a polite and calm manner, civilly and unquestioning. It must be remembered that the judge is not going to make comparisons, rating one dog *against* another, but can, if he chooses, give a brief explanation as to how he evaluated *your* dog. More often than not, on the way home in the car, or back at the bench, when you have given the decisions some thought,

it will occur to you why the judge did what he did without your having to have asked.

It is always advisable to remember that no one wins every show. You will win some and lose some no matter how good your dog is. Judges are human and, while no one is perfect, each has earned the title of "judge" for some mighty good reasons. Try to recall that it is a sport and should be fun, and tomorrow is another day—and another show!

THE GAMES PEOPLE PLAY

If you are new to the game of dog show exhibiting, there are a few things you should know about how to protect yourself and your dog so that you do not get too discouraged and disillusioned right at the start.

For example, the first time Joan Brearley exhibited in the show ring she was convinced, with good reasons, that she had a wonderful dog because so many of the competitors in the class with her tried so hard to make the dog look bad! The fact of the matter was, it *was* a good dog and posed a threat to the others competing, and they decided to try to do something about it. It was nothing personal at first (she hadn't been around long enough for the other exhibitors to either like her or dislike her), but the beautiful dog was an obvious contender for the ribbons, and *that* they thought they *could* do something about!

Two of the old-time breeders decided they would "initiate" Joan and really gave the dog "the business." One got ahead of her and the other behind her in the lineup. While gaiting around the ring, one ran up on top of the dog and the other stopped short in front of him. This followed an episode at ringside earlier when, under the pretense of going over the dog and saying (so quietly that no one else could hear the compliment) that the dog had "nice hindquarters," another exhibitor squeezed her dog's testicles! It was hoped that this would make the dog spook in the ring when the judge checked him out.

Another trick was that while stacking the dogs as the judge came down the line to look at them, they would block Joan's dog by walking in front of him, all the while pretending to get their dog ready for the judge to look at next. While supposedly giving the judge a better look at her dog, the woman next to Joan "accidentally" stepped on her dog's back foot! The second time she saw it coming and gave the woman a nudge with her hip and threw her off balance before she could come down hard enough to make the dog go lame and get it excused from the ring. Joan might have been new in the game, but the woman soon got the

196

Janiric's Jamb-O-Laya pictured winning Best Puppy out of an entry of 7 at the Huronia Kennel Club show under American judge Joseph Faigel. He is handled by Mr. Richard Logie of Ontario, Canada.

Dutch import Ch. Hayohan v Buruf winning Best of Breed under judge Roy Cowan at the 1975 Council Bluffs Kennel Club show. Owner-handled by Dr. Roland Wicks of Kansas City, Kansas, the dog was bred by S.E. Burema, a niece of Eta Pauptit.

Best in Show winner Ch. Emperor's Quapaw Quarter Emp, handled by John Murdock for owners Juanita S. Core and Wilma J. McCarthy, Quapaw Quarter Shih Tzu, Little Rock, Arkansas. This Toy Group win was in 1974.

Bon D'Art Aramus of Parwins finished his championship in six shows with handler Rena Martin. Owned by Carol R. Bogner, Highland House Shih Tzu, Wooster, Ohio. Bred by Bonnie and Len Guggenheim, Aramus was whelped in October 1971, and was the first champion for the Bon D'Art Kennel.

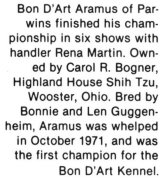

A Canadian Best In Show win went to Ch. Chumulari Li Liang in June 1973 under American judge William Kendrick. Less than 36 hours later tragedy struck and this marvelous little dog was drowned in a flash flood in the Rockies. Liang was the third Best in Show winning son of Can. and Am. Ch. Chumulari Ying Ying, and his loss brought a great sadness to both the handler, Pat Tripp, and his breeders, the Eastons.

message and never tried it again. Fortunately, a very discerning and "show-wise" judge saw what had been going on and gave Joan and her dog Best of Winners anyway!

Before Joan's next appearance in the show ring for the next points toward her dog's championship, a youngster poured beer all over her almost-white dog. The girl was prompted by a parent who happened to be entered in Joan's class at the show that day. Just so you do not think it was only Joan's misfortune that day, the incident was witnessed by another woman who had also been a victim of this vicious woman. She had had a cigarette rubbed out in her dog's coat; the singeing left a gaping hole there.

Over the years there have been fatal and near fatal poisonings, and dog thefts as well. We cannot emphasize too strongly the need to look after your dogs at the shows. We all know that the more winning a dog does, the more jealous the competitors become. As Shakespeare once wrote,

"Jealousy is the green-eyed monster which doth make the meat it feeds upon!" So, protect your dogs against the green-eyed monsters!

Needless to say, most judges are aware of these nasty tricks people play and do not tolerate them. For instance, a judge will ask the handler to move his dog aside so he can observe another dog without interference, or he will inform the handlers to keep enough space between the dogs as they gait around the ring if he sees there is crowding. A judge may ask a handler to pull his dog out of the line so that he might get an unobstructed view. *You* must also be aware of those around you that might be trying to make you and your dog look bad. Be pleasant at ringside and at the benches, but in the ring you must remember it is "all business" and the competition is keen. You have to think of everything, including showing your dog. Some of the professional handlers can be guilty of these practices also, so stay on your toes and always keep in mind the *games people play.*

CHILDREN IN THE SHOW RING

No one is more approving than we are of children learning to love and to care for animals. It is beautiful to see a child and an animal sharing complete rapport and companionship, or performing as a team in the show ring. Those of us who have been around dog shows for any length of time have all been witness to some remarkable performances by children and their dogs. Junior Showmanship is one example; dogs virtually caring for or standing guard over babies and infants is another example.

However, there is nothing "cute" about a child being allowed to handle a dog where both the welfare of the child and the general public is in danger. We have been witness to scraped faces when large dogs have pulled children to the floor and dragged them along behind as they pursued another dog. We have seen a male take off after a bitch in season, and we have had the horrible experience of seeing a child unable to restrain a large dog simply let go of the leash allowing the dog to attack another dog. Worse still was the incident where the child itself became entangled in the dropped leash and became the central figure in a three way battle that left all three of them scarred for life in spite of the wonders of today's plastic surgery. Children have been known to let small dogs wander, causing people to trip over them and fall. Also, small dogs tend, unfortunately, to fall victim to attacks by large dogs left momentarily unattended.

If a child shows the natural desire to exhibit a dog after having attended handling classes where they are taught to show the dog, they must also be taught ring procedure. It is not fair to expect other exhibitors to show patience while a judge or the steward informs the child where to stand, or waits for them to gait the dog several times before they do it in the formation requested. Lack of knowledge and repeated requests delay the judging, look bad to the ringside crowds and certainly don't make the dog look good.

If necessary, parents might stay late after dog

Best in Show winner Ch. Gin-Doc's Champane Ladi pictured here at the 1976 Saginaw Valley Kennel Club winning the Toy Group under judge Henry Stoecker.

199

Rondelay Glowyn DaZee, foundation bitch at the Pine Haven Kennels in Windsor, Maine. DaZee is the dam of Ch. Pine Haven's Chu Tzi Tzu.

Ch. Johmar's Yankee Doodle finished his championship in record time . . . four weekends. The sire was Ch. Johmar's Pahko ex Ch. Johmar's Doodle Bug. Owner-breeder Marion C. Potis of Reisterstown, Maryland.

Chumulari Sasha-San is owned by Jean Johnson of Decatur, Illinois. The sire was Ch. Willows the Golden Fleece ex Chumulari Chin Yu.

Sue Miller pictured showing Canadian Ch. Gin Doc's Pocohanas. This photo was taken in June 1976, when the dog was four years old. Mrs. Miller is from Green, South Carolina.

Ch. Windsor Gayelyn Ra-Sa-Ruck pictured winning on the way to championship. The sire was Curson Colcock ex Ch. Chumulari Mei Mei. Bred by Kathleen Kolbert, the owner is Jacqueline Hager.

Our favorite Christmas present: a Shih Tzu puppy. Largyn Luuz Mai Aim of Nanjo was a Christmas present for lucky Virginia Smigley, Phoenixville, Pennsylvania.

American Champion Conwynn's Tabetha, owned by Del and Connie Smart, Conwynn Shih Tzu, Akron, Ohio. Tabetha was Best of Winners and Best of Opposite Sex at the Westminster Kennel Club show in 1973.

Anlean's Yuan Shih Kai of Cas Yu pictured at nine weeks of age. Bred and owned by Ralph and Florence Zidanowicz of Bogota, New Jersey.

Happy wins Best in show at the 1975 Terry-All Kennel Club show. Happy's owner: Mrs. Frank E. Dinelli of Poplar Bluffs, Missouri.

shows are over, and actually train the children in an empty ring. This can help. Parents might sit at ringside near the judge's table with their young handlers to explain each process to them as it is performed. Doing this a few times will certainly acquaint the child with the proper procedures that they will have to follow once they enter the ring.

We have to assume that any small child that wishes to show a dog at a show is a bit precocious, so make sure you channel this tendency in the right direction. Many match show appearances should certainly precede any appearance in a regular show where serious contenders are vying for those important points. Even if the child doesn't actually win, their presence can still delay matters and detract from normal procedure. Certainly no parent could possibly expect a judge to give them a win just because they are a cute pair—even though they very well may be!

BAITING

No matter how one feels about baiting a dog in the ring, we must acknowledge that almost everyone at one time or another has resorted to it in the show ring. Certain breeds are particularly responsive to it, and others show little or no interest in baiting with so much going on all around them.

There is no denying that baiting is an aid to basic training and there is no rule against it. Aside from the fact that it is disconcerting to observe exhibitors wagging small bits of boiled liver about in the air before popping it into their dog's mouth, baiting is an indication that the training of the dog for the show ring is not yet complete. It becomes obvious to the judge that the dog still needs an incentive to respond to what other dogs are doing in the name of performance and showmanship.

Also, so many of the exhibitors are inept at handling the bait that more often than not pieces of liver end up all over the ring floor and turn out to be a distraction for other dogs that can't help but pick up the scent. We have found that the Shih Tzu, which aren't always the most enthusiastic eaters in the world anyway, are more responsive to squeaky toys, though I disapprove of these as well. If you are in the habit of talking to your dog you have surely come to recognize certain sounds you can make that will bring a genuine response, even in the show ring, without resorting to the toy chest or the kitchen stove.

DOUBLE HANDLING

While it may not seem probable, you can rest assured that the competent judge becomes aware

Ch. Car-Lyn's Kung Fu, finishing with owner-handler Glenda Wicks of Kansas City, under judge Edd Bivin.

A nine week old little lion dog owned by Ralph and Florence Zidanowicz of Bogota, New Jersey poses with oriental lions, part of an impressive collection of Chinese art owned by the couple.

Ch. Hajji Baba of Floridonna, owned by Donna F. and Edgar D. Ellis. The sire was Ch. Paisley Ping Pong; the dam was Mariljac Monsy Bonsy Colwell.

Ch. Highlandell Sun's A Blazin, pictured winning Best of Breed under judge Kay Finch in 1975.

Ch. Jaisu Ling-Ho X-Rated of Lainee, owned by Elaine Meltzer of New York City and bred by Carol Walsh and Jay Ammon.

Capa's Sol-Del-Oro pictured winning under judge Keke Blumberg. "Tubby" is owned by Mr. and Mrs. Paul Arcuragi, Capa Kennels, Camden, Ohio.

of any double handling to which some of the more desperate exhibitors may resort.

Double handling is unfair and frowned upon by the American Kennel Club. Nonetheless, some owners go to all sorts of ridiculous lengths to get their apathetic dogs to perform in the ring. They hide behind trees or posts at ringside, or may lurk behind the ringside crowd until the exact moment when the judge is looking at or gaiting their dog and then pop out in full view emitting some familiar whistle or make some sort of clucking noise, or wave a crazy hat, or squeak a pet toy, all in the hopes that the dog will suddenly become alert and express a bit of animation.

It calls to mind early days in dancing school, when during recitals some of the children couldn't remember the time step until they spotted their mothers in the front row keeping time with their feet and clapping hands to the music. Double-handling, no matter what form it takes, is against the rules and is stupid. Many of us can recall the woman who sneaked her dog's favorite companion—the family cat—to ringside to encourage a spirited gait. She had neglected to inform her handler about what she intended to do and the dog took off to greet the cat, leaving the surprised handler in the ring by himself!

If your dog needs you as a security blanket in order to go through a few formations in a show ring, it shouldn't be shown. Don't be guilty of double handling. The day may come when you finally have a great show dog, and the reputation of an owner guilty of double handling lives on forever. You will always be accused of the same shady practices and your new show dog is apt to suffer for it.

APPLAUSE, APPLAUSE

Another "put-on" by some insecure exhibitors is the practice of bringing their own cheering section to applaud vigorously every time the judge happens to cast an eye on their dog.

The judge that is truly dedicated and concentrating on what he is doing will not be influenced by the claques set up by those trying to push their dogs over the top by "popular approval." One of Joan Brearley's earliest revelations at the dog shows was her sheer astonishment at one woman who was instructing in a loud whisper a little cluster of assorted friends and relatives as to where to stand at ringside during the judging. "Spread out," she told them, "so it doesn't look as if you are a group of my friends." During the actual judging, she looked around the crowd to check and see if everyone was in their designated position and ready to burst forth with appropriate

Am. and Mex. Ch. Dynasty's Toi-Ying, pictured winning at the 1975 Guadalajara, Mexico, show. Bred by Fredric M. Alerman, he is owned by N. Sherri Newkirk.

applause. By the time the judge was ready to make his final placements the situation had almost gotten out of hand . . . the applause was more than obvious and included whistles and yeas from children who were trying to become part of the drama.

As far as we are concerned the only legitimate time for applause is during a Parade of Champions, during the gaiting of an entire Specialty Best of Breed class, or during the gaiting of an entire Stud Dog, Brood Bitch or Veteran Class. At these thrilling moments the tribute of applause—and the tears—are understandable and well received. Trying to prompt a win or stir up interest in a particular dog during the normal course of judging is amateurish. If you have ever observed this practice you will almost always see that the dogs being applauded are the poorest specimens in the class. Their owners seem to subconsciously realize that they cannot win under normal conditions.

Here is a list to check before entering the show ring:

CARDINAL SINS WHEN SHOWING YOUR DOG

1. *Don't* forget to exercise your dog before entering the ring! Do it before grooming if you are afraid the dog will get wet or dirty after getting off the grooming table.
2. *Don't* be late for your class, causing you to enter the ring with both you and your dog in a nervous state.
3. *Don't* drag the dog around in the ring on a short lead and destroy his proud carriage.

4. *Don't* talk to the judge in the ring. Watch the judge closely and follow instructions. Don't talk to people at ringside, or the other exhibitors in the ring with you.
5. *Don't* strike or abuse your dog in any way—espcially not in the ring! The time and place for training and discipline is at home and not in front of the judge or the public. Even outside the ring we know that the reward system, not punishment, is the most successful method of training a dog.
6. *Don't* be a bad loser! Whether you win or lose, be a good sport. You can't win them all, so if you win be gracious, and if you lose, be happy for the winner.
7. *Don't* shove your dog in a crate or leave him on the bench after you come out of the ring and forget about him until it's time to go home. A drink of water, something to eat and a little companionship will go a long way toward making dog shows more enjoyable for him so that he will show even better next time.

Ch. Aagalynn Lion of Joppa is pictured going Best of Winners under judge George Payton at the 1972 Kennel Club of Pasadena Show. Daisy Austad handled for owner Gordon K. Kellogg of Stanton, California.

Ch. Royale White Tie and Tails pictured winning under judge Emma Stephens. Handled by Warren Lee for owner Lucille E. Huntsman of Windsor, Maine.

Ch. Chumulari Mei-Mei pictured winning under judge Edith Nash Hellerman at a 1971 show. The sire was Chumulari Mr. Shih ex Int. Ch. Tangra V Tschomo Lung Ma. Bred by the Eastons, Mei-Mei's owner is Kathleen Kolbert, Windsor Gayelyn, Oxford, Connecticut.

Ch. Mar Del's Ring-A-Ding Ding pictured going Best in Show at the 1971 Hunterdon Hills Show with handler John Marsh. Judge was Emma Stephens. Sire was American and Bermudian Ch. Mar Del's Chow Mein ex Mar Del's Snow Pea. Bred and owned by Margaret Edel MacIntosh, Millersville, Maryland.

Ch. Lau Rin Destiny of Shang T'ou owned by Laura Riney, and bred by Eleanore Eldredge of Easton, Washington.

Jondalin Peek-A-Boo photographed winning at nine months of age for a 3-point major at the 1974 Silver State Kennel Club show. Peke-A-Boo is handled by John Thornton for owners Madeline Thornton and Laurie Battey of Torrence, California.

Ju Shig's Lemonade enjoys the company of her friend, Michelle Miller, of Green, South Carolina.

Yum Yum of Ssu Chi, owned by Judie B. Merrill of Alexandria, Virginia. Yum Yum was whelped in December 1966.

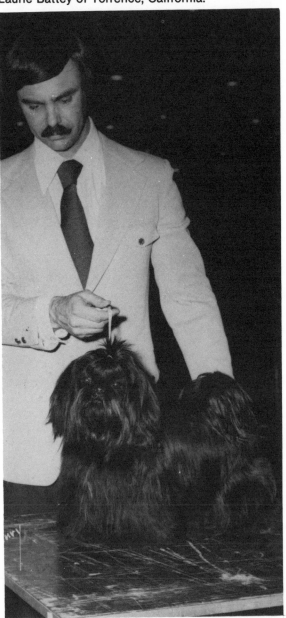

Ch. Lau Rin Poke A Long, owned by Laura Riney, is pictured winning Best of Breed over specials. The judge pictured here is the late Miss Frances Angela. This win completed Poke's championship at less than one year of age, with Edna Voyles the handler.

Ch. Malones Le-Jil-Mop owned by Clarence and Jennie Malone of Lexington, Kentucky. "Mop" is the dam of the Malones' Ch. Cinnabar's Golden Pirate.

Ch. Chumulari Tzu Yu is handled by Vernelle Hartman for owner Sandra O. Harris of Falls Church, Virginia. This win was under the late judge, Clara M. Alford.

Char-Nick's Gotcha of Davanik, foundation bitch of Peggy Angelastro's Davanik Shih Tzu kennels in Runnemede, New Jersey.

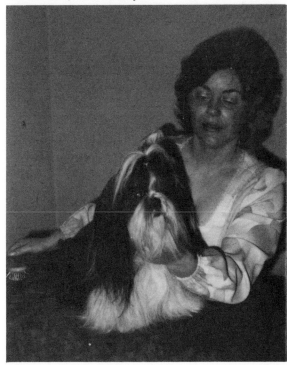

Omar Play Boy, U.D. and Canadian C.D. owned and trained by Mary Hollingsworth of Lancaster, Ohio. Omar was the second Shih Tzu to earn a C.D.X. title and the first Utility Dog titlist in the breed. Omar is pictured here going over the bar jump in the utility directed jumping exercise.

Chapter 12
THE SHIH TZU IN OBEDIENCE

There are those obedience buffs who will tell you that Shih Tzu—or any other Toy breed—are not too well suited to obedience training. In some instances this is true. There is nothing more frustrating than trying to train a dog that just doesn't "get the call." It is uphill work all the way to train them, and there is always the doubt lingering in the back of your mind whether they will do it or won't do it in the ring, which is far from the satisfaction one gets from *knowing* that your dog is as anxious as you are to put on a perfect show!

More and more Shih Tzu are receiving their degrees and more and more training methods and devoted owners are succeeding where others have failed, proving that Shih Tzu are intelligent and can be trained—especially if they want to be. Some Shih Tzu do seem to take a special delight in convincing their owners that they aren't suited for obedience, when actually it is just that they don't *want* to and have convinced their owners that it is a hopeless cause. Others just need to be coaxed.

While it is not advisable to force a dog into working for a degree, basic training is good for every dog just for the sake of good manners. If approached correctly, training will not make the dog dislike taking orders. Those who wish to go further should make sure that their dog displays a natural desire to "please" its owner and then both the owner and the dog can take pleasure from the experience of obedience training.

Those of us who have owned or observed Shih Tzu at work are the first to admit that it is a delight to see, and proves that titles can be won by these highly intelligent and independent dogs when approached in the right manner. It was our original intent to list all the obedience titlists in the breed, but we are happy to say, if only to prove our point, that they are too numerous to mention!

FIRST SHIH TZU C.D. TITLIST

The first Shih Tzu to earn a Companion Dog title was Si-Kiangs Say It Again, owned by Herbert W. Kellogg of Joliet, Illinois. "Hey Boy" finished at the show held May 1, 1966, in Decatur, Il-

linois. He is co-owned by Eloise B. Craig, but Mr. Kellogg, a former obedience columnist for *Shih Tzu News* magazine, trained and handled the dog to his title.

The second Shih Tzu to earn the C.D. title was Susan Clinch's Si-Kiang's Puddy-Kat, who finished at the Chester Valley Kennel Club Show on May 14, 1966, handled by his owner. Both these dogs were bred by Ingrid Colwell.

The third C.D. title was earned by Da-Lu of Brahania, also in 1966. An impressive list of title holders were to follow these three beginners and the names are too numerous to list in a book such as this. However, we are proud of them all and hope the list continues to grow. Our little dogs are highly intelligent and take to this training with amazing results. It was in April, 1972, that Tohatsu of Sherilyn made his mark as being the recipient of the first Companion Dog Excellent title in our breed. He was owned by Sherry Heldman of Florida.

FIRST UTILITY DOG SHIH TZU

The first Shih Tzu to earn this top obedience degree was named Omar Play Boy and his very proud owner and trainer, Mary Hollingsworth, took him all the way through his three obedience titles.

Ms. Hollingsworth originally decided to try obedience training with Omar out of curiosity in March, 1971. While obviously intelligent, Omar did have his stubborn moments and two of the C.D. exercises were especially difficult for him to perform, but after five shows Omar ended up second out of a class of 35. This was encouragement enough for Mary Hollingsworth to move on to the next step up.

Omar completed his Companion Dog Excellent title in August, 1972, in four shows, placing all three times. He went right into his Utility Dog training after becoming the second C.D.X. title holder in the breed, amassing scores of 196, 197 and 196½. The U.D. title was won in record time. Omar did it all—training and showing—in just three months, at the age of two, and in just six shows. This is a tremendous record, since most dogs are over three and often take a dozen or more

Top: Three Fang Chu Shih Tzu puppies, (from l.) Sin Dee, Shurman, and Pogo, belonging to Mary Hollingsworth of Lancaster, Ohio. **Bottom:** House of Wu Boi named Tzu, bred and owned by Mrs. Charles R. Eckes of Denver.

tries before being awarded this advanced title.

PAT McCANN AND PAT-TEZ

While Omar was the first to win a U.D. title, he was quickly followed by numerous other Shih Tzu, many of which were owned by Mrs. Pat McCann of Spokane, Washington. A February, 1976, issue of *Shih Tzu News* featured a story on her group with a list of title-holders that is most impressive.

Mrs. McCann's Pat-tez Fu Yen Ce was the first Shih Tzu to receive both an American and Canadian U.D. title. Her Pat-tez Chin Pu was the third Shih Tzu to attain both these U.D. titles and Pat-tez Aloha was the first Shih Tzu bitch and the second Shih Tzu to attain the Utility Dog degree. Aloha has also been awarded a Canadian U.D. Another of Mrs. McCann's dogs, Pat-tez Po Go, is an American and Canadian C.D. title holder and has one leg on his C.D.X. as of February, 1976.

Pat-Tez Lu Yence, an American and Canadian Utility dog owned by Mrs. McCann, has won Washington's first Obedience Trial Championship. At the Electric City Kennel Club show in Great Falls, Montana, held June 24, Yence won a first in utility under Judge Virginia Miller. This outstanding Shih Tzu is the Northwest's second Obedience Trial champion and quite possibly the third OT champion in the nation.

Mrs. McCann has bred, trained and shown Pekingese for many years, and Yence has won for her proud owner seven High in Trial awards. Yence has the distinction of being the number 2 Toy in the latest Delaney final standings. Another of Mrs. McCann's Shih Tzu, Pat-Tez Yoshiko, is the number two Shih Tzu in the nation.

Mrs. McCann now owns two of the five Pat-Tez Shih Tzu on the Delaney list of the top ten of the breed.

EARLY BASIC TRAINING

There are few things in the world a dog would rather do than please his master. Therefore, obedience training, or even the initial basic training, will be a pleasure for your dog, if taught correctly, and will make him a much nicer animal to live with for the rest of his life.

Omar Play Boy, Utility Dog and Canadian Companion Dog, is owned by John Hollingsworth. Omar received his thorough training from Mary Hollingsworth. The Hollingsworths, of Lancaster, Ohio, are quite proud of the fact that Omar is the first Shih Tzu to be awarded the title of Utility Dog.

WHEN TO START TRAINING

The most frequently asked question by those who consider training their dog is, naturally, "What is the best age to begin training?" The answer is "not before six months." A dog simply cannot be sufficiently or permanently trained before this age and be expected to retain all he has been taught. If too much is expected of him, he can become seriously frustrated and it may ruin him completely for any serious training later on, or even jeopardize his disposition. Most things a puppy learns and repeats before he is six months of age should be considered habit rather than training.

THE REWARD METHOD

The only proper and acceptable kind of training is the kindness and reward method which will build a strong bond between dog and owner. A dog must have confidence in and respect for his teacher. The most important thing to remember in training any dog is that the quickest way to teach, especially the young dog, is through repetition. Praise him when he does well and scold him when he does wrong. This will suffice. There is no need or excuse for swinging at a dog with rolled up newspapers or flailing hands because this will only tend to make the dog hand shy the rest of his life. Also, make every word count. Do

Overleaf:
Top: Encore Ming Huang Wing Tai, finishing at the 1976 Kern County Kennel Club Show under judge Frank Haze Burch. "Bunny" is handled by Madeline Thornton for owners Clifton and Marion Browne of Santa Barbara. Breeder, Jane Fitts. **Bottom:** Ch. Emperor's Thing-Ah-Ma-Ying pictured winning Best in Show under judge Sally Keyes at a recent Lewis-Clark Kennel Club show. Eddie Boyes handled for owner Mrs. Frank E. Dinelli of Poplar Bluff, Missouri.

This is Nellie, Can. Ch. Ken Mor's Kwan Yen, an obedience champion in America, Canada and Bermuda. Bred by Ken Falconi and W.G. Murton, the sire was Am. Can. Bda. Ch. Carrimount Ah-Tiko-Tiko ex Char-Nick's Kim Shu. Owned by Mary K. Dullinger of Weymouth, Massachusetts.

not give a command unless you intend to see it through. Pronounce distinctly with the fewest possible words, and use the same words for the same command every time.

Include the dog's name every time to make sure you have his undivided attention at the beginning of each command. Do not go on to another command until he has successfully completed the previous one and is praised for it. Of course, you should not mix play with the serious training time. Make sure the dog knows the difference between the two.

In the beginning, it is best to train without any distractions whatsoever. After he has learned to concentrate and is older and more proficient, he should perform the exercises with interference, so that the dog learns absolute obedience in the face of all distractions. Needless to say, whatever the distractions, you never lose control. You must be in command at all times to earn the respect and attention of your dog.

HOW LONG SHOULD THE LESSONS BE?

The lessons should be brief with a young dog, starting at five minutes, and as the dog ages and becomes adept in the first lessons, increase the time all the way up to one-half hour. Public training classes are usually set for one hour, and this is acceptable since the full hour of concentration is

not placed on your dog alone. Working under these conditions with other dogs, you will find that he will not be as intent as he would be with a private lesson where the commands are directed to him alone for the entire thirty minutes.

If you should notice that your dog is not doing well, or not keeping up with the class, consider putting off training for awhile. Animals, like children, are not always ready for schooling at exactly the same age. It would be a shame to ruin a good obedience dog because you insist on starting his training at six months rather than at, say, nine months, when he would be more apt to be receptive both physically and mentally. If he has a particular difficulty in learning one exercise, you might do well to skip to a different one and come back to it again at another session. There are no set rules in this basic training, except, "don't push!"

WHAT YOU NEED TO START TRAINING

From three to six months of age, use the soft nylon show leads, which are the best and safest. When you get ready for the basic training at six months of age, you will require one of the special metal-link choke chains sold for exactly this purpose. Do not let the word "choke" scare you. It is a soft, smooth chain and should be held slack whenever you are not actually using it to correct

Overleaf:
Top: Heavenly Dynasty's Tapersty pictured at almost six months of age. Owned by Victor and Leslie Morales, Fortune Cookie Kennels, Brooklyn. Tapersty took his first major at eight months and was undefeated in the Puppy Classes at the time of this writing. **Bottom:** Imua's Five-O of Alethra, handled by Randi Schmidt to this win under judge Anna Cowie. Bred and owned by Ginger Schedlbauer, Martinsville, New Jersey.

BEST OF WINNERS
MOUNTAINEER
KENNEL CLUB SHOW
JUNE 27 1976
PHOTOS BY D ALVERSON

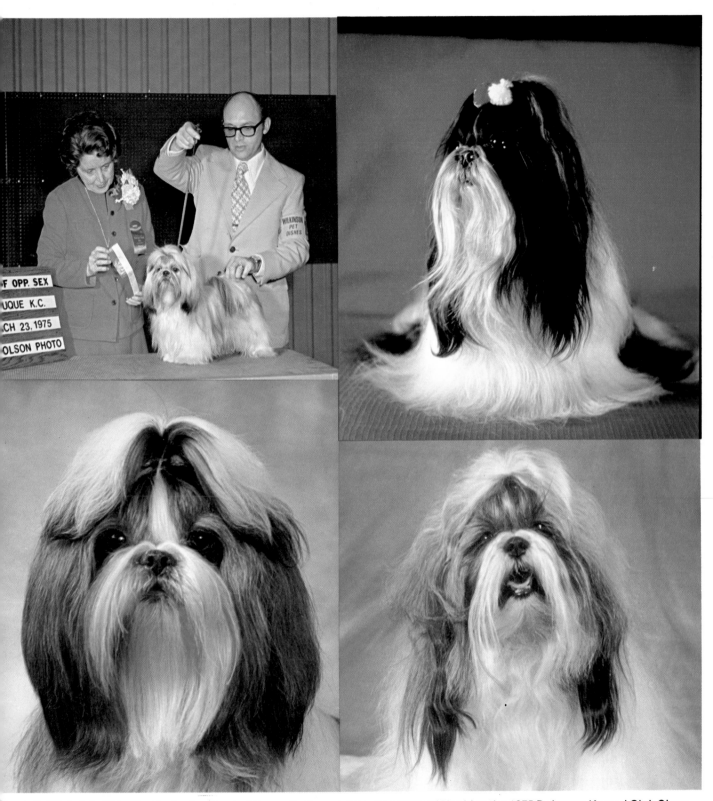

Top left: Misty Isle Chin Mo Li winning Best of Opposite Sex under judge Mildred Heald at the 1975 Dubuque Kennel Club Show with owner-handler Mike Heigert, who co-owns with Sharron Heigert, White Pine, Brentwood, Missouri. **Top right:** Shadaar's Sin Yih of Thompson, bred by Mary Smithburn and owned by Linda Miller of Belton, Missouri. Whelped in October, 1967, the sire was Ch. Silver Nymph's Top Secret ex Shaadar's Hi Tibetan Goddess. This photograph was taken in January, 1973. **Bottom left:** Ch. Wenrick's Tini Tina, first homebred champion for Wendy and Richard Paquette of Ontario, Canada. This little lady pictured here at 11 months of age, finished for her championship before she was a year old. She has a Group First and several Group Placements to her credit. She was born in April, 1973. **Bottom right:** Ch. Fang's Chang Tzu of Shang T'ou, owned by Mary Hollingsworth of Lancaster, Ohio.

Chumulari Woo Muh, C.D., one of the first Shih Tzu to succeed in the obedience ring. Trainer was Marvel Runkel of Spokane, Washington.

Wild Meadow's Shanghai Happy, C.D. owned by Ginny Mills, Honeoye Falls, New York.

the dog. This chain should be put over the dog's head so that the lead can be attached over the dog's neck rather than underneath against his throat. It is wise when you buy your choke collar to ask the sales person to show you how it is put on. Those of you who will be taking your dog to a training class will have an instructor who can show you.

To avoid undue stress on the dog, use both hands on the lead. The dog will be taught to obey commands at your left side, and therefore, your left hand will guide the dog close to his collar on a six-foot training lead. The balance of the lead will be held in your right hand. Learn at the very beginning to handle your choke collar and lead correctly. It is as important in training a dog as is the proper equipment for riding a horse.

WHAT TO TEACH FIRST

The first training actually should be to teach the dog to know his name. He can, of course, learn this at an earlier age than six months just as he can learn to walk nicely on a leash or lead. Many puppies will at first probably want to walk around with the leash in their mouths. There is no objection to this if the dog will walk while doing it. Rather than cultivating this as a habit, you will find that if you don't make an issue of it, the dog will soon realize that carrying the lead in his

mouth is not rewarding and he'll let it fall to his side where it belongs.

Let the puppy walk around by himself for awhile with the lead around his neck. If he wants to chew on it a little, that's all right too. In other words, let it be something he recognizes and associates with as readily as he does a collar. Do not let the lead be just something he is "pulled around on" from the first moment it is put around his neck.

If the dog is at all bright, chances are he has learned to come on command when you call him by name. This is relatively simple with sweet talk and a reward. On lead, without a reward, and on command without a lead is something else again. If there has been, or is now, a problem, the best way to correct it is to put on the choke collar and the six foot lead. Then walk away from the dog and call, "Pirate, come!" and gently start reeling him in until the dog is in front of you. Give him a pat on the head and/or a reward.

Walking, or heeling, next to you is also one of the first and most important things for him to learn. With the soft lead training starting very early, he should soon take up your pace at your left side. At the command "heel" he should start off with you and continue alongside until you stop. Give the command, "Pirate, sit!" This is taught by leaning over and pushing down on his hind-

216

quarters until he sits next to you, while pulling up gently on the collar. When you have this down pat on the straightaway, start practicing it in circles, with turns and figure eights. When he is an advanced student, you can look forward to the heels and sits being done neatly, spontaneously, and off lead as well.

THE "DOWN" COMMAND

One of the most valuable lessons or commands you can teach your dog is to lie down on command. Some day it may save his life, and is invaluable when travelling with a dog or visiting, if behavior and manners are required even beyond obedience. While repeating the words, "Pirate, down!" lower the dog from a sitting position in front of you by gently pulling his front legs out in front of him. Place your full hand on him while repeating the command "Pirate, down!" and hold him down to let him know you want him to *stay* down. After he gets the general idea, this can be done from a short distance away on a lead along with the command, by pulling the lead down to the floor. Perhaps you can slip the lead under your shoe (between the heel and sole) and pull it directly to the floor. As the dog progresses in training, a hand signal with or without verbal command, or with or without lead, can be given from a considerable distance by raising your arm and extending the hand palm down.

THE "STAY" COMMAND

The stay command eventually can be taught from both a sit and a stay position. Start with the sit. With the dog on your left side in the sitting position give the command, "Pirate, stay!" Reach down with the left hand and open palm side to the dog and sweep it in close to his nose. Walk a short distance away and face him. He will, at first, having learned to heel immediately as you start off, more than likely start off with you. The trick in teaching this is to make sure he hears "stay" before you start off. It will take practice. If he breaks, sit him down again, stand next to him, and give the command all over again. As he masters the command, let the distance between you and your dog increase while the dog remains seated. Once the command is learned, advance to the stay command from the down position.

THE STAND FOR EXAMINATION

If you have any intention of going on to advanced training in obedience with your dog, or if you have a show dog which you feel you will enjoy showing yourself, a most important command which should be mastered at six months of age is

Patrick of Tasmania, an obedience trained Shih Tzu owned by Patricia Trescott Ripley of Ranchos de Taos, New Mexico.

Ch. Nanjo Happi Yakki, C.D. pictured winning with his handler Barbara Alderman. Happi is owned by Virginia Smigley of Phoenixville, Pennsylvania.

Overleaf
Top: Ch. Lau Rin Jasmine of Shang T'ou winning Best of Opposite Sex at the 1971 Chicago International show under the late judge Winifred Heckmann. Edna Voyles handled for owner Laura Riney of Louisville, Kentucky. Breeder was Eleanore Eldredge. **Bottom:** Mei San Saki Tuo Mee Babe winning Best of Breed at a 1975 show with handler Daryl Martin. Owned by Betty Meidlinger of the Mei San Shih Tzu, St. Paul, Minnesota.

217

Mount Archer's Moppet, C.D., whelped in August of 1967, received her title in November 1972. She is owned and trained by Mrs. Charles W. Jewett of Lyme, Connecticut.

the stand command. This is essential for a show dog since it is the position used when the show judge goes over your dog. This is taught in the same manner as the stay command, but this time with the dog remaining up on all four feet. He should learn to stand still, without moving his feet and without flinching or breaking when approached by either you or strangers. The hand with palm open wide and facing him should be firmly placed in front of his nose with the command, "Pirate, stand!" After he learns the basic rules and knows the difference between stand and stay, ask friends, relatives and strangers to assist you with this exercise by walking up to the dog and going over him. He should not react physically to their touch. A dog posing in this stance should show all the beauty and pride of being a sterling example of his breed.

FORMAL SCHOOL TRAINING

We mentioned previously about the various training schools and classes given for dogs. Your local kennel club, newspaper, or the yellow pages of the telephone book will put you in touch with organizations in your area where this service is performed. You and your dog will learn a great deal from these classes. Not only do they offer formal training, but the experience for you and your dog in public, with other dogs of approximately the same age and with the same purpose in mind, is excellent. If you intend to show your dog, this training is valuable ring experience for later on. If you are having difficulty with the training, remember, it is either too soon to start—or *you* are doing something wrong.

ADVANCED TRAINING AND OBEDIENCE TRIALS

The A.K.C. obedience trials are divided into three classes: Novice, Open and Utility.

In the Novice class, the dog will be judged on the following basis:

TEST	MAXIMUM SCORE
Heel on lead	40
Stand for examination	30
Heel free—on lead	40
Recall (come on command)	30
One-minute sit (handler in ring)	30
Three-minute sit (handler in ring)	30
Maximum total score	200

If the dog "qualifies" in three shows by earning at least 50% of the points for each test, with a total of at least 170 for the trial, he has earned the Companion Dog degree and the letters C.D. are entered after his name in the A.K.C. records.

After the dog has qualified as a C.D., he is judged eligible to enter the Open Class competition, where he will be judged on this basis:

TEST	MAXIMUM SCORE
Heel free	40
Drop on Recall	30
Retrieve (wooden dumbell) on flat	20
Retrieve over obstacle (hurdle)	30
Broad jump	20
Three-minute sit (handler out of ring)	30
Five-minute down (handler out of ring)	30
Maximum total score	200

Overleaf:
Top: Ch. Happi Showing Bandit winning a 5-point major to finish his championship, August, 1976, under judge Martha Jane Ablett. Ferd Rent handled for owner Susan E. Archer, Happi Shih Tzu, Richland, Michigan. **Bottom:** Ch. Pine Haven's Chu Tzi Tzu winning Best of Breed over Specials from Puppy Class under judge Merrill Cohen at the 1976 North Shore Kennel Club show. Bred, owned and handled by Lucille E. Huntsman, Pine Haven Kennels, Windsor, Maine.

Hidden Coves Change of Pace gets in some early show training while still a puppy. Owner is Barbara Ward of Revere, Massachusetts.

These seven exercises must be executed to achieve the C.D.X. degree, and the percentages for achieving these are the same as for the C.D. degree. Candidates must qualify in three different obedience trials, under three different judges and must have received scores of more than 50% of the available points in each exercise, with a total of 170 points or more out of the possible 200. At that time they may add the letters C.D.X. after their name. He is then eligible for the Utility Class, where he can earn the Utility Dog (U.D.) degree in these rugged tests:

TEST	MAXIMUM SCORE
Scent discrimination (Article #1)	30
Scent discrimination (Article #2)	30
Direct retrieve	30
Signal exercise (heeling, etc., on hand signal)	40
Directed jumping (over hurdle and bar jump)	40
Group examination	30
Maximum total score	200

The Utility Dog degree is awarded to dogs which have qualified by successfully completing these six exercises under three different judges at three different obedience trials, with a score of more than 50% of available points in each exercise, and with a score of 170 or more out of a possible 200 points.

For more complete information about these obedience trials, write for the American Kennel Club's *Regulations and Standards for Obedience Trials*. Dogs that are disqualified from breed shows because of alteration or physical defects are eligible to compete in these trials.

THE TRACKING DOG DEGREE

The Tracking Dog trials are not held, as the others are, with the dog shows, and need be passed only once.

The dog must work continuously on a strange track at least 440 yards long and with two right angle turns. There is no time limit, and the dog

Hidden Coves Pennys from Hev'n, also owned by Barbara Ward, is shown taking a Best Opposite Sex during show career. Judge Betty Dullinger awarded the win.

Overleaf:
Top: Topper of Shang T'ou at 10 weeks of age, bred by Eleanore Eldredge, Easton, Washington and owned by Mrs. Glae Bickford of Las Vegas. **Bottom:** Ch. House of Wu Highland Ray-Sin De De winning from the Puppy Class under judge Frank Oberstar at the 1976 Mahoning Shenango Kennel Club Show. Bred by Mrs. Charles Eckes and owned by Carol R. Bogner, Highland House Shih Tzu, Wooster, Ohio, who is pictured handling.

BEST OF
WINNERS

PHOTO
BY BOOTH

BEST OF
BREED

GILBERT PHOTO

must retrieve an article laid at the other end of the trail. There is no score given; the dog either earns the degree or fails. The dog is worked by his trainer on a long leash, usually in harness.

THE NEW OBEDIENCE TRIAL CHAMPIONSHIP TITLES

The Board of Directors of the American Kennel Club has approved the following addition to the Obedience Regulations, effective July 1, 1977.

Obedience Trial Championship

Section 1. Dogs That May Compete. Championship points will be recorded only for those dogs which have earned the Utility Dog Title. Any dog that has been awarded the Title of Obedience Trial Champion may continue to compete, and if such a dog earns a First or Second place ribbon, that dog shall also earn the points.

Section 2. Championship Points. Championship points will be recorded for those dogs which have earned a First or Second place ribbon competing in the Open B or Utility Class (or Utility B, if divided), according to the schedule of points established by the Board of Directors of The American Kennel Club. In counting the number of eligible dogs in competition, a dog that is disqualified, or is dismissed, excused or expelled from the ring by the judge shall not be included.

Requirements for the Obedience Trial Champion are as follows:

1. Shall have won 100 points; and
2. shall have won a First place in Utility (or Utility B, if divided) provided there are at least three dogs in competition; and
3. shall have won a First place in Open B, provided there are at least six dogs in competition; and
4. shall have won a third First place under the conditions of 2 or 3 above; and
5. shall have won these three First places under three different judges.

Section 3. O.T. Ch. Title Certificate. The American Kennel Club will issue an Obedience Trial Championship Certificate for each registered dog and will permit the use of the letters O.T. Ch. preceding the name of each dog that meets these requirements.

Section 4. Ineligibility and Cancellation. If an ineligible dog has been entered in any licensed or member obedience trial or dog show, or if the name of the owner given on the entry form is not that of the person or persons who actually owned the dog at the time entries closed, or if shown in a class for which it had not been entered, or if its entry form is deemed invalid or unacceptable by the American Kennel Club, all resulting awards shall be cancelled. In computing the championship points, such ineligible dogs, whether or not they have received awards, shall be counted as having competed.

Section 5. Move Ups. If an award in any of the regular classes is cancelled, the next highest scoring dog shall be moved up and the award to the dog moved up shall be counted the same as if it had been the original award. If there is no dog of record to move up, the award shall be void.

Section 6. Return of Awards. If the win of a dog shall be cancelled by The American Kennel Club, the owner of the dog shall return all ribbons and prizes to the show-giving club within ten days of receipt of the notice of cancellation from the American Kennel Club.

Section 7. Point Schedule

Number Competing	Points For First Place	Points For Second Place
6-10	2	0
11-15	4	1
16-20	6	2
21-25	10	3
26-30	14	4
31-35	18	5
36-40	22	7
41-45	26	9
46-50	30	11
51-56	34	13

Overleaf:
Top: Chumulari Ho Feng going Best of Winners on the way to championship at a recent Superstition Kennel Club show under judge Buelah Hatch. Ho Feng was shown by Ellen Keenan for owner Nessa Gale, Phoenix. **Bottom:** Ch. Moon Ling's Wu Tai Shan winning Best of Breed under Mildred Heald from the classes over Specials. Whelped in 1973, the sire was Ch. Longs Chiny Chin Ah Chop Chop ex Moon Ling's Tang Lee of Tien Tan. Bred by Frances Heller, handled by Bill Zervoulis who co-owns with Janine Zervoulis, Basking Ridge, New Jersey.

Ch. Windsor My Rimpoche, bred and owned by Kathleen Kolbert of Oxford, Connecticut and pictured winning under judge Winifred Heckmann at a 1971 Holyoke show. The sire was Ch. Ying Ying ex Ch. Chumulari Mei Mei.

UTILITY CLASS

Number Competing	Points For First Place	Points For Second Place
3-5	2	0
6-9	4	1
10-14	6	2
15-19	10	3
20-24	14	4
25-29	18	5
30-34	22	7
35-39	26	9
40-44	30	11
45-48	34	13

Zervlistan Tai Wun On, better known as "Boozer," at 12 weeks old in this Bill Zervoulis photo. Boozer is owned by Janine R. Zervoulis.

Town Hall Stardust O'Moon Ling with her litter of eight-week-old puppies bred by Sara L. Weinberg and Jan Zervoulis. The puppies are (l. to r.) Mahjong Legacy v Zervlistan, owned by Florence Veniey, Baltimore; Zervlistan Renegade, owned by Mary Buresh, Ogdensburg, NJ; Zervlistan Impact owned by the Zervoulis'; and Zervlistan Tornade, owned by Sara L. Weinberg, East Orange, NJ.

Ch. Winemakers E'Zee Luvin pictured going Winners Bitch under English judge Edna Joel at the 1976 Framingham District Kennel Club show. Owner is Barbara Ward, Revere, Mass.

Ch. Emperor's Quapaw Dakota Sioux being shown going Best of Winners at the 1974 Piedmont Kennel Club show with handler John Murdock. Owners are Juanita S. Core and Wilma J. McCarthy, Quapaw Quarter Shih Tzu.

Ch. House of Wu Hai-U, owned by Max Kerrfoot, is pictured winning a Best In Show in 1976. The breeder was Mrs. Charles Eckes of Denver.

Bda., Am., Can. Ch. Chen Yu, owned by the Zidanowiczes. Chen Yu is pictured winning at the 1974 Providence show. William Trainor handles for this win.

Overleaf:
Top: Ch. Shaadar's Yankee Doll, bred by Mary Smithburn and owned by Mrs. Charles R. Eckes. Doll was Best in Show at the 1972 Metro Mile Hi Kennel Club Show. **Bottom:** Zervlistan Impact, sired by Ch. Moonling's Wu Tai Shan ex Town Hall Stardust O'Moonling. Impi is here winning Best Puppy in Match at the Shih Tzu Club of Northern New Jersey first A Match under Mrs. Donna Steapp, owner of the Bomshu Kennels in Texas. Handled by Janine Zervoulis who co-owns with Bill Zervoulis.

Encore A I Jen pictured winning at a recent show. The owner is Jane Fitts.

Ch. Elfann Golden Puff Ball, owned by Gilbert S. Khan and Jorge N. Sanchez of Coral Gables, Florida. Bred in England by Miss E. M. Evans, he is shown here taking a 5-point major at the 1976 St. Petersburg show under judge Dr. Harry Smith. Jean Lade handled.

Hidden Coves Golden Tiffany pictured winning under judge Robert Graham at a 1975 show. L. Garrett Lambert handles and co-owns Tiffany with Barbara Ward.

Ch. Carrimount Ah Flip-Flop, owned by L. Garrett Lambert and Joseph R. Repice of North Miami Beach, Florida. Flip-Flop is pictured going Winners Dog at the Westminster Kennel Club show.

Overleaf:
Top: Int. Ch. Irkoe Shu van de Oranje Manege, a Dutch import from the famous kennels of Eta Pauptit. Judge Robert Waters gave the dog Best of Breed and Group Third at a recent Tuscon show. Irkoe is shown by owner Ellen M. Keenan of Phoenix. **Bottom:** Ch. Mar Del's U Betcha winning on the way to championship at the 1976 Lancaster Kennel Club Show. The sire was Ch. Char Nick's I Gotcha ex Ch. Mar Del's Samantha. Owned by Joe Cannon, Cannonade, Reg., Potomac, Md.

Kloeber

BEST OF
WINNERS

GILBERT PHOTO

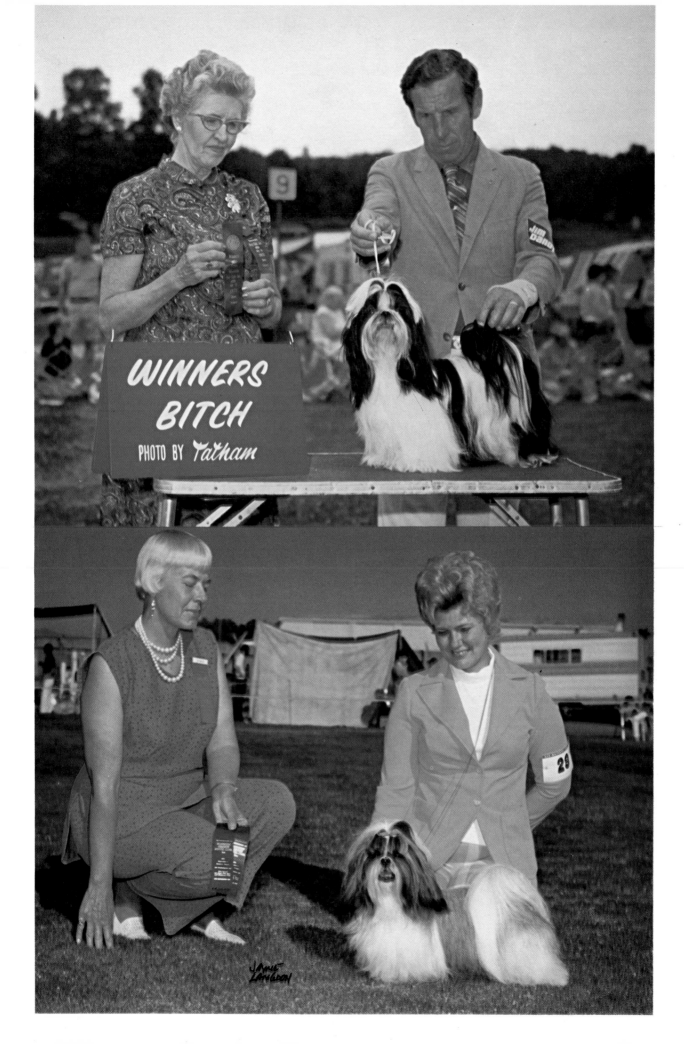

Overleaf:
Top: Am., Can. Ch. Brownhills Yolan of Greenmoss, owned by J.G. Carrique of Quebec and shown with handler William Trainor. **Bottom:** Ch. Hei Lein's Mr. Bo Jangles winning under judge Bess Pickens at a recent show. Bred, owned and handled by Lois Frank, Hei Lein Kennels, Chico, California.

Chapter 13
GENETICS

No one can guarantee the workings of nature. But, with facts and theories as guides, you can plan, at least on paper, a litter of puppies that should fulfill your fondest expectations. Since the ultimate purpose of breeding is to try to improve the breed, or maintain it at the highest possible standard, such planning should be earnestly undertaken, no matter how uncertain particular elements may be.

There are a few terms with which you should become familiar to help you understand the breeding procedure and the workings of genetics. The first thing that comes to mind is a set of formulae known as the Mendelian Laws. Gregor Mendel was an Austrian cleric and botanist born July 22, 1822 in what is now named Jyncice and is in Czechoslovakia. He developed his theories on heredity by working for several years with garden peas. A paper on his work was published in a scientific journal in 1866, but for many years it went unnoticed. Today the laws derived from these experiments are basic to all studies of genetics and are employed by horticulturists and animal breeders.

To apply these laws to the breeding of dogs, it is necessary to understand the physical aspects of reproduction. First, dogs possess reproductive glands called gonads. The male gonads are the testicles where the sperm (spermatozoa) that impregnate the female are produced. Eggs (ova) are produced in the female gonads (ovaries). When whelped, the bitch possesses in rudimentary form all the eggs that will develop throughout her life, whereas spermatozoa are in continual production within the male gonads. When a bitch is mature enough to reproduce, she periodically comes in heat (estrus). Then a number of eggs descend from the ovaries via the fallopian tubes and enter the two horns of the uterus. There they are fertilized by male sperm deposited in the semen while mating, or they pass out if not fertilized.

In the mating of dogs, there is what is referred to as a tie, a period during which anatomical features bind the male and female together and about 600 million spermatozoa are ejected into the female to fertilize the ripened eggs. When a sperm penetrates a ripe egg, zygotes are created and these one-celled future puppies descend from the fallopian tubes, attach themselves to the walls of the uterus, and begin the developmental process of cell production known as mitosis. With all inherited characteristics determined as the zygote was formed, the dam then assumes her role as an incubator for the developing organisms. She has been bred and is in whelp; in these circumstances she also serves in the exchange of gases and in furnishing nourishment for the puppies.

Let us take a closer look at what is happening during the breeding process. We know that the male deposits millions of sperm within the female and that the number of ripe eggs released by the female will determine the number of puppies in the litter. Therefore, those breeders who advertise a stud as a "producer of large litters" do not know the facts or are not sticking to them. The bitch determines the size of the litter; the male sperm determines the sex of the puppies. Half of the millions of sperm involved in a mating carry the characteristic that determines development of a male and the other half carry the factor which triggers development of a female, and distribution of sex is thus decided according to random pairings of sperm and eggs.

Each dog and bitch possesses 39 pairs of chromosomes in each body cell; these pairs are split up in the formation of germ cells so that each one carries half of the hereditary complement. The chromosomes carry the genes, approximately 150,000 like peas in a pod in each chromosome, and these are the actual factors that determine inherited characteristics.

As the chromosomes are split apart and rearranged as to genetic pairings in the production of ova and spermatozoa, every zygote formed by the joining of an egg and a sperm receives 39 chromosomes from each parent. This union will

Ch. Fang of Shang T'ou, pictured with comedienne Phyllis Diller. Fang was bred by Eleanor Eldredge and owned by Mary Hollingsworth.

Above: Ch. Nanjo's Oh Mai Gosh of Char Nick pictured winning the Toy Group at the 1975 Ashtabula Kennel Club show with handler Barbara Alderman. Judge was Anne Rogers Clark. Owned by Joan Cowie of Kimberton, Penn., this Shih Tzu's sire was Ch. Char Nicks I Gotcha ex Ch. Sesame of Sam Chu. **Left:** American and Canadian Ch. Greenmoss Gilligan, owned by Faye and Ray Wine. The sire was Int., Eng. Ch. Golden Peregrine of Elfann, ex Jasmine of Greenmoss.

Overleaf:
Top: Li Ming's Cha Meng going Winners Bitch at a 1976 show under judge Ruth Turner. Daryl Martin handles for owners Bob and Dawn Perretz Tendler of Ridgefield, Connecticut. **Bottom:** Ch. Char Nick's Be-Wit-Ching of Copa, Best in Show-winning bitch owned by Carol S. Davis, here winning under judge Kenneth Miller with Jean Lade handling. "The Witch" was bred by the Louis Sanfilippos.

form the pattern of 78 chromosomes inherited from dam and sire, which will be reproduced in every cell of the developing individual, determining what sort of animal it will be.

To understand the procedure more clearly, we must know that there are two kinds of genes—dominant and recessive. A dominant gene is one of a pair whose influence is expressed to the exclusion of the effects of the other. A recessive gene is one of a pair whose influence is subdued by the effects of the other, and characteristics determined by recessive genes become manifest only when both genes of a pairing are recessive. Most of the important qualities we wish to perpetuate in our breeding programs are carried by the dominant genes. It is the successful breeder who becomes expert at eliminating recessive or undesirable genes and building up the dominant or desirable gene patterns.

We have merely touched upon genetics here to point out the importance of planned mating. Any librarian can help you find further information, or books may be purchased offering the very latest findings on canine heredity and genetics. It is a fascinating and rewarding program toward creating better dogs.

THE POWER IN PEDIGREES

Once you have considered the basics of genetics and realize the strong influence heredity has on your breeding program, you will find yourself compelled to delve into pedigrees of dogs which you may be considering for stud service for your bitches, especially if you intend to breed show dogs.

Someone in the dog fancy once remarked that the definition of a show prospect puppy is one third the pedigree, one third what you see and one third what you *hope* it will be! Well, no matter how you break down your qualifying fractions, we all agree that good breeding is essential if you have any plans at all for a show career for your dog. Many breeders will buy on pedigree alone, counting largely on what they themselves can do with the puppy by way of feeding, conditioning and training. Needless to say, that very important piece of paper commonly referred to as the pedigree is mighty reassuring to a breeder or

Witch's Yum Yum pictured winning Best in Show at the 1971 Kittanning Kennel Club show under judge Mrs. Cass. Handler was John M. Murdock for owners Dr. and Mrs. J. Wesley Edal.

buyer new at the game, or to one who has a breeding program in mind and is trying to establish his own bloodline.

One of the most fascinating aspects of tracing pedigrees is the way the names of the really great dogs of the past keep appearing in the pedigrees of the great dogs of today—positive proof of the strong influence of heredity and witness to a great deal of truth in the statement that great dogs frequently reproduce themselves, though not necessarily in appearance only. A pedigree represents something of value when one is dedicated to breeding better dogs.

To the novice buyer or one who is perhaps merely switching to another breed and sees only a frolicking, leggy, squirming bundle of energy in a fur coat, a pedigree can mean everything! To those of us who believe in heredity, a pedigree is more like an insurance policy—so always read them carefully and take heed!

For the even more serious breeder of today who wishes to make a further study of bloodlines in relation to his breeding program, the American Kennel Club library stud books can and should be consulted.

Overleaf:
Top: Best in Show over an entry of 103 dogs at the Shih Tzu Fanciers of Southern California show in January, 1975, was Ch. Jilga Shu van de Oranje Manege. This Dutch import was bred by Eta Pauptit and is shown and owned by Ellen M. Keenan of Phoenix. The judge is Derek Rayne. Jilga is just 13 months of age at the time of this impressive win. **Bottom:** Ch. Windsor Gayelyn Jade of Nika, bred by Kathleen Kolbert and owned by Mrs. Ruth B. Hager of Madison, Connecticut, winning under judge Edna Ackerman at the 1975 Connecticut Kennel Club Show.

Chumulari Hih-Hih winning the Miscellaneous Class at the Mid-Hudson Kennel Club Show in June 1969 before AKC breed championship recognition had been approved. Judge James Trullinger officiated. Owner-handler of Hih-Hih is Richard Bauer. Hih-Hih was the top-winning bitch in the United States in 1967 and 1968. She was bred by the Eastons.

Overleaf:
Top: Can., Am. Champion Carrimount Ah Chun-Ki, winning the Group at the 1972 Kars Show where he later went on to win Best in Show. The judge is Eve Whitmore; handling is L. Garret Lambert for owners Mrs. K.T. Johnstone of Quebec.
Bottom: Ch. Mistybank Ouzo v Zervoulis (winning Best of Breed) and Bomshu Contessa v Zervlistan, co-owned and shown by Bill and Janine Zervoulis are shown at a 1975 show under judge Florence Gamburg. Contessa was bred by the late Jean W. Gadberry, owner of the Bomshu Kennels.

Greylocks Sassy Seducer photographed at twelve weeks of age. Sire was Ch. Paisley Ping Pong ex Astrids Shih Ling. Breeder-owner is Judith Goldberg of North Tonawanda, New York.

Ch. Maui's Ping Kan celebrates St. Valentine's Day at the Karmicki Kennels in Alberta, Canada. This photograph appeared in the local paper in 1977. Owner is Mrs. Mary Ellen Baker.

Dragonseed Wen-U-Hot-U-Hot pictured winning on way to championship. John J. March handled at the 1976 Camden County Kennel Club Show. The sire was Ch. Chumulari Ying Ying ex Ch. Chumulari Yu Lo.

BEST OF WINNERS

GILBERT PHOTO

Hodari Imperial Lin, co-owned by Laurie Battey and Helen McClarnon, is pictured winning a 4-point major under judge Peter Federico at the 1977 Orange Empire show. Handler is Madeline Thornton. Lin was Best in Sweepstakes at eleven months at the Shih Tzu Fanciers of Southern California Specialty show in 1977 and was Winners Bitch for a 4-point major at the 1977 Westminster Kennel Club show.

Pencil drawing by Gladys Ray of Ch. Bomshis Olletime Gorgeous and Town Halls Dragon Blossom, owned by Betty R. Winters, Walpole, Massachusetts.

Copa Swing to Ma Foo pictured under judge Georgina Lane at the 1976 Warrenton Kennel Club Show. Ma Foo was bred and is owned and handled by Coni Nickerson of Richmond, Virginia.

Above:
Jennifer Winship of Greenville, Mississippi did this marvelous water color of a Shih Tzu puppy during the "crysanthemum" stage.

Right, Top:
Artist Arne Besser's oil painting of Ch. Change of Kandu. This dog was bred in England by Mrs. I. Lorisson and imported by Gilbert S. Khan and Jorge N. Sanchez of Coral Gables, Florida.

Opposite:
A lovely portrait of Ch. Luv-Tzu Shazam, owned by Mary Marxen of Van Wert, Ohio.

Right, Bottom:
Am. Can. Ch. Bamboo Sassy Saboo, owned by Shirley Pearson. In September 1969 at his first point show he went Best of Breed and completed his American title with three majors.

Below:
Ch. Bobbie's Hunk I Dor I Do, handled by Dee Shepherd for owner Bobbie Franklin of Kansas City, Missouri.

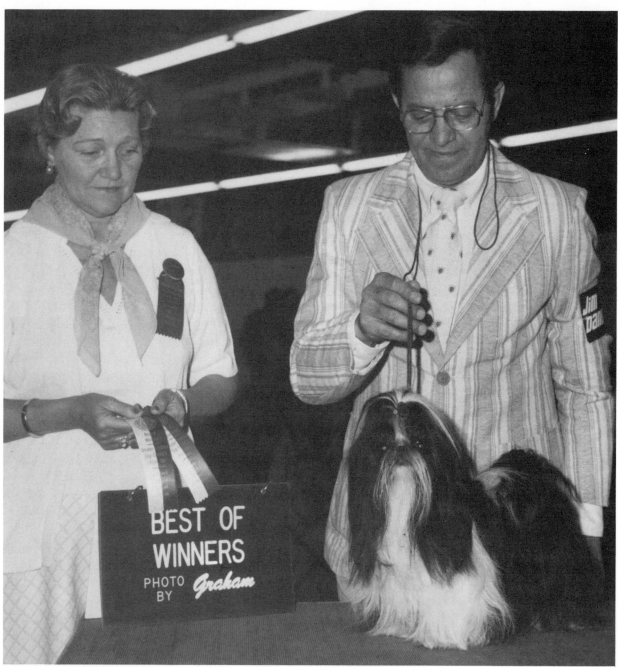

Ch. Whitethroat Shih T'sai, bred in England by Mrs. E.J. Fox. This lovely bitch finished for her championship in 1976 with four majors, three Bests of Breed over Specials and two group Fourths. She is pictured here winning a 4-point major as Best of Winners under judge Mrs. George Wanner. She is handled by Dr. Jorge Sanchez, who co-owns with Gilbert S. Kahn of Coral Gables, Florida.

Chapter 14
BREEDING YOUR SHIH TZU

Let us assume the time has come for your dog to be bred, and you have decided you are in a position to enjoy producing a litter of puppies that you hope will make a contribution to the breed. The bitch you purchased is sound, her temperament is excellent and she is a worthy repesentative of the breed.

You have taken a calendar and counted off the ten days since the first day of red staining and have determined the tenth to fourteenth day, which will more than likely be the best days for the actual mating. You have additionally counted off 60 to 65 days before the puppies are likely to be born to make sure everything necessary for their arrival will be in good order by that time.

From the moment the idea of having a litter occurred to you, your thoughts should have been given to the correct selection of a proper stud. Here again the novice would do well to seek advice on analyzing pedigrees and tracing bloodlines for the best breedings. As soon as the bitch is in season and you see color (or staining) and a swelling of the vulva, it is time to notify the owner of the stud you selected and make appointments for the breedings. There are several pertinent questions you will want to ask the stud owners after having decided upon their pedigree. The owners, naturally, will also have a few questions they wish to ask you. These questions will concern your bitch's bloodlines, health, age, how many previous litters if any, and the like.

THE HEALTH OF
THE BREEDING STOCK

Some of your first questions should concern whether or not the stud has already proved himself by siring a normal healthy litter. Inquire as to whether or not the owners have had a sperm count made to determine just exactly how fertile or potent the stud is. Determine for yourself whether the dog has two normal testicles.

When considering your bitch for this mating, you must take into consideration a few important points that lead to a successful breeding. You and the owner of the stud will want to recall whether she has had normal heat cycles, whether there were too many runts in the litter and whether

Caesarean section was ever necessary. Has she ever had a vaginal infection? Could she take care of her puppies by herself or was there a milk shortage? How many surviving puppies were there from the litter, and what did they grow up to be in comparison to the requirements of the breed Standard?

Don't buy a bitch that has problem heats and has never had a live litter, but don't be afraid to buy any healthy maiden bitch since chances are, if she is healthy and from good stock, she will be a healthy producer. Don't buy a monorchid male, and certainly not a cryptorchid. If there is any doubt in your mind about a stud's potency, get a sperm count from the veterinarian. Older dogs that have been good producers and are for sale are usually not too hard to find at good established kennels. If they are not too old and have sired quality show puppies, they can give you some excellent show stock from which to establish your own breeding lines.

WHEN TO BREED A GROWN BITCH

The best advice used to be to not breed a bitch until her second heat. Today with our new scientific knowledge we have become acutely aware of such things as hip dysplasia, juvenile cataracts and other congenital diseases. The best advice now seems to be not to breed before two years of age when both the bitch and the sire have been examined by qualified veterinarians and declared—in writing—free and clear of these conditions.

THE DAY OF THE MATING

Now that you have decided upon the proper male and female combination to produce what you hope will be, according to the pedigrees, a fine litter of puppies, it is time to set the date. You have selected the two days (with a one day lapse in between) that you feel are best for the breeding, and you called the owner of the stud. The bitch always goes to the stud, unless, of course, there are extenuating circumstances. You set the date and the time and arrive with the bitch *and* the money.

Standard procedure is payment of a stud fee at

Two adorable Shih Tzu puppies whelped in 1966 at Daniece Greggans' Kathway Shih Tzu Kennels in LaVerne Heights, California.

the time of the first breeding, if there is a tie. For a stud fee, you are entitled to two breedings with ties. Contracts may be written up with specific conditions on breeding terms, of course, but this is general procedure. Often a breeder will take the pick of a litter to protect and maintain his bloodlines. This can be especially desirable if he needs an outcross for his breeding program or if he wishes to continue his own bloodlines if he sold you the bitch to start with, and this mating will continue his line-breeding program. This should all be worked out ahead of time and written and signed before the two dogs are bred. Remember that the payment of the stud fee is for the services of the stud—not for a guarantee of a litter of puppies. This is why it is so important to make sure you are using a proven stud. Bear in mind also that the American Kennel Club will not register a litter of puppies sired by a male that is under eight months of age. In the case of an older dog, they will not register a litter sired by a dog over 12 years of age, unless there is a witness to the breeding in the form of a veterinarian or other responsible person.

Many studs over 12 years of age are still fertile and capable of producing puppies, but if you do not witness the breeding there is always the danger of a "substitute" stud being used to produce a litter. This brings up the subject of sending your bitch away to be bred if you cannot accompany her.

The disadvantages of sending a bitch away to be bred are numerous. First of all, she will not be herself in a strange place, so she'll be difficult to handle. Transportation by air, while reasonably safe, is still a traumatic experience, and there is

the danger of her being put off at the wrong airport, not being fed or watered properly, etc. Some bitches get so upset that they go out of season and the trip, which may prove expensive, especially on top of a substantial stud fee, will have been for nothing.

If at all possible, accompany your bitch so that the experience is as comfortable for her as it can be. In other words, make sure before setting this kind of schedule for a breeding that there is no stud in the area that might be as good for her as the one that is far away. Don't sacrifice the proper breeding for convenience, since bloodlines are so important, but put the safety of the bitch above all else. There is always a risk in traveling, since dogs are considered cargo on a plane.

HOW MUCH DOES
THE STUD FEE COST?

The stud fee will vary considerably—the better the bloodlines, the more winning the dog does at shows, the higher the fee. Stud service from a top winning dog could run up to $500.00. Here again, there may be exceptions. Some breeders will take part cash and then, say, third pick of the litter. The fee can be arranged by a private contract rather than the traditional procedure we have described.

It is wise to get the details of the payment of the stud fee in writing to avoid trouble.

Hullaballou 'n Briar Hill Too, otherwise known as "Louie," is co-owned by Jay and Linda Ballou of Tulsa, Oklahoma.

A marvelous group photo of the Shih Tzu belonging to members of the Twin City Area Shih Tzu Club in Minnesota. This charming photograph was submitted on behalf of the club by Betty Meidlinger, Mei San Shih Tzu, St. Paul.

THE ACTUAL MATING

It is always advisable to muzzle the bitch. A terrified bitch may out of fear bite the stud or even one of the people involved, and the wild or maiden bitch may snap or attack the stud, to the point where he may become discouraged and lose interest in the breeding. Muzzling can be done with a lady's stocking tied around the muzzle with a half knot, crossed under the chin and knotted at the back of the neck. There is enough "give" in the stocking for her to breathe or salivate freely and yet not open her jaws far enough to bite. The bitch should be placed in front of her owner, who holds onto her collar, talks to her and calms her as much as possible.

If the male will not mount on his own initiative, it may be necessary for the owner to assist in lifting him onto the bitch, perhaps even guiding him to the proper place. Usually, the tie is accomplished once the male gets the idea. The owner should remain close at hand, however, to make sure the tie is not broken before an adequate breeding has been completed. After a while the stud may get bored, and try to break away. This could prove injurious. It may be necessary to hold him in place until the tie is broken.

We must stress at this point that while some bitches carry on physically and vocally during the tie, there is no way the bitch can be hurt. However, a stud can be seriously or even permanently damaged by a bad breeding. Therefore, the owner of the bitch must not be alarmed by any commotion. All concentration should be devoted to the stud and properly executed service.

Many people believe that breeding dogs is simply a matter of placing two dogs, a male and a female, in close proximity, and letting nature take its course. While often this is true, you cannot count on it. Sometimes it is hard work, and in the case of valuable stock it is essential to supervise to be sure of the safety factor, especially if one or both of the dogs are inexperienced. If the owners are also inexperienced it may not take place at all!

ARTIFICIAL INSEMINATION

Breeding by means of artificial insemination is usually unsuccessful, unless under a veterinarian's supervision, and can lead to an infection for the bitch and discomfort for the dog. The American Kennel Club requires a veterinarian's certificate to register puppies from such a breeding. Although the practice has been used for over two decades, it now offers new promise, since research has been conducted to make it a more feasible procedure for the future.

Great dogs may eventually look forward to reproducing themselves years after they have left this earth. There now exists a frozen semen concept that has been tested and found successful. The study, headed by Dr. Stephen W.J. Seager, M.V.B., an instructor at the University of Oregon Medical School, has the financial support of the American Kennel Club, indicating that organization's interest in the work. The study is being monitored by the Morris Animal Foundation of Denver, Colorado.

Dr. Seager announced in 1970 that he had been able to preserve dog semen and to produce litters

247

with the stored semen. The possibilities of selective world-wide breedings by this method are exciting. Imagine simply mailing a vial of semen to the bitch! The perfection of line-breeding by storing semen without the threat of death interrupting the breeding program is exciting, also.

As it stands today, the technique for artificial insemination requires the depositing of semen (taken directly from the dog) into the bitch's vagina, past the cervix and into the uterus by syringe. The correct temperature of the semen is vital, and there is no guarantee of success. The storage method, if successfully adopted, will present a new era in the field of purebred dogs.

THE GESTATION PERIOD

Once the breeding has taken place successfully, the seemingly endless waiting period of about 63 days begins. For the first ten days after breeding, you do absolutely nothing for the bitch—just spin dreams about the delights you will share with the family when the puppies arrive.

Around the tenth day it is time to begin supplementing the diet of the bitch with vitamins and calcium. We strongly recommend that you take her to your veterinarian for a list of the necessary supplements and the correct amounts of each for your particular bitch. Guesswork, which may lead to excesses or insufficiencies, can ruin a litter. For the price of a visit to your veterinarian, you will be confident that you are properly feeding your bitch.

The bitch should be free of worms, of course, and if there is any doubt in your mind, she should be wormed before the third week of pregnancy. Your veterinarian will advise you on the necessity of this and proper dosage as well.

PROBING FOR PUPPIES

Far too many breeders are over-anxious about whether the breeding "took' and are inclined to feel for puppies or persuade a veterinarian to radiograph or X-ray their bitches to confirm it. Unless there is reason to doubt the normalcy of a pregnancy, this is risky. Certainly 63 days are not too long to wait, and why risk endangering the litter by probing with your inexperienced hands? Few bitches give no evidence of being in whelp, and there is no need to prove it for yourself by trying to count puppies.

ALERTING YOUR VETERINARIAN

At least a weak before the puppies are due, you should telephone your veterinarian and notify him that you expect the litter and give him the date. This way he can make sure that there will be

Tigher Tail of Shang T'ou pictured at 4½ months of age. Tigher was bred by Ruth Ragle, and owned by Eleanore Eldredge, Shang T'ou Kennels in Easton, Washington.

Int. Sc. Ch. In-Cheng, top-winning Shih Tzu dog in Sweden for 1975 and 1976. Bred by Rose Akersten of Stockholm, Sweden, he is owned by Mrs. Anita Carlsson, Horby, Sweden.

Int. Dutch, World, German, Belgian, Lux., Can., and Am. Ch. Quang-Te van de Blauwe Mammouth is shown winning a 4-point major under judge James W. Trullinger on the way to earning his American Championship.

Ch. Long's Hi Sacke Ah Chop-Chop, co-owned by L. Garrett Lambert and Joseph R. Repice, pictured handling him at the 1974 Queensboro Kennel Club show under judge Dr. Harry Smith.

someone available to help, should there be any problems during the whelping. Most veterinarians today have answering services and alternate vets on call when they are not available themselves. Some veterinarians suggest that you call them when the bitch starts to labor so that they may further plan their time, should they be needed. Discuss this matter with your veterinarian when you first take the bitch to him for her diet instructions, etc., and establish the method which will best fit in with his schedule.

DO YOU NEED A VETERINARIAN IN ATTENDANCE?

Even if this is your first litter, I would advise that you go through the experience of whelping without panicking and calling desperately for the veterinarian. Most animal births are accomplished without complications, and you should call for assistance only if you run into trouble.

When having her puppies, your bitch will appreciate as little interference and as few strangers around as possible. A quiet place, with her nest, a single familiar face and her own instincts are all that is necessary for nature to take its course. An audience of curious children squealing and questioning, other family pets or strange adults nosing around should be avoided. Many a bitch which has been distracted in this way have been known to devour their young. This can be the horrible result of intrusion into the bitch's privacy. There are other ways of teaching children the miracle of birth, and there will be plenty of time later for the whole family to enjoy the puppies. Let them be born under proper and considerate circumstances.

LABOR

Some litters—many first litters—do not run the full term of 63 days. So, at least a week before the puppies are actually due, and at the time you alert your veterinarian as to their arrival, start observing the bitch for signs of the commencement of labor. This will manifest itself in the form of ripples running down the sides of her body, which will come as a revelation to her as well. It is most noticeable when she is lying on her side—and she will be sleeping a great deal as the arrival date comes closer. If she is sitting or walking about, she will perhaps sit down quickly or squat peculiarly. As the ripples become more frequent, birth

Ch. House of Wu Hai-U, bred by Mrs. Charles R. Eckes and owned by Max Kerrfoot. Hai-U is shown going Best in Show.

time is drawing near; you will be wise not to leave her. Usually within 24 hours before whelping, she will stop eating, and as much as a week before she will begin digging a nest. The bitch should be given something resembling a whelping box with layers of newspaper (black and white only) to make her nest. She will dig more and more as birth approaches, and this is the time to begin making your promise to stop interfering unless your help is definitely required. Some bitches whimper and others are silent, but whimpering does not necessarily indicate trouble.

THE ARRIVAL OF THE PUPPIES

The sudden gush of green fluid from the bitch indicates that the water or fluid surrounding the puppies has "broken" and they are about to start down the canal and come into the world. When the water breaks, birth of the first puppy is imminent. The first puppies are usually born within minutes to a half hour of each other, but a couple of hours between the later ones is not uncommon. If you notice the bitch straining constantly without producing a puppy, or if a puppy remains partially out for too long, it is cause for concern. Breech births (puppies born feet first instead of head first) can often cause delay or hold things up, and this is often a problem which requires veterinarian assistance.

BREECH BIRTHS

Puppies are normally delivered head first. However, some are presented feet first, or in other abnormal positions, and this is referred to as a "breech birth." Assistance is often necessary to get the puppy out of the canal, and great care must be taken not to injure the puppy or the dam.

Aid can be given by grasping the puppy with a piece of turkish towelling and pulling gently during the dam's contractions. Be careful not to squeeze the puppy too hard; merely try to ease it out by moving it gently back and forth. Because even this much delay in delivery may mean the puppy is drowning, do not wait for the bitch to remove the sac. Do it yourself by tearing the sac open to expose the face and head. Then cut the cord anywhere from one-half to three-quarters of an inch away from the navel. If the cord bleeds excessively, pinch the end of it with your fingers and count to five. Repeat if necessary. Then pry open the mouth with your finger and hold the puppy upside-down for a moment to drain any fluids from the lungs. Next, rub the puppy briskly with turkish or paper towels. You should get it wriggling and whimpering by this time.

If the litter is large, this assistance will help to conserve the strength of the bitch and will probably be welcomed by her. However, it is best to allow her to take care of at least the first few

Mexican Ch. Mei Lu Ming So Tzu of Kathways, owned by Daniece Greggans of LaVerne Heights, California. "Si An" was the first American bitch in the breed to win a championship certificate. Here, she is winning at a 1965 Mexican show with handler Betty Francis.

herself to preserve the natural instinct and to provide the nutritive values obtained by her consumption of the one or more of the afterbirths as nature intended.

DRY BIRTHS

Occasionally the sac will break before the delivery of a puppy and will be expelled while the puppy remains inside, thereby depriving the dam of the necessary lubrication to expel the puppy normally. Inserting vaseline or mineral oil via your finger will help the puppy pass down the birth canal. This is why it is essential that you be present during the whelping—so that you can count puppies and afterbirths and determine when and if assistance is needed.

FEEDING THE BITCH AFTER WHELPING

Usually the bitch will not be interested in food as long as two or three days after the pups' arrival. The placenta which she cleans up after each puppy is high in food value and will be more than ample to sustain her. This is nature's way of allowing the mother to feed herself and her babies without having to leave the nest and hunt for food during the first crucial days. The mother always cleans up all traces of birth in the wilds so as not to attract other animals to her newborn babies.

However, there are those of us who believe in making food available should the mother feel the need to restore her strength during or after delivery—especially if she whelps a large litter. Raw chopped meat, beef bouillon and milk are all acceptable and may be placed near the whelping box during the first two or three days. After that, the mother will begin to put the babies on a sort of schedule. She will leave the whelping box at frequent intervals, take longer exercise periods and begin to take interest in other things. This is where the fun begins for you. Now the babies are no longer soggy little pinkish blobs. They begin to crawl around and squeal and hum and grow before your very eyes!

It is at this time, if all has gone normally, that the family can be introduced gradually and great praise and affection given to the mother.

THE TWENTY-FOUR HOUR CHECKUP

It is smart to have a veterinarian check the mother and the puppies within 24 hours after the last puppy is born. The vet can check the puppies for cleft palates or umbilical hernia and may wish to give the dam—particularly if she is a show dog—an injection of Pituitin to make sure of the expulsion of all afterbirths and to tighten up the

Ch. Mei San Saki Tuo Mee Babe and Ch. Greenmoss Jezebel, the black and white, are pictured after winning a recent show. They are owned by Betty Meidlinger, Mei San Shih Tzu, St. Paul, Minnesota.

uterus. This can prevent a sagging belly after the puppies are weaned and the bitch is being readied for the show ring.

FALSE PREGNANCY

The disappointment of a false pregnancy is almost as bad for the owner as it is for the bitch. She goes through the gestation period with all the symptoms—swollen stomach, increased appetite, swollen nipples—even makes a nest when the time comes. You may even take an oath that you noticed the ripples on her body from the labor pains. Then, just as suddenly as you have made up your mind that she was definitely going to have puppies, you will know that she definitely is not! She may walk around carrying a toy as if it were a puppy for a few days, but she will soon be back to normal and acting just as if nothing happened—and nothing did!

CAESAREAN SECTION

Should the whelping reach the point where there is complication, such as the bitch's not being able to whelp the puppies herself, the "moment of truth" is upon you, and a Caesarean section may be necessary. The bitch may be too small or too immature to expel the puppies herself; her cervix may fail to dilate enough to allow the young to come down the birth canal. In some cases there may be torsion of the uterus, a dead or monster puppy, a sideways puppy blocking the canal or perhaps toxemia. A Caesarean section

251

Ch. Floridonna Lucky Seven, shown winning with handler Wendell J. Sammet at the 1976 Chagrin Valley Kennel Club show under judge Tory Lankenan. The sire was Ch. Chumulari Ying Ying ex Ch. Floridonna Sexa Peal. Sandra P. Adshead of East Greenwich, Rhode Island is the owner.

Two typical 10 week old gold and white puppies, both illustrating the desired "chrysanthemum" look at its best.

Sitting pretty: Chumulari Phola photographed at 12 years of age on February 23, 1977. Dam of many champions, including Canadian and American Ch. Willows Golden Fleece, sire of Chumulari Tai Tai, owned by Joan Brearley.

Ono-Ne-Ko-Pi, Tee-Nee Ne-Ko-Pie and Tee-Nee MiTu Ne Ko Pi Tulee, whelped in 1975 and bred by the Jack Scardinos and the Van Wormers in Milwaukee, Wisconsin.

Ch. Elfann Golden Sunmaiden, owned by Del and Connie Smart of Akron, Ohio. Sunmaiden is part of the breeding program at the Smarts' Conwynn Shih Tzu kennels.

Ch. Echodale Flower Power poses with her first litter of Shih Tzu puppies sired by Am. Can. Bda. Ch. Carrimount Ah-Tiko-Tiko. The owners are Katherine and Michael Mooney Jr., of Bethel Park, Penn. Photo by Marie O'Hanlon.

Just eight days old! The white blaze on the forehead and paws, highly prized in China, are clearly evident, while the "chrysanthemum look" is just beginning to fill in around the nose. Shih Tzu puppies weigh from two to four ounces at birth.

This pair of five month old puppies from the Chumulari Kennels illustrate the need, even at this young age, for a top knot to keep the hair out of the pup's eyes.

Chumulari Ying Su and her mistress, Gail Marcus of Manhattan. Ying Su and Gail were featured in a special story in *Life* magazine in July, 1969.

Ch. Gem's Leonardo de Visconti, owned by Barbara Johnson, is pictured winning at a 1976 show with handler Jean Lade. Breeder was Jon C. Ferante.

Ch. Bomshu Born Flee is being shown by Jan Zervoulis, who co-owns with Bill Zervoulis. Judging at this Westchester Kennel Club show was Irene K. Schlintz. Whelped in January, 1974, the sire was Ch. Lakoya Momotaro Asian Peach ex Ch. Imperial Ping Tan. Born Flee attained his championship shortly after this important win.

Ginger Schedlbauer with Imua's Wicked Wahine and Imua's Guava Jam. These four month old puppies were sired by Ch. Loto's Panda Bear of Nanjo ex Ch. Nanjo's Haiku Dragon Bear.

254

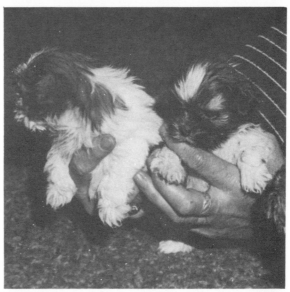

Ch. Mariljac Joey of Jubilation, bred by Mary Wood and owned by Garrett R. Crissman. Co-owned and handled by Linda A. Miller of Belton, Missouri. The sire was Best in Show Ch. Mariljac Maripet ex Ch. Mariljac Tinkertown Toi.

Typical six week old parti-color Shih Tzu puppies bred by Edythe Kennedy of Barnstable, Massachusetts.

Ch. Hodari Fuchsia Lin pictured winning Best of Breed at the 1976 Terry-All Kennel Club show. Handling for owners Laurie Battey and Helen McClarnon is Madeline Thornton. The judge was C.L. Savage. Fuchsia finished her championship in less than a month.

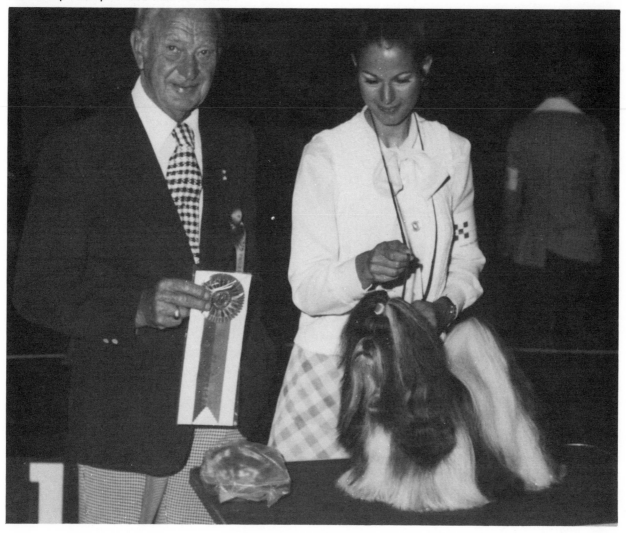

will be the only solution. No matter what the cause, get the bitch to the veterinarian immediately to insure your chances of saving the mother and/or the puppies.

The Caesarean section operation involves the removal of the unborn young from the uterus of the dam by surgical incision into the walls through the abdomen. The operation is performed when it has been determined that for some reason the puppies cannot be delivered normally. While modern surgical methods have made the operation itself reasonably safe, with the dam being perfectly capable of nursing the puppies shortly after the completion of the surgery, the chief danger lies in the ability to spark life into the puppies immediately upon their removal from the womb. If the mother dies, the time element is even more important in saving the young, since the oxygen supply ceases upon the death of the dam, and the difference between life and death is measured in seconds.

After surgery, when the bitch is home in her whelping box with the babies, she will probably nurse the young without distress. You must be sure that the sutures are kept clean and that no redness or swelling or ooze appears in the wound. Healing will take place naturally, and no salves or ointments should be applied unless prescribed by the veterinarian, for fear the puppies will get it into their systems. If there is any doubt, check the bitch for fever, restlessness (other than the natural concern for her young) or a lack of appetite, but do not anticipate trouble.

EPISIOTOMY

Even though most dogs are generally easy whelpers, any number of reasons might occur to cause the bitch to have a difficult birth. Before automatically resorting to Caesarean section, many veterinarians are now trying the technique known as episiotomy.

Used rather frequently in human deliveries, episiotomy (pronounced A-PEASE-E-*OTT*-O-ME) is the cutting of the membrane between the rear opening of the vagina back almost to the opening of the anus. After delivery it is stitched together, and barring complications, heals easily, presenting no problem in future births.

SOCIALIZING YOUR PUPPY

The need for puppies to get out among other animals and people cannot be stressed enough. Kennel-reared dogs are subject to all sorts of idiosyncrasies and seldom make good house dogs or normal members of the world around them when they grow up.

Pretty Posh of Shang T'ou, bred by Eleanore Eldredge, is owner-handled by Charmalee Cookingham of West Linn, Oregon. Judging for this Group win was Beulah Koontz at a 1973 Fun Match.

Absom Tashi is described by his owners as bright, merry and beautiful! Whelped in December of 1972, this darling white and gold is owned by Dr. and Mrs. H. Michelson of Paterson, New Jersey.

The crucial age, which determines the personality and general behavior patterns which will predominate during the rest of the dog's life, are formed between the ages of three and ten weeks. This is particularly true during the 21st to 28th day. It is essential that the puppy be socialized during this time by bringing him into family life as much as possible. Walking on floor surfaces, indoor and outdoor, should be experienced; handling by all members of the family and visitors is important; preliminary grooming gets him used to a lifelong necessity; light training, such as setting him up on tables and cleaning teeth and ears and cutting nails, etc., has to be started early if he is to become a show dog. The puppy should be ex-

Dashi's My My, bred and handled by Catherine F. Pouliot and co-owned by her and Mary K. Dullinger.

posed to car riding, shopping tours, a leash around its neck, children—your own and others—and in all possible ways the pup should develop relationships with humans.

It is up to the breeder, of course, to protect the puppy from harm or injury during this initiation into the outside world. The benefits reaped from proper attention will pay off in the long run with a well-behaved, well-adjusted grown dog capable of becoming an integral part of a happy family.

REARING THE FAMILY

Needless to say, even with a small litter there will be certain considerations which must be adhered to in order to secure successful rearing of the puppies. For instance, the diet for the mother should be appropriately increased as the puppies grow and take more and more nourishment from her. During the first few days of rest while the bitch just looks over her puppies and regains her strength, she should be left pretty much alone. It is during these first days that she begins to put the puppies on a feeding schedule and feels safe enough about them to leave the whelping box long enough to take a little extended exercise.

It is cruel, however, to try to keep the mother away from the puppies any longer than she wants to be because you feel she is being too attentive or to give the neighbors a chance to peek in at the puppies. The mother should not have to worry about harm coming to her puppies for the first few weeks. The veterinary checkup will be enough of an experience for her to have to endure until she is more like herself once again.

EVALUATING THE LITTER

A show puppy prospect should be outgoing, (probably the first one to fall out of the whelping box!) and all efforts should be made to socialize the puppy which appears to be the most shy. Once the puppies are about three weeks old, they can and should be handled a great deal by friends and members of the family.

The crucial period in a puppy's life occurs when the puppy is from 21 to 28 days old, so all the time you can devote to him at this time will reap rewards later on in life. This is the age when several other important steps must be taken in a puppy's life. Weaning should start if it hasn't already, and it is time to check for worms. Do not worm unnecessarily. A veterinarian should advise on worming and appropriate dosage and can also discuss with you at this time the schedule for serum or vaccination, which will depend on the size of the puppies as well as their age.

Exercise and grooming should be started at this time, with special care and consideration given to the diet. You will find that the dam will help you wean the puppies, leaving them alone more and more as she notices that they are eating well on their own. Begin by leaving them with her during the night for comfort and warmth; eventually, when she shows less interest, keep them separated entirely.

By the time the fifth week of their lives arrives you will already be in love with every one of them and desperately searching for reasons to keep them all. They recognize you—which really gets to you—and they box and chew on each other and try to eat your finger and perform a million other captivating antics which are special with puppies. Their stomachs seem to be bottomless pits, and their weight will rise steadily. At eight to ten weeks, the puppies will be weaned and ready to go.

SPAYING AND CASTRATING

A wise old philospher once said, "Timing in life is everything." No statement could apply more readily to the age-old question which every dog owner is faced with sooner or later . . . to spay or not to spay.

For the one-bitch pet owner, spaying is the most logical answer, for it solves many problems. The pet is usually not of top breeding quality, and therefore there is no great loss to the bloodline; it takes the pressure off the family if the dog runs free with children and certainly eliminates the

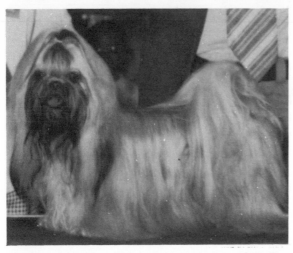

Ki Lin of Chasmu, who was whelped in 1970. The breeder was Mrs. Audrey Fowler of London, England. The sire was Cherholmes Garson of Chasmu ex Mara of Chasmu. Owners: Camille Beranti and Marie Beranti of Bethpage, New York.

Lingchoo Woochin, a C.D. owned by Shirley L. Arnold of Masillon, Ohio.

Ch. Mistybank Ouzo v Zervlistan, bred by M.E. Banga and owned by Janine R. Zervoulis. Whelped in 1973, Ouzo is pictured at 5 months of age. Photo by Bill Zervoulis.

problem of repeated litters of unwanted puppies or a backyard full of eager males twice a year.

But for the owner or breeder, the extra time and protection which must be afforded a purebred quality bitch can be most worthwhile—even if it is only until a single litter is produced after the first heat. It is then not too late to spay, the progeny can perpetuate the bloodline, the bitch will have been fulfilled—though it is merely an old wives' tale that bitches should have at least one litter to be "normal"—and she may then be retired to her deserved role as family pet once again.

With spaying the problem of staining and unusual behavior around the house is eliminated, as is the necessity of having to keep her in "pants" or administering pills, sprays or shots . . . which most veterinarians do not approve of anyway.

In the case of males, castration is seldom contemplated, which to me is highly regrettable. The owner of the male dog merely overlooks the dog's ability to populate an entire neighborhood, since they do not have the responsibility of rearing and disposing of the puppies. When you take into consideration all the many females the male dog can impregnate it is almost more essential that the males be taken out of circulation than that the female be. The male dog will still be inclined to roam but will be less frantic about leaving the grounds, and you will find that a lot of the wanderlust has left him.

STERILIZING FOR HEALTH

When considering the problem of spaying or castrating, the first consideration after the population explosion should actually be the health of the dog or bitch. Males are frequently subject to urinary disease, and sometimes castration is a help. Your veterinarian can best advise you on this problem. Another aspect to consider is the kennel dog which is no longer being used at stud. It is unfair to keep him in a kennel with females in heat when there is no chance for him to be used. There are other more personal considerations for both kennel and one-dog owners, but when making the decision remember that it is final. You can always spay or castrate, but once the deed is done there is no return.

San Yen-Won Wei tang, owned by Susan D. Barr, San Yen Shih Tzu, Salt Lake City, Utah.

Canadian Champion Chumulari Sheng-Li Che, gold and white dog photographed at seven months of age. Bred and owned by the Eastons. The sire was Ch. Chumulari Ying Ying ex Chumulari Trari.

Winner of a Utility Group at the 1969 Ladies Kennel Association show in England was Mr. and Mrs. K.B. Rawling's Ch. Fleeting Yu-Sing of Antarctica.

Ch. Lainee X-Tra Amorous, whelped in May, 1975. Breeder was Elaine Meltzer of New York. She is co-owned by Ms. Meltzer and Pat Gresham. The sire was Ch. Jaisu Ling-Ho X-Rated of Lainee ex Ch. Heavenly Dynasty's Olivia.

Chapter 15
FEEDING AND NUTRITION

FEEDING PUPPIES

There are many diets today for young puppies, including all sorts of products on the market for feeding the newborn, for supplementing the feeding of the young and for adding this or that to diets, depending on what is lacking in the way of a complete diet.

When weaning puppies, it is necessary to put them on four meals a day, even while you are tapering off with the mother's milk. Feeding at six in the morning, noontime, six in the evening and midnight is about the best schedule, since it fits in with most human eating plans. Meals for the puppies can be prepared immediately before or after your own meals, without too much of a change in your own schedule.

6 A.M.

Two meat and two milk meals serve best and should be served alternately, of course. Assuming the 6 A.M. feeding is a milk meal, the contents should be as follows: Goat's milk is the very best milk to feed puppies but is expensive and usually available only at drug stores, unless you live in farm country where it could be readily available fresh and still less expensive. If goat's milk is not available, use evaporated milk (powdered milk can be substituted later on), diluted two parts evaporated milk and one part water, along with raw egg yolk, honey or Karo syrup, sprinkled with high-protein baby cereal and some wheat germ. As the puppies mature, cottage cheese may be added or, at one of the two milk meals, it can be substituted for the cereal.

NOONTIME

A puppy chow which has been soaked in warm water or beef broth according to the time specified on the wrapper should be mixed with raw or simmered chopped meat in equal proportions with vitamin powder added.

6 P.M.

Repeat the milk meal—perhaps varying the type of cereal from wheat to oats, corn or rice.

MIDNIGHT

Repeat the meat meal. If raw meat was fed at noon, the evening meal might be simmered.

Please note that specific proportions on this suggested diet are not given. However, it's safe to say that the most important ingredients are the milk and cereal, and the meat and puppy chow which forms the basis of the diet. Your veterinarian can advise on the portion sizes if there is any doubt in your mind as to how much to use.

If you notice that the puppies are cleaning their plates you are perhaps not feeding enough to keep up with their rate of growth. Increase the amount at the next feeding. Observe them closely; puppies should each "have their fill," because growth is very rapid at this age. If they have not satisfied themselves, increase the amount so that they do not have to fight for the last morsel. They will not overeat if they know there is enough food available. Instinct will usually let them eat to suit their normal capacity.

If there is any doubt in your mind as to any ingredient you are feeding, ask yourself, "Would I give it to my own baby?" If the answer is no, then don't give it to your puppies. At this age, the comparison between puppies and human babies can be a good guide.

If there is any doubt at all in your mind, ask your veterinarian to be sure.

Many puppies will regurgitate their food, perhaps a couple of times, before they manage to retain it. If they do bring up their food, allow them to eat it again, rather than clean it away. Sometimes additional saliva is necessary for them to digest it, and you do not want them to skip a meal just because it is an unpleasant sight for you to observe.

This same regurgitation process holds true sometimes with the bitch, who will bring up her own food for her puppies every now and then. This is a natural instinct on her part which stems from the days when dogs were giving birth in the wilds. The only food the mother could provide at weaning time was too rough and indigestible for her puppies. Therefore, she took it upon herself to pre-digest the food until it could be taken and retained by her young. Bitches today will sometimes resort to this, especially bitches which love having litters and have a strong maternal instinct.

Canadian Ch. Kalidan Sang Chun Tse, bred, owned and handled by Elaine Mawson, is pictured winning under judge John Devlin, Jr. at a recent Canadian show. On the right is Chumulari Ai Jen, bred and owned by the Eastons, and handled by Ray Gaudet. Chun Tse's sire was American and Canadian Ch. Chumulari Ying Ying ex Ch. Filicia's Chin Te Nu Shen. Ai Jen's sire was American and Canadian Ch. Willows the Golden Fleece ex Canadian Ch. Chumulari Pao Mu.

Some dams will help you wean their litters and even give up feeding entirely once they see you are taking over.

ORPHANED PUPPIES

The ideal solution to feeding orphaned puppies is to be able to put them with another nursing dam who will take them on as her own. If this is not possible within your own kennel, or a kennel that you know of, it is up to you to care for and feed the puppies. Survival is possible but requires a great deal of time and effort on your part.

Your substitute formula must be precisely prepared, always served heated to body temperature and refrigerated when not being fed. Esbilac, a vacuum-packed powder, with complete feeding instructions on the can, is excellent and about as close to mother's milk as you can get. If you can't get Esbilac, or until you do get Esbilac, there are two alternative formulas that you might use.

Mix one part boiled water with five parts of evaporated milk and add one teaspoonful of dicalcium phosphate per quart of formula. Dicalcium phosphate can be secured at any drug store. If they have it in tablet form only, you can powder the tablets with the back part of a tablespoon. The other formula for newborn puppies is a combination of eight ounces of homogenized milk mixed well with two egg yolks.

You will need baby bottles with three-hole nipples. Sometimes doll bottles can be used for the newborn puppies, which should be fed at six-hour intervals. If they are consuming sufficient amounts, their stomachs should look full, or slightly enlarged, though never distended. The amount of formula to be fed is proportionate to the size, age, growth and weight of the puppy, and is indicated on the can of Esbilac or on the advice of your veterinarian. Many breeders like to keep a baby scale nearby to check the puppies' weights to be sure they are thriving on the formula.

At two to three weeks you can start adding Pablum or some other high protein baby cereal to the formula. Also, baby beef can be licked from your finger at this age, or added to the formula. At four weeks the surviving puppies should be taken off the diet of Esbilac and put on a more substantial diet, such as wet puppy meal or chopped

Shih Tzu figurine sculptured by Gini Evans, and photographed by her daughter, Sandra Sunner.

Nanjo Cinder-Ella of Largyn, owned by Joan E. Cowie of Kimberton, Pennsylvania. The sire was Ch. Lotos Panda Bear of Nanjo ex Ch. Nanjo Pings Patticake. Ella is pictured here winning Best of Winners on the way to championship under judge Anne Rogers Clark at a recent show.

Mrs. Aasta Hellisen Finstad, depicted in an oil painting with her first Shih Tzu, Bijou, whelped in 1934. The artist was Gerda Knudsen. Photo by Arne Laakso.

Ch. Willows Dan Di Lion, bred and owned by Consuelo Bolsaks, Redding, California. The sire of several champions, "Dan Di" is handled to this win under judge Winifred Nishimura by Lois Frank.

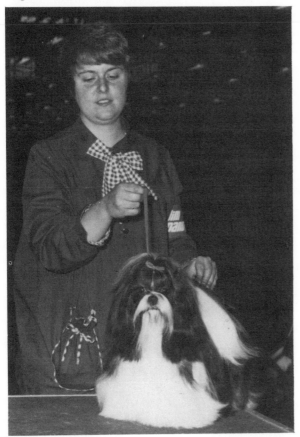

This litter of six week old puppies was whelped in November, 1976, and photographed by Bill Zervoulis. The sire was Ch. Moon Ling's Wu Tai Shan ex Bomshu Mei Kou.

Sleeping it off at Dino's Shih Tzu Kennels in Milwaukee, Wisconsin.

beef. However, Esbilac powder can still be mixed in with the food for additional nutrition. The jarred baby foods of pureed meats make for a smooth change over also, and can be blended into the diet.

HOW TO FEED THE NEWBORN PUPPIES

When the puppy is a newborn, remember that it is vitally important to keep the feeding procedure as close to the natural mother's routine as possible. The newborn puppy should be held in your lap in your hand in an almost upright position with the bottle at an angle to allow the entire nipple area to be full of the formula. Do not hold the bottle upright so the puppy's head has to reach straight up toward the ceiling. Do not let the puppy nurse too quickly or take in too much air and

possibly get the colic. Once in a while, take the bottle away and let him rest awhile and swallow several times. Before feeding, test the nipple to see that the fluid does not come out too quickly, or by the same token, too slowly so that the puppy gets tired of feeding before he has had enough to eat.

When the puppy is a little older, you can place him on his stomach on a towel to eat, and even allow him to hold on to the bottle or to "come and get it" on his own. Most puppies enjoy eating and this will be a good indication of how strong an appetite he has and his ability to consume the contents of the bottle.

It will be necessary to "burp" the puppy. Place a towel on your shoulder and hold the puppy there as if it were a human baby, patting and rubbing it gently. This will also encourage the puppy to defecate. At this time, you should observe for diarrhea or other intestinal disorders. The puppy should eliminate after each feeding with occasional eliminations between times as well. If the puppies do not eliminate on their own after each meal, massage their stomachs and under their tails gently until they do.

You must keep the puppies clean. If there is diarrhea or if they bring up a little formula, they should be washed and dried off. Under no circumstances should fecal matter be allowed to collect on their skin or fur.

All this—plus your determination and perseverance—might save an entire litter of puppies that would otherwise have died without their real mother.

Ch. Sikiang Jody's Tidbie Toodle, owned by Jody, Gloria and Louis Lieberman of Valley Stream, N.Y.

To Te Mei's Gatsby's Gad-A-Bout pictured at 8½ months of age winning the Toy Group at the Foothill Dog Fanciers Show under judge June Young. Bred and owned by Irene Caty of Glendora, California.

Tina in a tree! Jennifer Murphy's Hsi Jenni Tu, a bitch of Mariljac breeding is shown occupying one of her favorite resting places in her backyard in Jacksonville, Florida. This charming photo is by Gene Sukovich.

Chapter 16
THE BLIGHT OF PARASITES

Anyone who has ever spent hours peering intently at their dog's warm, pink stomach waiting for a flea to appear will readily understand why we call this chapter the "blight of parasites." It is that dreaded onslaught of the pesky flea that heralds the subsequent arrival of worms.

If you have seen even one flea scoot across that vulnerable expanse of skin, you can be sure that there are more lurking on other areas of your dog. They seldom travel alone. So, it is now an established fact that *la puce*, as the French refer to the flea, has set up housekeeping on your dog! It is going to demand a great deal of your time before you manage to evict them—probably just temporarily at that—no matter which species your dog is harboring.

Fleas are not always choosy about their host, but chances are your dog has what is commonly known as *Ctenocephalides canis*, the dog flea. If you are a lover of cats also, your dog might even be playing host to a few *Ctenocephalides felis*, the cat flea, or vice versa! The only thing you can be really sure of is that your dog is supporting an entire community of them, all hungry and sexually oriented, and you are going to have to be persistent in your campaign to get rid of them.

One of the chief reasons fleas are so difficult to catch is that what they lack in beauty and eyesight (they are blind at birth, throughout infancy, and see very poorly if at all during adulthood), they make up for in their fantastic ability to jump and scurry about.

While this remarkable ability to jump—some claim 150 times the length of their bodies—stands them in good stead with circus entrepreneurs and has given them claim to fame as chariot pullers and acrobats in side show attractions, the dog owner can be reduced to tears at the very thought of the onset of fleas.

Modern research has provided a panacea in the form of flea sprays, dips, collars and tags which can be successful to varying degrees. However, there are those who still swear by the good old-fashioned methods of removing them by hand, which can be a challenge to your sanity as well as your dexterity.

Since the fleas' conformation (they are built like envelopes, long and flat), with their spiny skeletal systems on the outside of their bodies, is specifically provided for slithering through forests of hair, they are given a distinct advantage to start with. Two antennae on the head select the best spot for digging and then two mandibles penetrate the skin and hit a blood vessel. It is also at this moment that the flea brings into play his spiny contours to prop himself against surrounding hairs to avoid being scratched off as he puts the bite on your dog. A small projecting tube is then lowered into the hole to draw out blood and another tube pumps saliva into the wound; this prevents the blood from clotting and allows the flea to drink freely. Simultaneously, your dog jumps into the air and gets one of those back legs into action, scratching endlessly and in vain, and sometimes ruining some coat at the same time!

You might be so lucky as to occasionally catch an itinerant flea as it mistakenly shortcuts across your dog's stomach, but the best hunting grounds in the world are actually in the deep fur all along the dog's back from neck to tail. However, the flea, like every other creature on earth, must have water, so several times during its residency it will make its way to the moister areas of your dog's anatomy such as the corners of the mouth, the eyes or the genital parts. This is when the flea collars and tags are useful. Their fumes prevent fleas from passing the neck to get to your dog's head.

Your dog can usually support several generations of fleas, if it doesn't scratch itself to death or go out of its mind in the interim. The propagation of the flea is insured by the strong mating instinct and the well-judged decision of the female flea as to the best time to deposit her eggs. She has the rare capacity to store semen until the time is right to lay the eggs after some previous brief encounter with a passing member of the opposite sex.

When that time comes for her to lay her eggs, she does so without so much as a backward glance and moves on. The dog shakes the eggs off during a normal day's wandering, and they remain on the ground until hatched and the baby fleas are ready to jump back onto a passing dog. If any of the eggs have remained on the original dog, chances are that in scratching an adult flea, he will help

House of Wu Jade Doll, breeder owned by Mrs. Charles R. Eckes, House of Wu Kennels, Denver, Colorado.

the baby fleas emerge from their shells.

Larval fleas are small and resemble slender maggots; they begin their lives eating their own shells until the dog comes along and offers them a return to the world of adult fleas, whose excrement provides the predigested blood pellets they must have to thrive. They cannot survive on fresh blood, nor are they capable at this tender age of digging for it themselves.

After a couple of weeks of this freeloading, the baby flea makes his own cocoon and becomes a pupa. This stage lasts long enough for the larval flea to grow legs, mandibles and sharp spines and to flatten out and in general become identifiable as the commonly known and obnoxious *Ctenocepha-*

lides canis. The process can take several weeks or several months, depending on weather conditions, heat, moisture, etc., but generally three weeks is all that is required to enable the flea to start gnawing your dog in its own right.

And so the life-cycle of the flea is renewed and begun again. If you don't have a plan to stem the tide, you will certainly see a population explosion. Getting rid of fleas can be accomplished by the aforementioned spraying of the dog, or the flea collars and tags, but air, sunshine, and a good shaking out of beds, bedding, carpets, cushions, etc., certainly must be undertaken to get rid of the eggs or larvae lying around the premises.

However, if you love the thrill of the chase, and

268

have the stomach for it, you can still try to catch them on safari across your dog's stomach. Your dog will love the attention, that is, if you don't keep pinching a bit of skin instead of that little blackish critter. Chances are great you will come up with skin rather than the flea and your dog will lose interest and patience.

Should you be lucky enough to get hold of one, you must either squeeze it to death, (which isn't likely) or break it in two with a sharp, strong fingernail (which also isn't likely) or you must release it *underwater* in the toilet bowl and flush immediately. This prospect is only slightly more likely.

There are those dog owners, however, who are much more philosophical about the flea, since, like the cockroach, it has been around since the beginning of the world. For instance, that old-time philosopher, David Harum, has been much quoted with his remark, "A reasonable amount of fleas is good for a dog. They keep him from broodin' on bein' a dog." We would rather agree with John Donne who in his *Devotions* reveals that "The flea, though he kill none, he does all the harm he can." This is especially true if your dog is a show dog! If the scratching doesn't ruin the coat, the inevitable infestation of parasites left by the fleas will!

We readily see that dogs can be afflicted by both internal and external parasites. The external parasites are known as the aforementioned fleas, plus ticks and lice; while all of the these are bothersome, they can be treated. However, the internal parasites, or worms of various kinds, are usually well-infested before discovery and require more substantial means of ridding the dog of them completely.

INTERNAL PARASITES

The most common worms are the round worms. These, like many other worms, are carried and spread by the flea and go through a life cycle within the dog host. They are excreted in egg or larval form and passed on to the dog in this manner.

Worm medicine should be prescribed by a veterinarian, and dogs should be checked for worms at least twice a year, every three months if there is a known epidemic in your area, and during the summer months when fleas are plentiful.

The prevalent worms are hookworms, whipworms, tapeworms (the only non-round worms in this list), ascarids (the "typical" round worms), heartworms, kidney and lung worms. Each can be peculiar to a part of the country or may be carried by a dog from one area to another. Kidney and

Mr. Bojangles, co-owned by Mrs. Julia Brown and Mable Cowgill of Pinconning, Michigan.

Ch. Gin Doc's Suzy of Shanguish, owned by Inez O'Brien of Findley, Ohio. Dorothy J. White handled Suzy to this Best of Breed win.

lung worms are fortunately quite rare; the others are not. Some symptoms of worm infestation are: vomiting intermittently, the eating of grass, lack of pep, bloated stomach, rubbing the tail along the ground, loss of weight, dull coat, anemia and pale gums, eye discharge, or unexplained nervousness and irritability. Also, a dog with worms will usually eat twice as much as he normally would.

Never administer worm medications to a sick dog, or to a pregnant bitch within two weeks of her mating. Too, never worm a constipated dog, as it will retain the strong medicine within the body for too long a time.

HOW TO TEST FOR WORMS

Worms can kill your dog, if the infestation is severe enough. Even light infestations of worms can debilitate a dog to the point where he is more susceptible to other serious diseases that can kill, if the worms do not.

Today's medication for worming is relatively safe and mild, and worming is no longer the traumatic experience for either the dog or owner, that it used to be. Great care must be given, however, to the proper administration of the drugs. Correct dosage is a "must" and clean quarters are essential to rid your kennel of these parasites. It is almost impossible to find an animal that is completely free of parasites, so we must consider worming as a necessary evil.

However mild today's medicines may be, it is inadvisable to worm a dog unnecessarily. There are simple tests to determine the presence of worms and this chapter is designed to help you learn how to make these tests yourself. Veterinarians charge a nominal fee for this service, if it is not part of their regular office visit examination. It is a simple matter to prepare fecal slides that you can read yourself on a periodic basis. Over the years it will save you much time and money, especially if you have more than one dog or a large kennel.

All that is needed by way of equipment is a microscope with 100X power. These can be purchased in a toy store or in the toy department of a department store for a few dollars. The basic, least expensive sets come with the necessary glass slides and attachments.

After the dog has defecated, take an applicator stick, a toothpick with a flat end or even an old-fashioned wooden matchstick and gouge off a piece of the stool about the size of a small pea. Have one of the glass slides ready with a large drop of water on it. Mix the two together until you have a cloudy film over a large area of the slide. This smear should be covered with another slide or a cover slip—though it is possible to obtain readings with just an open slide. Place your slide under the microscope and prepare to focus in on it. To read the slide you will find that your eye should follow a certain pattern. Start at the top and read from left to right, then right back to the left and then left over to the right side once again until you have looked at every portion of the slide from the top left to the bottom right side.

Make sure that your smear is not too thick or watery or the reading will be too dark and confused to make proper identification. If you decide you would rather not make your own fecal examinations, but would prefer to have the veteri-

A family of Shih Tzu lovers: the Raineys from Pensacola, Florida. Captain Gary Rainey, wife Shirlee, and son, David with Shir-Lee's Miss Muffet.

Ch. Wenrick's Sweet Jai Son, handled by breeder-owner Richard Paquette, Wenrick Kennels, Ontario, Canada. American judge Jay Schaeffere awarded the Best in Show win at the June 1976 Club VI Specialty Show.

narian do it, the proper way to present a segment of the stool for him to examine is as follows:

After the dog has defecated, a portion of the stool, say a square inch from different sections of it, should be placed in a glass jar or plastic container and labeled with the dog's name and the address of the owner. If the sample cannot be examined within three or four hours after passage, it should be refrigerated. Your opinions as to what variety of worms you suspect is sometimes helpful to the veterinarian and may be noted on the label of the jar you submit to him for the examination.

Checking for worms on a regular basis is advisable not only for the welfare of the dog but for the protection of your family, since most worms are transmissible, under certain circumstances, to humans.

Best Brace at the 1977 American Shih Tzu Club Specialty Show under judge Edd Bivin were China Chimes Jasmine N Jade and China Chimes Changsha Charm. Owner-handled by Kathryn L. Heilman of Fayetteville, North Carolina and co-owned by her mother, Irene E. Strapp.

Best in Show winner Champion House of Wu Hai-U, owned by Max Kerrfoot of Denver, Colorado. This multiple group, Best in Show and Specialty winner is owner-handled.

Ch. Gin Doc's Champagne Lady, a Best in Show winner at 17 months. Owned by Gini Evans of Bethel Park, Pennsylvania, the sire was Ch. Winemaker's Pla Boi ex Ch. Gin Doc's Suzy Wong.

Chapter 17
YOUR DOG, YOUR VETERINARIAN, AND YOU

The purpose of this chapter is to explain why you should never attempt to be your own veterinarian. Quite the contrary, we urge emphatically that you establish good liason with a reputable veterinarian who will help you maintain happy, healthy dogs. Our purpose is to bring you up to date on the discoveries made in modern canine medicine and help you work with your veterinarian by applying these new developments to your own animals.

We are providing in this chapter brief descriptions of many common conditions and accidental injuries that may occur to your dog. We feel that in such instances where treatment or first aid is warranted, the more prior knowledge you have, the better for your dog. Also, your part in first aid procedures gives the veterinarian all the more advantage when the dog then goes to him for complete attention to the problem.

Today's dog owner is a realistic, intelligent person who learns more and more about his dog—inside and out—so that he can care for and enjoy the animal to the fullest. He uses technical terms for parts of the anatomy, has a fleeting knowledge of the miracles of surgery and is fully prepared to administer clinical care to his animals at home. This chapter is designed for study and/or reference and we hope you will use it to full advantage.

We repeat, we do *not* advocate your playing "doctor." This includes administering medications without veterinary supervision, or even doing your own inoculations. General knowledge of diseases, their symptoms and side effects will assist you in diagnosing diseases for your veterinarian. He does not expect you to be an expert, but will appreciate your efforts in getting a sick dog to him before it is too late and he cannot save its life.

ASPIRIN: A DANGER

There is a common joke about doctors telling their patients, when they telephone with a complaint, to take an aspirin, go to bed and let him know how things are in the morning. Unfortunately, that is exactly the way it turns out with a lot of dog owners who think aspirins are cure-alls and give them to their dogs indiscriminately. They finally call the veterinarian when the dog has an unfavorable reaction.

Aspirins are not panaceas for everything—certainly not for every dog. In an experiment, fatalities in cats treated with aspirin in one laboratory alone numbered ten out of 13 within a two-week period. Dogs' tolerance was somewhat better, as far as actual fatalities, but there was considerable evidence of ulceration in varying degrees on the stomach linings when necropsy was performed.

Aspirin has been held in the past to be almost as effective for dogs as for people when given for many of the everyday aches and pains. The fact is however that medication of any kind should be administered only after veterinary consultation and a specific dosage suitable to the condition is recommended.

While aspirin is chiefly effective in reducing fever, relieving minor pains and cutting down on inflammation, the acid has been proven harmful to the stomach when given in strong doses. Only your veterinarian is qualified to determine what the dosage is, or whether it should be administered to your particular dog at all.

WHAT THE THERMOMETER CAN TELL YOU

You will notice in reading this chapter that practically everything a dog might contract in the way of sickness has basically the same set of symptoms: loss of appetite, diarrhea, dull eyes, dull coat, warm and/or runny nose and fever.

Therefore, it is most advisable to have a thermometer on hand for checking temperatures. There are several inexpensive metal rectal-type thermometers that are accurate and safer than the glass variety which can be broken. This may happen either by dropping, or perhaps even breaking off in the dog because of improper insertion or an aggravated condition with the dog that makes him violently resist the injection of the thermometer. Whichever type thermometer you use, it should first be sterilized with alcohol and then lubricated with petroleum jelly to make the insertion as easy as possible.

The normal temperature for a dog is 101.5° Fahrenheit, as compared to the human 98.6°. Excitement as well as illness can cause this to vary a degree or two, but any sudden or extensive rise in the body temperature must be considered as cause for alarm. Your first indication will be that your dog feels unduly "warm;" this is the time to take the temperature, not when the dog becomes very ill or develops additional serious symptoms. With a thermometer on hand, you can check temperatures quickly and perhaps prevent some illnesses from becoming serious.

COPROPHAGY

Perhaps the most unpleasant of all phases of dog breeding concerns a dog that takes to eating its stool. This practice, which is referred to politely as coprophagy, is one of the unsolved mysteries in the dog world. There is simply no confirmed explanation as to why some dogs do it.

However, there are several logical theories, any or all of which may be the cause. Some people cite nutritional deficiencies; others say that dogs that are inclined to gulp their food (which passes through them not entirely digested) find it still partially palatable. There is another theory that the preservatives used in some meat are responsible for an appealing odor that remains through the digestive process. Then again, poor quality meat can be so tough and unchewable that dogs swallow it whole and it passes through them in large undigested chunks.

There are others who believe the habit is strictly psychological, the result of a nervous condition or insecurity. Others believe the dog cleans up after itself because it is afraid of being punished as it was when it made a mistake on the carpet as a puppy. Some people claim boredom is the reason, or even spite. Others will tell you a dog does not want its personal odor on the premises for fear of attracting other hostile animals to itself or its home.

The most logical of all explanations and the one most veterinarians are inclined to accept is that it is a deficiency of dietary enzymes. Too much dry food can be bad and many veterinarians suggest trying meat tenderizers, monosodium glutamate or garlic powder to give the stool a bad odor and discourage the dog. Yeast or certain vitamins or a complete change of diet are even more often suggested. By the time you try each of the above you will probably discover that the dog has outgrown the habit anyway. However, the condition cannot

be ignored if you are to enjoy your dog to the fullest.

There is no set length of time that the problem persists, and the only real cure is to walk the dog on a leash, morning and night and after every meal. In other words, set up a definite eating and exercising schedule before coprophagy is an established pattern.

MASTURBATION

A source of embarrassment to many dog owners, masturbation can be eliminated with a minimum of training.

The dog which is constantly breeding anything and everything, including the leg of the piano or perhaps the leg of your favorite guest, can be broken by the habit of stopping its cause.

The over-sexed dog—if truly that is what he is—which will never be used for breeding can be castrated. The kennel stud dog can be broken of the habit by removing any furniture from his quarters or keeping him on leash and on verbal command when he is around people, or in the house where he might be tempted to breed pillows, people, etc.

Hormone imbalance may be another cause and your veterinarian may advise injections. Exercise can be of tremendous help. Keeping the dog's mind occupied by physical play when he is around people will also help relieve the situation.

Females might indulge in sexual abnormalities like masturbation during their heat cycle, or again, because of a hormone imbalance. But if they behave this way because of a more serious problem, a hysterectomy may be indicated.

A sharp "no!" command when you can anticipate the act, or a sharp "no!" when the dog is caught in the act will deter most dogs if you are consistent in your correction. Hitting or other physical abuse will only confuse a dog.

RABIES

The greatest fear in the dog fancy today is still the great fear it has always been—rabies.

What has always held true about this dreadful disease still holds true today. The only way rabies can be contracted is through the saliva of a rabid dog entering the bloodstream of another animal or person. There is, of course, the Pasteur treatment for rabies, which is very effective. There was of late an incident of a little boy bitten by a rabid bat having survived the disease. However, the Pasteur treatment is administered immediately to a bite victim if there is any question of the animal's having rabies. Even more than dogs being found to be rabid, we now know that the biggest carriers

Ch. Highlandell Truly Terrific, owned by Jack D. Russell and Joan Niedecken. Bred by Audrey M. Hansen, Terrific is pictured winning Best of Breed under judge Gwladys Groskin.

The typical "chrysathemum" stage of the Shih Tzu puppy. "Boozer," owned by Janine R. Zervoulis, was sired by Ch. Moon Ling's Wu Tai Shan ex Town Hall Stardust O'Moon Ling. Whelped in November 1976, Zervlistan Tai Wun On was photographed by Bill Zervoulis.

Ch. Lou Wan Casinova and his daughter Ch. Lou Wan Mariposa of Sarafin. They are pictured winning at the 1975 New Brunswick Kennel Club show under the distinguished English judge, Stanley Dangerfield. Bred and owned by Louis and Wanda Gec of Clifton, New Jersey.

Sad sack! 10 month old puppy owned by Will C. Mooney, dog editor of the *Dallas Time Herald*, looks as if he's had a bad day. This picture of Panda was taken in 1963.

are bats, skunks, foxes, rabbits and other warm-blooded animals, which pass it from one to another, since they do not have the benefit of inoculation. Dogs that run free should be inoculated for protection against these animals. For city or house dogs that never leave their owner's side, it may not be as necessary.

For many years, Great Britain, because it is an island and because of the country's strictly enforced six-month quarantine, was entirely free of rabies. But in 1969, a British officer brought back his dog from foreign duty and the dog was found to have the disease soon after being released from quarantine. There was a great uproar about it, with Britain killing off wild and domestic animals in a great scare campaign, but the quarantine is once again down to six months and things seem to have returned to a normal, sensible attitude.

Health departments in rural towns usually provide rabies inoculations free of charge. If your dog is outdoors a great deal, or exposed to other animals that are, you might wish to call the town hall and get information on the program in your area. One cannot be too cautious about this dreaded disease. While the number of cases diminishes each year, there are still thousands being reported and there is still the constant threat of an outbreak where animals roam free. Never forget: there is no cure for rabies.

Rabies is caused by a neurotropic virus which can be found in the saliva, brain and sometimes the blood of the afflicted warm-blooded animal. The incubation period is usually two weeks or as long as six months, which means you can be exposed to it without any visible symptoms. As we have said, while there is still no known cure, it *can* be controlled. It is up to every individual to help effect this control by reporting animal bites, educating the public to the dangers and symptoms and prevention of it, so that we may reduce the fatalities.

There are two kinds of rabies; one form is called "furious," and the other is referred to as "dumb." The mad dog goes through several stages of the disease. His disposition and behavior change radically and suddenly; he becomes irritable and vicious. The eating habits alter, and he rejects food for things like stones and sticks; he becomes exhausted and drools saliva out of his mouth almost constantly. He may hide in corners, look glassy eyed and suspicious, bite at the air as he races around snarling and attacking with his tongue hanging out. At this point paralysis sets in, starting at the throat so that he can no longer drink water though he desires it desperately; hence, the term hydrophobia is given. He begins to stagger and eventually convulse and death is imminent.

In "dumb" rabies paralysis is swift; the dog seeks dark, sheltered places and is abnormally quiet. Paralysis starts with the jaws, spreads down the body and death is quick. Contact by humans or other animals with the drool from either of these types of rabies on open skin can produce the fatal disease, so extreme haste and proper diagnosis is essential. In other words, you do not have to be bitten by a rabid dog to have the virus enter your system. An open wound or cut that comes in touch with the saliva is all that is needed.

The incubation and degree of infection can vary. You usually contract the disease faster if the wound is near the head, since the virus travels to the brain through the spinal cord. The deeper the wound, the more saliva is injected into the body, and the more serious the infection. So, if bitten by a dog under any circumstances—or any warm-blooded animal for that matter—immediately wash out the wound with soap and water, bleed it profusely, and see your doctor as soon as possible.

Also, be sure to keep track of the animal that bit, if at all possible. When rabies is suspected the public health officer will need to send the animal's head away to be analyzed. If it is found to be rabies-free, you will not need to undergo treatment. Otherwise, your doctor may advise that you

San Yen Ho-Chi Reali Sumting at three months of age. Owner is Tina Christenson of Pocatello, Idaho.

Ch. Hullaballou J. Ray of Nanjo won Best In Show at the 1976 Ft. Smith, Arkansas, Kennel club show under judge Florence Savage. Handling for owner Joan E. Cowie of Kimberton, Pennsylvania was Sandy Tremont. The sire was Ch. Paisley Ping Pong ex Nanjo Miss Wiggles. Dr. Braxton Sawyer presents the trophy.

Shente's Mo Moi Yu O'Chumulari twice won the Best Puppy In Show award at the Spring 1978 Bermuda circuit. Judges Robert Waters, pictured, and Irving Diamond officiated. Karolynne MacAteer handled for owners the Eastons.

Hadda Shu van de Oranje Manege, who was the dam of many American champions, including the first West Coast Shih Tzu champion. Owner of this Eta Pauptit-bred bitch was Eleanore Eldredge.

Ch. Willows Dandi-lion and daughter Willows Miss Muffet are pictured winning at a recent show. They are owned by Consuelo Bolsaks of Redding, California. Bennet Assoc. photo.

have the Pasteur treatment, which is extremely painful. It is rather simple, however, to have the veterinarian examine a dog for rabies without having the dog sent away for positive diagnosis of the disease. A ten-day quarantine is usually all that is necessary for everyone's peace of mind.

Rabies is no respecter of age, sex or geographical location. It is found all over the world from North Pole to South Pole, and has nothing to do with the old wive's tale of dogs going mad in hot summer months. True, there is an increase in reported cases during the summer, but only because that is the time of year for animals to roam free in good weather, and time of the mating season when a battle of the sexes is taking place. Inoculation and a keen eye for symptoms and bites on our dogs and other pets will help control the disease.

VACCINATIONS

If you are to raise a puppy, or a litter of puppies, successfully, you must adhere to a realistic and strict schedule of vaccination. Many puppyhood diseases can be fatal and all of them are debilitating. According to the latest statistics, 98 per cent of all puppies are being inoculated after 12 weeks of age against the dread distemper, hepatitis and leptospirosis, and manage to escape these horrible infections. Orphaned puppies should be vaccinated every two weeks until the age of 12 weeks. Distemper and hepatitis live-virus vaccine should be used, since they are not protected with the colostrum normally supplied to them through the mother's milk. Puppies weaned at six to seven weeks should also be inoculated repeatedly because they will no longer be receiving mother's milk. While not all will receive protection from the serum at this early age, it should be given and they should be vaccinated once again at both nine and 12 weeks of age.

Leptospirosis vaccination should be given at four months of age with thought given to booster shots if the disease is known in the area, or in the case of show dogs which are exposed on a regular basis to many dogs from far and wide. While annual boosters are in order for distemper and hepatitis, every two or three years is sufficient for leptospirosis, unless there is an outbreak in your immediate area. The one exception should be the pregnant bitch since there is reason to believe that inoculation might cause damage to the fetus.

Strict observance of such a vaccination schedule will not only keep your dog free of these debilitating diseases, but will prevent an epidemic in your kennel, or in your locality, or to the dogs which are competing at the shows.

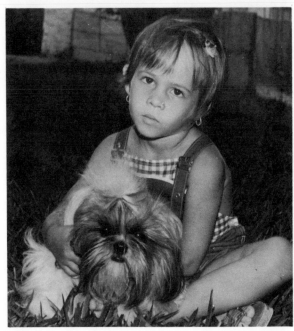

Int. Braz. Ch. Chumulari Wu Lai, with Eneida, daughter of Mr. and Mrs. Murilo Leite of Bahia, Brazil. Mr. Leite also owns Int. and Braz. Ch. Chumulari Sheng Tan Ling. Both of these imports are grandchildren of Chumulari Ying-Ying.

KIDNEY FAILURE

A great deal has been written about the problem of kidney failure in our breed. It is almost impossible to pick up a publication devoted to dogs without reading about the newest theories or practices uncovered in the relentless search for both cause and cure.

The pages of this book are hardly the place for discussion or review of already-published information that is better left to the medical authorities. We would, however, like to confirm that kidney failure is a serious affliction in our breed. As such, immediate veterinary consultation at the first indication of this insidious disease is essential in regards to the care of your dog and the future of your breeding program.

SNAKEBITE

As field trials and hunts and the like become more and more popular with dog enthusiasts, the incident of a snakebite becomes more of a likelihood. Dogs that are kept outdoors in runs, or dogs that work the fields and roam on large estates are also likely victims.

Most veterinarians carry snakebite serum, and snakebite kits are sold to dog owners for just such purposes. To catch a snakebite in time might mean the difference between life and death, and whether your area is populated with snakes or not, it behooves you to know what to do in case it happens to you or your dog.

Ch. Abacus' Little Red Waggin' photographed at nine months of age with handler J.D. Basil, who co-owns with co-breeder Steve R.C. Smith. Whelped in June, 1975, "Waggin's" sire was Ch. Char Nicks Executive Action ex Nanjo Pier Tuo.

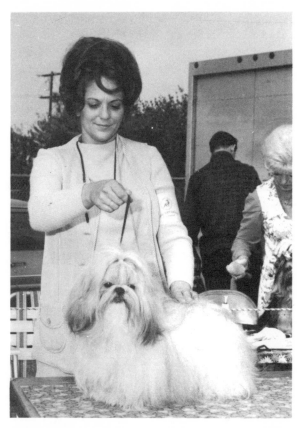

Ch. Kathaway's Too To is owner-handled and bred by Daniece Greggans.

A charming portrait: Lance and Susan Barr with two San Yen Shih Tzu in their native Salt Lake City, Utah.

Your primary concern should be to get to a doctor or veterinarian immediately. The victim should be kept as quiet as possible (excitement or activity spreads the venom through the body more quickly) and if possible the wound should be bled enough to clean it out before applying a tourniquet, if the bite is severe.

First of all, it must be determined if the bite is from a poisonous or non-poisonous snake. If the bite carries two horseshoe shaped pinpoints of a double row of teeth, the bite can be assumed to be non-poisonous. If the bite leaves two punctures or holes—the result of the two fangs carrying venom—the bite is very definitely poisonous and time is of the essence.

Recently, physicians have come up with an added help in the case of snakebite. A first aid treatment referred to as hypothermia, which is the application of ice to the wound to lower body temperature to a point where the venom spreads less quickly, minimizes swelling, helps prevent infection and has some influence on numbing the pain. If ice is not readily available, the bite may be soaked in ice-cold water. But even more urgent is the need to get the victim to a hospital or a veterinarian for additional treatment.

EMERGENCIES

No matter how well you run your kennel or keep an eye on an individual dog, there will almost invariably be some emergency at some

Victory ride! Misty Isle Chin Mo Li won Best in Match over 350 entries at a recent St. Charles Kennel Club show. Pulling the cart in this adorable photo are two Schipperkes owned and trained by Toni Strasburger, and handled by Rocky Volpp. Chin Mo Li is handled by owner Mike Heigert of Brentwood, Missouri.

time that will require quick treatment until you get the animal to the veterinarian. The first and most important thing to remember is to keep calm. You will think more clearly and your animal will need to know he can depend on you to take care of him. However, he will be frightened and you must beware of fear biting. Therefore, do not shower him with kisses and endearments at this time, no matter how sympathetic you feel. Comfort him reassuringly, but keep your wits about you. Before getting him to the veterinarian, try to alleviate the pain and shock.

If you can take even a minor step in this direction it will be a help toward the final cure. Listed here are a few of the emergencies which might occur and what you can do after you have called the vet and told him you are coming.

BURNS

If you have been so foolish as not to turn your pot handles toward the back of the stove—for your children's sake as well as your dog's—and the dog is burned, apply ice or ice-cold water and treat for shock. Electrical or chemical burns are treated the same, but with an acid or alkali burn, use, respectively, a bicarbonate of soda or vinegar solution. Check the advisability of covering the burn when you call the veterinarian.

DROWNING

Most animals love the water, but sometimes get in "over their heads." Should your dog take in too much water, hold him upside down and open his mouth so that water can empty from the lungs, then apply artificial respiration, or mouth-to-mouth resuscitation. With a large dog, hang the head over a step or off the end of the table while you hoist the rear end in the air by the back feet. Then treat for shock by covering him with a blanket, administering a stimulant such as coffee with sugar, and soothing him with your voice and hands.

FITS AND CONVULSIONS

Prevent the dog from thrashing about and injuring himself, cover with a blanket and hold down until you can get him to the veterinarian.

FROSTBITE

There is no excuse for an animal getting frostbite if you are on your toes and you care for the animal. However, should frostbite set in, thaw out the affected area slowly with a circulatory motion and stimulation. Use petroleum jelly to help keep the skin from peeling off and/or drying out.

HEART ATTACK

Be sure the animal keeps breathing by applying artificial respiration. A mild stimulant may be used and give him plenty of air. Treat for shock as well, and get to the veterinarian quickly.

SHOCK

Shock is a state of circulatory collapse that can be induced by a severe accident, loss of blood, heart failure or any injury to the nervous system. Until you can get the dog to the veterinarian, keep him warm by covering him with a blanket and administer a mild stimulant such as coffee or tea with sugar. Try to keep the dog quiet until the appropriate medication can be prescribed. Relapse is not uncommon, so the dog must be observed carefully for several days after initial shock.

SUFFOCATION

Administer artificial respiration and treat for shock, allowing the dog *plenty* of air.

SUN STROKE

Cooling the dog off immediately is essential. Ice packs, submersion in ice water, and plenty of cool air are needed.

WOUNDS

Open wounds or cuts which produce bleeding must be treated with hydrogen peroxide, and tourniquets should be used if bleeding is excessive. Also, shock treatment must be given, and the animal must be kept warm.

It would be sheer folly to try to operate a kennel or to keep a dog without providing for certain emergencies that are bound to crop up when there are active dogs around. Just as you would provide a first aid kit for people, you should also provide a first aid kit for the animals on the premises.

The first aid kit should contain the following items:

> medicated powder
> jar of petroleum jelly
> cotton swabs
> bandage—1″ gauze
> adhesive tape
> band-aids
> cotton
> boric acid powder

A trip to your veterinarian is always the safest route, but there are certain preliminaries for cuts and bruises of a minor nature that you can cure by yourself.

Cuts, for instance, should be washed out, medicated powder or petroleum jelly applied, and covered with a bandage. The lighter the bandage the better, so that the most air possible can reach the wound. Cotton swabs can be used for removing debris from the eyes, after which a mild solution of boric acid wash can be applied. As for sores, use dry powder on wet sores, and petroleum jelly on dry sores. Use cotton for washing out wounds and drying them.

Mary Marxen of Van Wert, Ohio and her Luv-Tzu Mai Fystee Wun.

All set for take-off for Saudi Arabia! Chumulari Ho T'ee is in the hands of stewardess Edwina Zimnowski for the 7,600-mile flight to new owner, Aline Boudreaux of the Arabia-American Oil Company in Dhahran. Ho T'ee, bred by the Eastons, arrived safely after the 19 hour journey by way of Paris, Rome and Cairo.

A particular caution must be given here on bandaging. Make sure that the bandage is not too tight to hamper the dog's circulation. Also, make sure the bandage is made correctly so that the dog does not bite at it trying to get it off. A great deal of damage can be done to a wound by a dog tearing at a bandage to get it off. If you notice the dog is starting to bite at it, do it over or put something on the bandage that smells and tastes bad to him. Make sure, however, that the solution does not soak through the bandage and enter the wound. Sometimes, if it is a leg wound, a sock or stocking slipped on the dog's leg will cover the bandage edges and will also keep it clean.

HOW NOT TO POISON YOUR DOG

"Just how dangerous are chemicals?"

In the animal fancy, where disinfectants, room deodorants, parasitic sprays, solutions and aerosols are so widely used, the question has taken on even more meaning. Veterinarians are beginning to ask, "What kind of disinfectant do you use?" or "Have you any fruit trees that have been sprayed recently?" When animals are brought to their offices in a toxic condition, or for unexplained death, or when entire litters of puppies die mysteriously, there is a good reason to ask such questions.

The popular practice of protecting animals against parasites has given way to their being exposed to an alarming number of commercial products, some of which are dangerous to their very lives. Even flea collars can be dangerous, especially if they get wet or somehow touch the genital regions or eyes. While some products are a great deal more poisonous than others, great care must be taken that they be applied in proportion to the size of the dog and the area to be covered. Many a dog has been taken to the vet with an unusual skin problem that was a direct result of having been bathed with a detergent rather than a proper shampoo. Certain products that are safe for dogs can be fatal for cats. Extreme care must be taken to read all ingredients and instructions carefully before use on any animal.

The same caution must be given to outdoor animals. Dog owners must question the use of fertilizers on their lawns. Lime, for instance, can be harmful to a dog's feet. The unleashed dog that covers the neighborhood on his daily rounds is open to all sorts of tree and lawn sprays and insecticides that may prove harmful to him, if not as a poison, then as a producer of an allergy.

There are various products found around the house which can be lethal, such as rat poison, boric acid, hand soap, detergents, car anti-freeze and insecticides. These are all available in the house or garage and can be tipped over easily and consumed. Many puppy fatalities are reported when they consume mothballs. All poisons should be placed on high shelves out of the reach of both children and animals.

Perhaps the most readily available of all household poisons are plants. Household plants are almost all poisonous, even if taken in small quantities. Some of the most dangerous are the elephant ear, the narcissus bulb, any kind of ivy leaves, burning bush leaves, the jimson weed, the dumb cane weed, mock orange fruit, castor beans, Scotch broom seeds, the root or seed of the plant called four o'clock and cyclamen. Also dangerous

Peggy Easton and a five week old Chumulari future champion.

Ting H'ao of Shang T'ou, with his famous movie star owner, Yul Brynner. Ting H'ou has an honorary co-pilot's license with T.W.A. so he can travel with his owner to movie locations. He was bred by Eleanore Eldredge of Easton, Washington.

are pimpernel, lily of the valley, the stem of the sweet pea, rhododendrons of any kind, spider lily bulbs, bayonet root, foxglove leaves, tulip bulbs, monkshood roots, azalea, wisteria, poinsetta leaves, mistletoe, hemlock, locoweed and arrowglove. In all, there are over 500 poisonous plants in the United States. Peach, elderberry and cherry trees can cause cyanide poisoning if the bark is consumed. Rhubarb leaves, either raw or cooked, can cause death or violent convulsions. Check out your closets, fields and grounds around your home, and especially the dog runs, to see what should be eliminated to remove the danger to your dogs.

SYMPTOMS OF POISONING

If you suspect that your dog has swallowed poison, be on the lookout for vomiting, hard or labored breathing, whimpering, stomach cramps, and trembling as a prelude to the convulsions. Any delay in a visit to your veterinarian can mean death. Take along the bottle or package or a sam-

Ch. Car-Lyn's Dynamo of Sanco pictured winning on the way to championship at the 1976 Clearwater Kennel Club Show. Annette Lurton handled for owner Sandy Cox, Sanco Shih Tzu, Lexington, Kentucky.

ple of the plant you suspect to be the cause to help the veterinarian determine the correct antidote.

The most common type of poisoning, which accounts for nearly one fourth of all animal victims, is staphylococcic-infected food. Salmonella is almost as common. These can be avoided by serving only fresh food and not letting it lie around in hot weather.

There are also many insect poisonings caused by animals eating cockroaches, spiders, flies, butterflies, etc. Toads and some frogs give off a fluid which can make a dog foam at the mouth—and even kill him—if he bites just a little too hard.

Some misguided dog owners think it is "cute" to let their dogs enjoy a cocktail with them before dinner. There can be serious effects resulting from encouraging a dog to drink—sneezing fits, injuries as a result of intoxication, and heart stoppage are just a few. Whiskey for medicinal purposes, or beer for brood bitches should be administered only on the advice of your veterinarian.

There have been cases of severe damage and death when dogs have emptied ash trays and consumed cigarettes, resulting in nicotine poisoning. Leaving a dog alone all day in a house where there are cigarettes available on a coffee table is asking for trouble. Needless to say, the same applies to marijuana. The narcotic addict who takes his dog along with him on "a trip" does not deserve to have a dog. All the ghastly side effects are as possible for the dog as for the addict, and for a person to submit an animal to this indignity is indeed despicable. Don't think it doesn't happen. Unfortunately, in all our major cities the practice is becoming more and more a problem for the veterinarian. Be on the alert and remember that in the case of any type of poisoning, the best treatment is prevention.

THE CURSE OF ALLERGY

The heartbreak of a child being forced to give up a beloved pet because he is suddenly found to be allergic to it is a sad but true story. Many families claim to be unable to have dogs at all; others seem to be able only to enjoy them on a restricted basis. Many children know animals only through occasional visits to a friend's house or the zoo.

While modern veterinary science has produced some brilliant allergists, the field is still working on a solution for those who suffer from exposure to their pets. As yet, there is no permanent cure.

Over the last quarter of a century there have been many attempts at a permanent cure, but none has proven successful, because the treatment was needed too frequently, or was too expensive to maintain over extended periods of time.

However, we find that most people who are allergic to their animals are also allergic to a variety of other things as well. By eliminating the other irritants, and by taking medication given for the control of allergies in general, many are able to keep pets on a restricted basis. This may necessitate the dog's living outside the house, being groomed at a professional grooming parlor instead of by the owner, or merely being kept out of the bedroom at night. A discussion of this "balance" factor with your medical and veterinary doctors may give new hope to those willing to try.

A paper presented by Mathilde M. Gould, M.D., a New York allergist, before the American Academy of Allergists in the 1960's, and reported in the September-October 1964 issue of the *National Humane Review* magazine, offered new hope to those who are allergic by a method referred to as hyposensitization. You may wish to write to the magazine and request the article for

Ch. Marya Winds Tie-Dye of Dynasty pictured winning at a 1976 show. Bred by Martha Coalina, Tie-Dye is owned by Frederic M. Alderman, Dynasty Kennels, Mundelein, Illinois. The sire was Ch. Mariljac Maripet ex Town Halls Gloria Gloria.

discussion with your medical and veterinary doctors on your individual problem.

ALLERGIES IN DOGS

It used to be that you recognized an allergy in your dog when he scratched out his coat and developed a large patch of raw skin, or sneezed himself almost to death on certain occasions. A trip to the veterinarian involved endless discussion as to why it might be an almost equally endless "hit and miss" cure of various salves and lotions with the hope that one of them would work. Many times the condition would correct itself before a definite cure was affected.

However, during this decade, preliminary findings at the University of Pennsylvania veterinary school evolved a diagnosis for allergies that eliminated the need for skin sensitivity tests. It is called RAST, and is a radioallergosobant test performed with a blood serum sample. It is not even necessary in all cases for the veterinarian to even see the dog.

A cellulose disc laced with a suspected allergen is placed in the serum, and if the dog is allergic to that particular allergen the serum will contain a specific antibody that adheres to the allergen on the disc. The disc is placed in a radioactively "labeled" antiserum that is attracted to that particular antibody. The antiserum binds with the antibody and can be detected with a radiation counter.

Furthermore, the scientists at the University of Pennsylvania also found that the RAST test has shown to be a more accurate diagnostic tool than skin testing because it measures the degree, and not merely the presence, of allergic reactions.

DO ALL DOGS CHEW?

The answer to the above question is an emphatic yes! Puppies and young dogs need something with resistance to chew on while their teeth and jaws are developing—for cutting the puppy teeth, to induce growth of the permanent teeth, to assure normal jaw development and to settle the permanent teeth solidly into the jaws.

The adult dog's desire to chew stems from the instinct for tooth cleaning, gum massage and jaw exercise—plus the need for an outlet from periodic doggie tensions. True, chewing can be destructive, even dangerous, if the dog practices on shoes, electrical wires, furniture or carpet corners, rather than something specifically designed for the purpose. It is very important that dogs not be permitted to chew on anything they can break, or indigestible things from which the dog can bite off sizeable chunks. Sharp pieces from a broken bone may pierce the intestine wall and kill the dog. Indigestible material which can be bitten off in chunks, such as toys made of rubber compound or cheap plastic, may cause an intestinal stoppage if not regurgitated, and immediate surgery must be performed to avoid death.

Nylon bones, especially those with natural meat and bone fractions added, such as Nylabone®, are probably the safest and most economical answer to the chewing need. Dogs cannot break Nylabone or bite off large chunks; hence, they are completely safe. Since Nylabones are longer lasting than other items offered for this purpose, they are economical, too.

Hard chewing raises little bristle-like projections on the surface of the nylon bones to provide effective tooth cleaning and vigorous gum massage. The toughness of Nylabone provides the strong chewing resistance needed for important jaw exercise and effective help for the teething functions—but there is no tooth wear because Nylabone is non-abrasive. Nylabone has been approved by the American Veterinary Medical Association, and can be purchased at most pet shops and department stores in petite, medium and large sizes, all reasonably priced.

SOME REASONS FOR CHEWING

Chewing can be a form of frustration or nervousness, or just plain spitefulness, which is why many dogs chew things when owners go out! Bitches will sometimes chew if their puppies are taken away from them too soon; insecure puppies often chew thinking that they're nursing. Puppies which chew wool, blankets, carpet corners or certain other types of materials may have a nutritional deficiency in their diet. They may be craving the starch that might be left in the material after washings. Perhaps the articles have been near something that tastes good and they have retained the odor of food.

The act of chewing has no connection with particular breeds or ages, any more than there is a logical reason for dogs to dig holes outdoors or dig on wooden floors indoors.

So we repeat, it is up to you to be on guard at all times until the need—or habit—passes.

HIP DYSPLASIA

Hip dysplasia, or HD, is one of the most widely discussed of all animal afflictions, since it has appeared in varying degrees in just about every breed of dog. True, the larger breeds seem most susceptible, but it has hit the small breeds and is beginning to be recognized in cats as well.

While HD in man has been recorded as far back as 370 B.C., HD in dogs was more likely referred to as rheumatism until veterinary research came into the picture. In 1935, Dr. Otto Schales, at Angell Memorial Hospital in Boston, wrote a paper on hip dysplasia and classified the four degrees of dysplasia of the hip joints as follows:

Grade 1: slight (poor fit between ball and socket)

Grade 2: moderate (moderate but obvious shallowness of the socket)

Grade 3: severe (socket quite flat)

Grade 4: very severe (complete displacement of head of femur at an early age)

HD is an incurable, hereditary, though not congenital disease of the hip sockets. It is transmitted as a dominant trait with irregular manifestations. Puppies appear normal at birth but the constant wearing away of the socket means the animal moves more and more on muscle, thereby presenting a lameness, a difficulty in getting up and severe pain in advanced cases.

The degree of severity can be determined

Chumulari Dorje is an important part of the Chumulari strain. Dorje is a daughter of Chumulari Trari by Jungfaltets Wu Po, bred by the Jungefeldts in Sweden and imported to the U.S. by Ingrid Colwell.

around six months of age, but its presence can be noticed from two months of age. The problem is determined by X-ray, and if pain is present it can be relieved temporarily by medication. Exercise should be avoided since motion encourages the wearing away of the bone surfaces.

Dogs with HD should not be shown or bred, if quality in the breed is to be maintained. It is essential to check a pedigree for dogs known to be dysplastic before breeding, since this disease can be dormant for many generations.

ELBOW DYSPLASIA

The same condition can also affect the elbow joints and is known as elbow dysplasia. This also causes lameness, and dogs so affected should not be used for breeding.

PATELLA DYSPLASIA

Some of the smaller breeds of dogs also suffer from patella dysplasia, or dislocation of the knee. This can be treated sugically, but the surgery by no means abolishes the hereditary factor. Therefore, these dogs should not be used for breeding.

All dogs—in any breed—should be X-rayed before being used for breeding. The X-ray should be

285

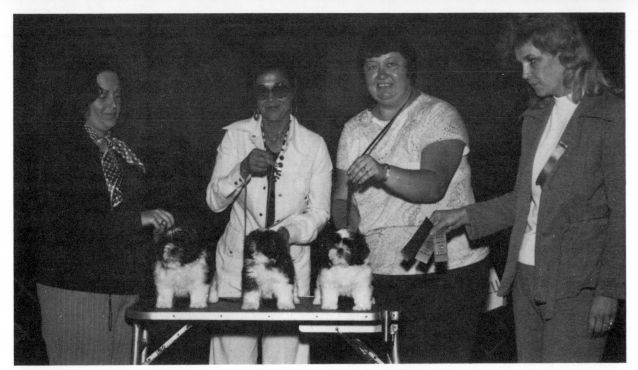

At the 1976 Penn-Ohio Fun Match, Carol Bogner's litter took from left to right, third, second and first places in their class. Highlands Devils Exorcist, Devils Due and Devils Advocate were all sired by Ch. Mariljac MeriPet ex Ch. Dunklehaven Luv-Li Ladee.

Best In Show-winner Ch. Emperor's Thing-Ah-Ma-Ying owned by Claralue Dinelli of Poplar Bluffs, Missouri.

Zizi's Chi-Ko Liang, owned by Mrs. Sonja Bai of Noway. Liang is a litter brother to the top winning bitch, Zizi's Tara. Liang's sire was Int., Nor. Ch. Marinas Muff-Lung-Feng ex Int., Nor., and Danish Ch. Zizi's Lhamo.

Rondelay Shi Kan Tu Wyn pictured at three months of age. Owned by Edythe B. Kennedy and photographed by William Kennedy.

Chumulari Hai Yang Kung Chu, pictured at four months of age, is owned by Leah Murray of Arcadia, Nova Scotia.

Canadian Ch. Greenmoss Casanova, owned by Ralph and Florence Zidanowicz.

Norwegian Champion Zizi's Buddha, bred by Ruth Laakso and owned by Mrs. Henny Langasdalen, Notodden, Norway. The sire was Nor. Ch. Zizi's Ching C'Hoo ex Swed. and Nor. Ch. Kwan-Jin van de Blauwe Mammouth. Photo by A. Laakso.

Ch. Dragonwycks the Great Gatsby, winner of the 1976 Ken-L Awards for winning the most Toy Groups that year. The sire was Am. Can. Ch. Chumulari Ying-Ying ex Ch. Mariljac Lotus Blossom. Owner is Robert Koeppel of New York City, and the handler is Peggy Hogg.

read by a competent veterinarian and the dog declared free and clear.

THE UNITED STATES REGISTRY

In the United States we have a central Hip Dysplasia Foundation, known as the OFA (Orthopedic Foundation for Animals). This HD control registry was formed in 1966. X-rays are sent for expert evaluation by qualified radiologists.

All you need do for complete information on getting an X-ray for your dog is to write to the Orthopedic Foundation for Animals at 817 Virginia Ave., Columbia, MO 65201, and request their dysplasia packet. There is no charge for this kit. It contains an envelope large enough to hold your X-ray film (which you will have taken by your own veterinarian), and a drawing showing how to position the dog properly for X-ray. There is also an application card for proper identification of the dog. Then, hopefully, your dog will be certified "normal." You will be given a registry number which you can put on his pedigree, use in your advertising, and then rest assured your breeding program is in good order.

We cannot urge strongly enough the importance of doing this. While it involves time and effort, the reward in the long run will more than pay for your trouble. To see the heartbreak of parents and children when their beloved dog has to be put to sleep because of severe hip dysplasia as the result of bad breeding is a sad experience. Don't let this happen to you or to those who will purchase your puppies!

Additionally, we should mention that there is a method of palpation to determine the extent of affliction. This can be painful if the animal is not properly prepared for the examination. There have also been attempts to replace the animal's femur and socket. This is not only expensive, but the percentage of success is small.

For those who refuse to put their dog down, there is a new surgical technique which can relieve pain, but in no way constitutes a cure. This technique involves the severing of the pectinius muscle, which for some unknown reason brings relief from pain over a period of many months—even up to two years. A few veterinary colleges in the United States are performing this operation at the present time. However, the owner must also give permission to "de-sex" the dogs at the time of the muscle severance. This is a safety measure to help stamp out hip dysplasia, since obviously the condition itself remains and can be passed on.

HD PROGRAM IN GREAT BRITAIN

The British Veterinary Association (BVA) has made an attempt to control the spread of HD by appointing a panel of members of their profession who have made a special study of the disease to read X-rays. Dogs over one year of age may be X-rayed and certified as HD-free. Forms are completed in triplicate to verify the tests. One copy remains with the panel, one copy is for the owner's veterinarian, and one for the owner. A record is also sent to the British Kennel Club for those wishing to check on a particular dog for breeding purposes.

GERIATRICS

If you originally purchased good healthy stock and cared for your dog throughout his life, there is no reason why you cannot expect your dog to live to a ripe old age. With research and the remarkable foods produced for dogs, especially in this past decade or so, his chances of longevity have increased considerably. If you have cared for him well, your dog will be a sheer delight in his old age, just as he was in his prime.

We can assume you have fed him properly if he is not too fat. As we mentioned earlier, fat people usually have fat dogs because they indulge their dog's appetite as they do their own. If there has been no great illness, then you will find that very little additional care and attention are needed to keep him well. Exercise is still essential, as is proper food, booster shots, and tender loving care.

Even if a heart condition develops, there is still no reason to believe your dog cannot live to an old age. A diet may be necessary, along with medication and limited exercise, to keep the condition under control. In the case of deafness, or partial blindness, additional care must be taken to protect the dog, but neither infirmity will in any way shorten his life. Prolonged exposure to temperature variances, overeating, excessive exercise, lack of sleep, or being housed with younger, more active dogs may take an unnecessary toll on the dog's energies and introduce more serious trouble. Good judgement, periodic veterinary checkups and individual attention will keep your dog with you for many added years.

When discussing geriatrics, the question of when a dog becomes old or aged usually is asked. We have all heard the old saying that one year of a dog's life is equal to seven years in a human. This theory is strictly a matter of opinion, and must remain so, since so many outside factors enter into how quickly each individual dog "ages." Recently, a new chart was devised which is more realistically equivalent:

DOG	MAN
6 months	10 years
1 year	15 years
2 years	24 years
3 years	28 years
4 years	32 years
5 years	36 years
6 years	40 years
7 years	44 years
8 years	48 years
9 years	52 years
10 years	56 years
15 years	76 years
21 years	100 years

It must be remembered that such things as serious illnesses, poor food and housing, general

Ch. San Yen Ming Ti Ja-Shu-Wa pictured winning under judge Mrs. Almos Oliver, with owner Susan Barr of the San Yen Kennels of Salt Lake City, Utah.

Ch. Floridonna Sexa Peal, whelped in 1972 and the dam of champions. Sexa Peal's co-owner/breeders are Donna and Edgar Ellis of Clearwater, Florida.

neglect and poor beginnings as puppies will take their toll on a dog's general health and age him more quickly than a dog that has led a normal, healthy life. Let your veterinarian help you determine an age bracket for your dog in his later years.

While good care should prolong your dog's life, there are several "old age" disorders to be on the lookout for no matter how well he may be doing. The tendency toward obesity is the most common, but constipation is another. Aging teeth and a slowing down of the digestive processes may hinder digestion and cause diarrhea. There is also the possibility of loss or impairment of hearing or eyesight which may also tend to make the dog

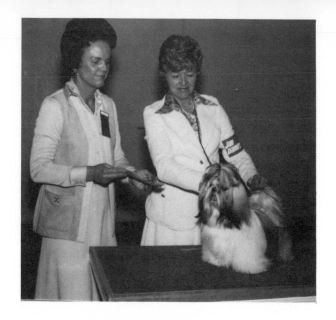

Left, top:
Ch. Marya Winds Gilded Lady is pictured winning under judge Michele Billings as she finished her championship in April 1976. Peggy Hogg handled for owner Martha Coalina of Valpariso, Indiana. The sire was Ch. Dragonwyck The Great Gatsby ex Ch. Mariljac Marilyn of Chusanho.

Left, middle: Alice Nystrom of Torrance, California is shown with her Shih Tzu, Patches, after his graduation from obedience novice class.

Left, bottom: Argentine Ch. Charing Cross Tang Too, bred by Gilbert S. Kahn and Jorge N. Sanchez, is owned by Sr. and Sra. Alberto Pettinari of Buenos Aires. Tang is shown winning the Bred by Exhibitor Class at the American Shih Tzu Club Specialty Show in Houston in 1975. Judge is Anne Rogers Clark, with Dr. Jorge N. Sanchez handling.

Below: Canadian Ch. Elfann Golden Adonis and American Ch. Elfann Golden Sunmaiden, owned by Del and Connie Smart of the Conwynn Shih Tzu, Akron, Ohio.

Car-Lyn's Gypsy Rose of Sanco pictured going Winners Bitch and Best of Opposite Sex from the Puppy Class for her first points toward championship under judge Dorothy Welse at the 1975 Stone City Kennel Club show. Gypsy Rose is owner-handled by Sandy Cox, Sanco Shih Tzu, Lexington, Kentucky.

wary and distrustful. Other behavioral changes may result as well, such as crankiness, loss of patience and lack of interest; these are the most obvious changes. Other ailments may manifest themselves in the form of rheumatism, arthritis, tumors and warts, heart disease, kidney infections, male prostratism and female disorders. Of course, all of these require a veterinarian's checking the degree of seriousness and proper treatment.

Take care to avoid all infectious diseases. When these hit older dogs, they can debilitate them to an alarming degree, leaving them open to more serious complications and shorter lives.

DOG INSURANCE

Much has been said for and against canine insurance, and much more will be said before this kind of protection for a dog becomes universal and/or practical. There has been talk of establishing a Blue Cross-type plan similar to the one now existing for humans. However, the best insurance for your dog is YOU! Nothing compensates for tender loving care. Like the insurance policies for humans, there will be a lot of fine print in the contracts revealing that the dog is not covered after all. These limited conditions usually make the acquisition of dog insurance expensive and virtually worthless.

Blanket coverage policies for kennels or establishments which board or groom dogs can be an advantage, especially in transporting dogs to and from their premises. For the one-dog owner, however, whose dog is a constant companion, the cost of limited coverage is not necessary.

THE HIGH COST OF BURIAL

Pet cemeteries are increasing in number across the nation. Here, as with humans, the sky can be the limit for those who wish to bury their pets ceremoniously. The costs of plots and satin-lined caskets, grave stones, flowers, etc., run the gamut of prices to match the emotions and means of the owner. This is strictly a matter of what the bereaved owner wishes to do.

IN THE EVENT OF YOUR DEATH

This is a morbid thought perhaps, but ask yourself the question, "If death were to strike at this moment, what would become of my dogs?"

Perhaps you are fortunate enough to have a spouse, children, a relative or friend who would take over immediately, even if only on a temporary basis. Perhaps you have already left instructions in your will for your pet's dispensation, as well as a stipend for its care.

Luv-Tzu Yummee Wun and Rockee Vollee Kim-Ko of Luv-Tzu are young puppies from Mary Marxen's Luv-Tzu Kennels in Van Wert, Ohio.

Provide definite instructions before a disaster occurs and your dogs are carted off to the pound to be destroyed, or stolen by commercially minded neighbors with "re-sale" in mind. It is a simple thing to instruct your lawyer about your wishes in the event of sickness or death. Leave instructions as to feeding, etc., posted on your kennel room or kitchen bulletin board, or wherever your kennel records are kept. Also, tell several people what you are doing and why. If you prefer to keep such instructions private, merely place them in sealed envelopes in a known place with directions that they are to be opened only in the event of your death. Eliminate the danger of your animals suffering in the event of an emergency that prevents your personal care of them.

KEEPING RECORDS

Whether you have one dog or a kennel full of them, it is wise to keep written records. It takes only a few moments to record dates of inoculations, trips to the vet, tests for worms, etc. It can avoid confusion or mistakes, or having your dog not covered with immunization if too much time elapses between shots because you have to guess at the last shot.

Make the effort to keep all dates in writing rather than trying to commit them to memory. A rabies injection can be a problem if you have to recall that "Fido had the shot the day Aunt Mary got back from her trip abroad, and, let's see, I guess that was around the end of June."

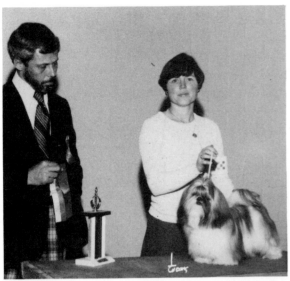

Wix Willy Woo pictured winning under judge Edd Bivin. Peggy Lloyd is handling for owners Glenda Wicks and Glenn Sands of Kansas City, Kansas.

Brotherly love: three month old Tiffany seeks the protection of her "big brother," an Afghan Hound. Both are owned by Susan Bell of Shreveport, Louisiana.

Marion Browne of Santa Barbara, California, with her eight week old Encore Princess Wing Ti Wei.

An impressive study of San Yen Won Wei Tang, owned by Susan Barr, San Yen Kennels, Salt Lake City.

Copa Centerfold is pictured going Best of Winners and Best of Opposite sex over Best In Show champions at the 1974 Boardwalk Kennel Club Show for a 5-point major under judge Merrill Cohen. This 11-month-old bitch won over an entry of 65 Shih Tzu. She was handled by Becky Brandon, who co-owns with Coni Nickerson of Richmond, Virginia. Copa Centerfold is a Ping Pong granddaughter and a Ying Ying great granddaughter.

Four-and-a-half-month-old puppy poses with two oriental foo dogs. This pup is owned by the Baroness van Panthaleon van Eck-Kalsing of the Netherlands.

Ch. Chekenda Lady Gay, a brindle and white female, is pictured here winning under judge Edd Bivin with her handler, Dee Sheper. Lady Gay's owner is Bobbie Franklin of Kansas City, Missouri.

A Shih Tzu family gathering! This merry group of Chumulari Shih Tzu was assembled for a charming photo portrait at the home of the Eastons in Gardiner, New York.

Sin-A-Bar's Duwacky Du, shown taking the ribbons with handler Lois Davis. Duwacky's owner is Bobbie Franklin of Kansas City, Missouri.

Pine Haven's Bo-Chu Hua, a bitch pictured here as an 11-month-old puppy. Bo-Chu Hua was whelped at Lucille E. Huntsman's Pine Haven Kennels in Windsor, Maine. The sire was Ch. Royale White Tie and Tails ex Rondelay Glowyn DaZee.

Frankay's Ah So Peking Pearl, owned by K. Coffee, Minot, North Dakota.

An impressive head study of Gor-Jus Jorg of San Yen, owned by Susan Barr.

In an emergency, these records may prove their value if your veterinarian cannot be reached and you have to use another, or if you move and have no case history on your dog for the new veterinarian. In emergencies, you do not always think clearly or accurately, and if dates, and types of serums used, etc., are a matter of record, the veterinarian can act more quickly and with more confidence.

TATTOOING

Ninety per cent success has been reported on the return of stolen or lost dogs that have been tattooed. More and more, this simple, painless, inexpensive method of positive identification for dogs is being reported all over the United States. Long popular in Canada, along with nose prints, the idea gained interest in this country when dognapping started to soar as unscrupulous people began stealing dogs for resale to research laboratories. Pet dogs that wander off, and lost hunting dogs have always been a problem. The success of tatooing has been significant.

Tattooing can be done by the veterinarian for a minor fee. There are several dog "registries" that will record your dog's number and help you locate it should it be lost or stolen. The number of the dog's American Kennel Club registration is most often used on thoroughbred dogs, or the owner's Social Security number in the case of mixed breeds. The best place for the tattoo is the groin. Some prefer the inside of an ear, and the American Kennel Club has rules that judges officiating at the AKC dog shows should not penalize the dog for the tattoo mark.

A boy and his dog: David Rainey and a Shir-Lee Shih Tzu.

The tattoo mark serves not only to identify your dog should it be lost or stolen, but offers positive identification in large kennels where several litters of the same approximate age are on the premises. It is a safety measure against unscrupulous breeders "switching" puppies. Any age is a proper age to tattoo, but for safety's sake, the sooner the better.

The buzz of the needle might cause your dog to be apprehensive, but the pricking of the needle is virtually painless. The risk of infection is negligible when done properly, and the return of your beloved pet may be the reward for taking the time to insure positive identification for your dog. Your local kennel club will know of a dog registry in your area.

296

Norwegian Ch. Zizi's Foo won his title from the junior class in just three shows! Bred by Ruth Laakso, he is sired by Int., Nor. Ch. Marinas Muff-Lung-Feng ex Int., Nor. and Danish Ch. Zizi's Lhamo. Owner, Sonja Bai, Arendal, Norway.

Ch. Yosha Toddi Mikko Bear, owned by the San Yen Kennels of Susan Barr.

Champion Barbara's Mr. Tu Ling Sing pictured going Winners Dog. Owned by Mrs. Barbara Henderson of Richmond, Virginia, he was sired by Sintez of Parquins out of Stumpy Acres Jade Idol.

INDEX

San Yen-Won Wei Tang,
owned by Susan D. Barr of
Salt Lake City, Utah.